Presidential Campaigns and Elections

PRESIDENTIAL CAMPAIGNS AND ELECTIONS

Issues, Images, and Partisanship

MYRON A. LEVINE

Albion College

F. E. PEACOCK PUBLISHERS, INC.   **Itasca, Illinois**

Cover art:
Stephen Kroninger, *Smile,* 1991
Montage, 6¼ by 10 inches
Reproduced by courtesy of the artist and
Mother Jones (July/August 1991 issue)

Library of Congress Catalog Card No. 91-76459

ISBN 0-87581-357-7

Printed in the United States of America

Printing: 10 9 8 7 6 5 4 3 2 1

Year: 96 95 94 93 92

To my mother and father,
Dorothy and David,
for their sacrifice, love, and
belief in education

CONTENTS

FIGURES AND TABLES

FIGURES

TABLES

POLITICAL ADS

PREFACE

Throughout the various stages of the quadrennial race for the American presidency, the strategic goal for a candidate and his political advisers is to construct winning campaign appeals. Presidential campaigns are increasingly run by candidate-centered organizations, not political parties. Although national campaigns continue to use newspapers, radios, and other traditional campaign media, especially to reach narrow, specified audiences, television has become the dominant medium in the presidential race.

But which appeals work best in influencing Americans' voting behavior? In choosing a President, do Americans respond primarily to partisan, personal image, or substantive issue appeals? The only part of the answer to this question that political scientists know for certain is that the influence of partisanship is on the decline. While still of great significance in a presidential election, political party identification no longer exerts the great pull on Americans that it once did. For presidential campaigners, the key strategic question is how to reach an increasingly independent American electorate. Is it personal image or substantive issue appeals that win presidential elections?

This book seeks to provide an answer to this question by examining presidential elections at two different levels: trends in American voting behavior and the conduct of individual presidential campaigns. In early chapters, we examine the evidence provided by the large volume of political science studies on voting behavior. But this book argues that such studies alone do not provide a full understanding of American elections. American voting behavior can only be understood in the context of individual presidential elections. Hence, in later chapters we will review recent elections with special attention to the televised campaign—that part of the presidential campaign that most Americans see. We will analyze political advertisements for the content of their messages. Transcriptions of many spots are included in the text. Only after reviewing both voting behavior and political advertising can we begin to judge the degree to which a particular presidential election turned on partisanship, personal imagery, or substantive policy considerations.

Such a review of voting behavior and the key events during the presidential election process should help dispel the popular misperception that presidential campaigns are won solely by the actions of professional image wizards. While personal leadership imagery is still important and political advertising has become increasingly sophisticated, presidential campaigns are won on substance as well. Oftentimes the most effective advertisements in a campaign communicate issue-based images, not just personality-based images. Voters may vary in their sophistication, but they are capable of choosing candidates they see as closer to themselves on key issues.

Neither voter's reactions to candidates nor the candidate's use of media may be divorced from the modern changes in American politics. The developments we discuss in this book include the rise of the consultant industry, campaign finance reform, the changed nature of the nominating system, and voter realignment. We will also discuss whether negative campaigning is as bad as alleged.

The book also seeks to address the question of how Democrats and Republicans can conduct winning presidential campaigns if voters respond to substantive concerns more than is commonly believed. As Republicans have succeeded in recent years in constructing winning presidential campaign appeals, the book largely represents an argument about what the Democratic party should and should not do if it hopes to regain the White House.

An overriding set of political theory questions helps to guide this examination of presidential campaigns and elections. Does

American democracy work in the age of television? Can Americans use elections to hold their government accountable? Are Americans offered a choice of candidates based on manufactured personal images or on more substantive policy concerns?

The author wishes to thank the following: Glenn Perusek for the many helpful comments he provided after reading an early draft of this manuscript; reviewers Emmett H. Buell, Jr., of Denison University, James E. Campbell of Louisiana State University, Thomas Holbrook of University of Wisconsin-Milwaukee, and James Hutter of Iowa State University, for their detailed and thoughtful suggestions that helped to make this a much better book; Ruth Ann Boyd for her invaluable assistance (especially during times of crisis entailed by "blown" computer disks); Albion College for the award of a sabbatical that allowed the completion of this book; and Walter Dean Burnham for his teachings. Leo Wiegman and Ted Peacock were outstanding as usual. An author could not ask for a more supportive or helpful publisher. Dana Gould was a meticulous editor. Both Leo and Dana contributed to and improved the manuscript in many ways. My thanks and love also go to Nancy, Alex, and Evie, who were always there to help me through the many downs that a prolonged writing project always entails.

THE ECONOMY, THE GULF WAR, AND THE PROLOGUE TO THE 1992 ELECTION

I n mid-1990, halfway through George Bush's presidential term, the United States was facing an economic recession. Confronting the prospects of ever-rising budget deficits and faced with a Democratic-controlled Congress, President Bush abandoned his 1988 campaign vow of "no new taxes." Conservative activists were outraged. Some even discussed the possibility of running conservative columnist and former Reagan speechwriter Patrick Buchanan for president. George Bush's presidential honeymoon was clearly over. His presidential approval rating scores began to decline. News commentators began to speculate that the President was in serious political trouble. Several even suggested that he consider dropping Vice President Dan Quayle from the Republican ticket to improve his electability in 1992.

But events in the Persian Gulf changed the political situation considerably. The Persian Gulf nations control vast oil reserves critical to the petroleum-hungry economies of the industrialized nations, including the United States, Western Europe, and Japan. A six-month military buildup placed more than 500,000 American and allied troops in the Gulf region to oppose Iraq's occupation of neighboring Kuwait. Following this buildup, a six-week air war demonstrated the vast technological superiority of the American-led forces. A 100-hour ground war followed, bringing operations Desert Shield and Desert Storm to a close in late February 1991. The scope of the American-led coalition's victory was as stunning as it was swift. American and allied casualties were very light. The United States was bathed in a sea of American flags and yellow ribbons.

News stories of Iraq's suppression of Kurdish rebels and Shi'ite factions did, however, dampen America's postwar euphoria. In a televised interview, General Norman Schwarzkopf revealed that President Bush had not allowed him to continue the war and pursue the destruction of Iraq's armed forces. As a result, Saddam Hussein remained in power. The United States stood by while Iraq used its remaining airplanes, helicopters, and armored vehicles to inflict death upon the Kurds. President Bush stated that he did not want to endanger American lives by embroiling American troops in what was essentially a civil war. Eventually, however, the President did order American troops to enter northern Iraq to set up relief camps and protect the Kurds.

In the wake of the initial military victory, prominent Republican officials began to use the war as an electoral weapon against Democrats. The congressional resolution authorizing President Bush to use force in the Gulf region had passed the Senate by a very narrow 52-to-47 vote. The vote had been pretty much along party lines; 45 of 55 Democrats opposed the use of force. In the House, where Democrat Stephen Solarz of New York helped steer the use-of-force resolution through the floor, the vote was only somewhat less partisan; 179 of 265 House Democrats voted to deny the President the right to use force in the Gulf. Democrats damaged their claims to being the party of leadership by hesitating on the war. As Republican Senator Phil Gramm of Texas elaborated:

> On the most important foreign-policy vote in years, the entire leadership and the vast majority of the membership on the Democratic side voted to deny the President his request for authority to use force against Saddam Hussein. That is something they have to explain.[1]

Democratic National Committee Chairman Ron Brown immediately cried foul. Brown accused the Republicans of playing dirty politics in attempting to make a political issue of what he said had clearly been a vote of conscience.

Brown was wrong in at least one regard. It was not that the Republicans were *attempting* to make the war a political issue. By the end of February 1991, the Gulf War *had already become* an important issue that changed the shape of the 1992 presidential race.

Brown was attempting damage control. Unless something new and dramatic occurred to greatly alter the public's perceptions, it seemed quite probable that voters would reward Bush in 1992 for his Gulf War victory. A number of Democrats who voted against the war were no longer intent on making the presidential race. Other prominent Democrats were reluctant to take on Bush and his newfound heights of popularity. Some news commentators even began to discuss the possibility that the Democrats might draft General Schwarzkopf to escape the war issue.

Even before the brief war ended, Operation Desert Storm had changed the context of the presidential race. The preliminary rounds of the 1992 election were unlike any other presidential campaign of recent memory. As the war drew to a close in February 1991, with the Iowa caucuses and New Hampshire primaries only a year off, virtually none of the expected Democratic candidates were found visiting Iowa and New Hampshire or setting up campaign organizations in these states with their early nominating contests.*

In part, the candidates had learned the lessons of the last presidential campaign; in 1988 a victory in Iowa did not lead to the nomination in either party. But more significantly, no Democrat wanted to be out on the campaign trail, the focus of reporters' attentions, while the outcome of the Gulf situation was still in doubt. Any statement by a Democratic hopeful in support of the Gulf War would have alienated the party's more liberal activists who saw the war as imprudent, unnecessary, and immoral. These activists make up an important constituency in Democratic primary and caucus electorates. But to criticize the war or the President's

---

*In recent years the Iowa caucuses and the New Hampshire primary have formally marked the start of the presidential race. As each state conducts its party caucuses or primary under slightly different rules, generalizations are difficult to make. A *caucus* is a precinct-level or other local meeting during which participants choose representatives to attend county, congressional district, or state conventions. The district or state convention then chooses delegates who will attend the party's national convention to select a presidential nominee. Caucuses and conventions often conduct other items of party business in addition to presidential selection. A *primary* is a day-long event during which voters go to the polls to directly vote for a candidate. The results of a primary greatly determine how many national convention delegates a state awards to each presidential aspirant. Generally speaking, any person who is willing to declare himself or herself a party member can now participate in a caucus or primary. As Chapter 2 recounts, this was not always the case. Also, it should be noted that primaries tend to attract much greater public participation than do caucuses. As we further describe in Chapter 2, candidates win a party's presidential nomination by establishing momentum and winning delegates in state caucuses and primaries. Nowadays, national party conventions simply reflect the choices that voters made during the caucus and primary stage of the nominating process.

policies would incur an even greater political risk. The Democrat who raised such criticisms could be accused of dividing the nation and failing to support American troops in a time of crisis. If the war turned out well, as it did, a candidate who voiced such criticisms would be unelectable. Faced with this conundrum, Democratic candidates were profiles in caution; they chose not to begin their active campaigns until the outcome of the Gulf War was known.

On August 20, 1991, a second foreign policy event further strengthened President Bush's reelection position. Hardliners in the Soviet Union attempted a coup to oust Soviet President Mikhail Gorbachev. But the coup proved badly organized and was short-lived. Bush was restrained and cautious in his initial response to the coup attempt. But his response quickly changed as the resistance of the Soviet people to the coup became increasingly evident. By the second day, Bush placed a series of phone calls to world leaders and to Russian President Boris Yeltsin, the head of resistance forces. Gorbachev was returned to power. Yeltsin and the forces of democracy were ascendant. Communism in the Soviet Union clearly was in decline.

Bush earned great praise for his handling of the situation. Once again, Bush looked presidential. The "status gap" between Bush and his potential Democratic rivals was widened. The outcome of events only reinforced the disadvantage suffered by Democrats in the foreign policy arena. As Democratic political consultant and former Carter aide Greg Schneiders remarked, "I said a while ago that our best strategy on foreign policy, when it comes up, is to change the subject."[2] Democrats could only hope that the public would turn its attention to new concerns, especially economic and domestic concerns, as the road to the 1992 election continued.

THE GULF WAR AND THE DEMOCRATIC PRESIDENTIAL FIELD

The Gulf War reshaped the field of Democratic presidential contenders. Senate House Armed Services Committee chairman Sam Nunn of Georgia, a moderate-conservative Democrat, had clearly been positioning himself for a presidential run by dropping his membership in an all-male suburban Washington country club and by relaxing his long-time opposition to abortion. When it came to the critical votes authorizing American action in the Gulf, Nunn rallied Senate Democrats in support of the continued application of economic sanctions and against the use of force. Nunn was a highly respected defense expert; he had worried greatly about the ramifications of further American involvement in the Gulf region's conflicts.

Nunn's leadership on the war resolutions won him increased respect from liberal Democrats who had previously distrusted the Georgian as an unreconstructed, militaristic hawk on defense matters. But Nunn improved his standing among liberal Democrats at the cost of hurting his electability in November. Compared to Bush, Nunn no longer looked presidential; Nunn had expressed his reservations while the President marched off to victory. When the Gulf War reached its conclusion, Nunn was no longer talking about a possible presidential bid.

House Majority Leader Richard Gephardt was another contender who had maneuvered to put himself in position for a possible 1992 presidential bid. Gephardt, an unsuccessful 1988 candidate, had built considerable elite support for another presidential effort by appearing at various dinners and fundraising efforts for Democrats across the nation. But like Nunn in the Senate, Gephardt had rallied House Democrats against the congressional authorization to give the President the ability to use force in the Gulf. He, too, would have to justify his actions to voters in a presidential contest.

Texas Senator Lloyd Bentsen, an often-mentioned possible contender because of his popularity as Michael Dukakis's 1988 running mate, was another prominent Democrat who voted against the use-of-force resolution. He, too, was now vulnerable to charges that he lacked the forceful leadership necessary in the international arena.

Even New York Governor Mario Cuomo was handicapped by the war issue. Cuomo had expressed his ambivalence on American involvement but still came out against the war. He declared that he agreed with a number of American war aims, but had he been in Congress he still would have voted for the Nunn resolution not to go to war.[3]

But Cuomo's political liabilities went beyond the war question. As the governor of New York, Cuomo suffered from a national image of being a big-spending liberal. In this vein Republican ads could easily paint Cuomo as another Dukakis. New York State's fiscal problems would also likely be used as ammunition against a Cuomo presidential candidacy. But in a shortened primary season, Cuomo also possessed considerable advantages. He enjoyed both national visibility and the big advantage of being able to raise large sums of money quickly—valuable assets for any candidate who decided to join the presidential race at the last minute.

Of those Democrats whom the press at the time generally mentioned as possible 1992 contenders, only Tennessee Senator Al Gore and Virginia Senator Charles Robb voted to support the use of force in the Gulf region. Of the two, Gore was more actively considering making the presidential race.

Gore had run unsuccessfully for the presidential nomination in 1988 as a "different" sort of Democrat, one who supported a strong national defense. His vote in favor of the use of force in the Gulf region helped to insulate him from attack on the war issue in a 1992 race. As a result, of all the prominently mentioned Democratic contenders, only Gore had the potential of carrying the attack to Bush and shifting the debate to economic issues and other Bush weak points without having it diverted back to the war and leadership questions. Gore could campaign on a platform advocating strength both abroad and at home.

Gore's presidential star rose as his use-of-force vote helped to differentiate him from other Democratic presidential hopefuls. But this differentiation also placed new obstacles in his path to the Democratic nomination. Now more than ever, liberal Democratic constituencies were suspicious of Gore. They argued that the Democrats could not hope to beat Bush by offering voters a pale imitation of the President. Instead, they argued, Democrats should run a candidate true to the party's progressive traditions.

Given the heights of Bush's popularity, Gore, like all other Democrats, was hesitant to enter the 1992 race. Finally, at the end of August 1991, Gore announced that he would not be a candidate. Gore's announcement came on the very same day that the attempted coup d'etat in the Soviet Union collapsed.

Jesse Jackson had been less constrained than other presidential Democrats in his politicking and criticisms of the Gulf War. In his media appearances and in his speech at a march on Washington against the war, Jackson declared that the resort to war was evidence of George Bush's failed diplomacy. Jackson also vigorously attacked the administration for ignoring domestic problems—for going to war overseas with troops that were disproportionately minority in composition, while at the same time failing to mount a war against pressing social problems at home. Jackson also paid an early visit to New Hampshire at a time when other Democrats were reluctant to go.

But Jackson's outspokenness came at the cost of raising further qualms among voters who thought that he lacked essential presidential leadership qualities in the foreign policy arena. Many voters questioned Jackson's lack of experience. Despite his recent election as "shadow Senator" from the District of Columbia, Jackson had never really occupied elective public office. Further, like Gore, Jackson feared that another unsuccessful run would earn him the sobriquet of perpetual candidate, effectively undermining his political credibility.

Jackson was not popular among more moderate Democrats who believed that the party needed to tone down its liberal image if it were to recapture the political center and regain the presidency. The Democratic Leadership Council (DLC), an association of centrist Democrats, invited other presidential aspirants, but not Jackson, to its spring 1991 meeting. Jackson and others were infuriated by the snub.

In the end, Jackson decided to forego a 1992 race but announced that he would still remain an active voice in the Democratic party for the causes of equality and justice.

The Gulf War played such havoc with the Democratic presidential field that it encouraged candidates with little name recognition to begin explorations for a possible presidential race. They hoped to identify new campaign themes that would appeal to middle-class Americans and win back those votes that had provided Reagan and Bush with their margins of victory.

Former Massachusetts Senator Paul Tsongas was the first to announce. Tsongas ran on a platform of economic growth, urging Democrats to stop their antagonistic criticisms of the business community. Tsongas had retired from the Senate when it was discovered that he had a form of cancer.

For a while, West Virginia Senator John D. "Jay" Rockefeller IV considered entering the race. He emphasized children's and health issues in his brief exploratory campaign.

Arkansas Governor Bill Clinton sought to appeal to the Democratic party's more traditional constituencies. Clinton spoke of the need to offer voters a "new choice" that would represent the needs of middle-class Americans without abandoning the party's traditional commitment to civil rights and the poor. Clinton was chair of the DLC, the organization of centrist Democrats which had snubbed Jesse Jackson at its convention and sponsored a debate on the subject of racial quotas. More liberal elements in the party viewed Clinton's candidacy with caution.

Former California Governor Edmund G. "Jerry" Brown, Jr., ran on a platform of political reform that criticized established elites and the role played by money in politics. Brown hoped to tap popular resentment against the political system. Brown carried the burden of having to overcome his image of being a "flake" from California.

Only Iowan Tom Harkin remained true to the party's liberal traditions. But even here, the outspoken Harkin sought to dress his candidacy in the garb of "populism" instead of big-government liberalism. Harkin cast himself as the voice of the average American whose educational, job, and economic concerns were forgotten by a President preoccupied with foreign-policy and free-trade matters. Harkin also sharply criticized the growing concentration of wealth during the Reagan and Bush years.

Harkin's message was well-received by organized labor and the party's more liberal Democratic activists. Attractive to key constituencies in the Democratic primaries, Harkin's unabashed liberalism would likely prove to be a problem in the general election. Harkin had also voted against the Gulf War. But he hoped that his record as a Navy flier in the Vietnam era would insulate him against adverse public reaction on the issue.

Of all the Democratic contenders, perhaps Nebraska Senator Robert Kerrey was least vulnerable on the Gulf War issue. Kerrey had been an outspoken critic of President Bush's haste to shift the United States from a defensive to an offensive military posture in the Gulf region. Kerrey had vigorously questioned the Bush administration's policies in the Gulf region at a time when other Democrats cautiously chose to remain silent. Kerrey's opponents could attack him for lacking essential leadership vision when it came to the Gulf War. But they could not charge him with lacking the courage to go to war. A Medal of Honor winner, Kerrey had lost a leg while serving in Vietnam.

In pursuing the presidency in 1992, Kerrey outlined a platform that sought to meet the health and economic concerns of middle-class voters. Political commentators saw Kerrey as the Democrat most likely to reassemble the coalition put together by Colorado's Gary Hart in his earlier presidential bids.

One active and somewhat unexpected contestant in the 1992 race was the newly elected Governor of Virginia, Douglas Wilder, an African-American. Even at a time when others practiced caution, Wilder visited New Hampshire, set up an exploratory committee to begin raising funds for a possible presidential bid, and undertook other actions to raise his national profile. Wilder, a fiscal conservative, represented a more moderate or centrist alternative black candidate to Jesse Jackson. By the end of summer 1991, Wilder had also taken a verbal potshot at the liberal record of New

York's Governor Cuomo, in effect offering himself to the party as a more pragmatic and winnable presidential alternative. Because Virginia's constitution prohibited his running for a second consecutive term as governor, Wilder had little to lose from a presidential effort. A presidential bid could only increase his national prominence.

Like Cuomo, Wilder suffered the liability of being less-than-overwhelmingly popular in his home state as the consequence of the fiscal stringency measures he imposed as governor. Wilder also lacked a strong political organization in key primary states. When Jackson withdrew from the race, Wilder increased the intensity of his campaigning in the African-American community in an effort to win a greater share of that community's vote.

A REAWAKENED ECONOMIC ISSUE

By mid-1991 neither a liberal nor a centrist Democrat appeared to have much of a chance in the 1992 election. The only real hope for the Democrats was that the quick resolution of the war would allow the public to shift its attention to issues where Bush was more vulnerable. Also, history shows that the successful conduct of a war does not guarantee a head of state popularity and easy reelection. President Harry Truman's popularity fell steeply only months after the end of World War II as the public shifted its attention to new concerns. In 1948 Truman survived an extremely close reelection battle. Similarly, in Great Britain Winston Churchill was ousted just months after leading his nation to victory in World War II. The British rejected Churchill's Conservative party platform and instead voted for a Labour government committed to more socialist health and welfare policies.

Economic problems continued to plague the United States after the Gulf War. The recession continued. The Southwest faced an economic downturn because of the "bust" in the "oil patch." The Northeast suffered an unrelenting slowdown in real estate sales. Cities such as New York, Philadelphia, and Detroit suffered serious fiscal problems. Bridgeport, Connecticut, went bankrupt and filed for court protection.

Bush's approval ratings could not continue at their stratospheric highs of the immediate postwar period. As they began to fall, commentators noted the President's increased political vulnerability. Bush's heart fibrillation even momentarily raised the "Quayle factor"—the public's doubt that Vice President Dan

Quayle possessed the capacity to serve as President. But the President's quick return to work and well-publicized program of vigorous physical activity put the Quayle factor to rest.

As the recession continued, Democrats sensed the President's political vulnerability and pushed the economic issue. They charged that the President was more interested in pursuing a Middle East peace settlement than in improving the lives of Americans at home.

In late 1991, Democrat Harris Wofford upset former Attorney General Richard Thornburgh in the Senate race in Pennsylvania. Thornburgh had run as a defender of the policies of the Bush administration. Wofford, in contrast, promised a new program of national health insurance to protect working-class and middle-class Americans. Suddenly, all the Democrats were stressing the need for a new program of national health protection. President Bush delayed a scheduled trip to Japan and Asia in order to pay more attention to domestic affairs. Presidential Chief of Staff John Sununu resigned amidst charges that the White House had failed to formulate an adequate game plan to jump-start the economy.

But the war issue still gave the President substantial reelection advantages. Even if economic bad times persisted through 1992, voters were still likely to remember America's success in the Gulf War. Prompting from Republican advertisers would help remind the public of the President's skill in conducting the war and the sense of national pride and joy the nation felt when American troops returned home in victory. The Republicans would build positively on the euphoria of the Gulf War victory. But if their polls showed the need to do so, the Republicans could also take a negative approach. Republican advertising would remind voters who acted to stop Saddam Hussein in the Gulf and who voted against the action—who hesitated when Saddam Hussein threatened his Gulf neighbors. Also, any upturn in the economy would only improve the President's already excellent chances of reelection.

The 1991 elections also showed that the tax issue could work to the Republicans' advantage. Voters in New Jersey ousted the Democratic state legislature as a result of the tax issue. In Connecticut, angered citizens demonstrated to protest the imposition of new taxes.

ISSUES, IMAGES, AND PARTISANSHIP IN PRESIDENTIAL ELECTIONS

The Gulf War changed presidential and partisan images. As a result of his strong and successful leadership, Bush looked undeniably presidential. No longer could media commentators seriously characterize him as a "wimp"—the dreaded label that had hounded him throughout the 1988 campaign. The Democrats, in contrast, suffered a serious image problem. They looked increasingly like a party that could not be entrusted with handling the difficult job of the presidency, especially in the crucial arena of foreign affairs.

When it came to handling the economy, Bush looked less presidential. Polls in late 1991 showed that voters no longer had great confidence in Bush's ability to manage the economy. Nor, however, did they have any great faith in the managerial abilities of the Democrats.

These politically relevant images that dominated the beginning of the 1992 presidential race were not the creation of professional image merchants or media consultants. Rather, they were perceptions that voters derived from substance, from the candidates' and the parties' past records and performances. Bush had skillfully garnered the support of the international community, the United States Congress, and the American public behind a course of military action. He had organized a successful war effort. It was a victory that looked easy only after it had been achieved, after the air war had destroyed the killing power of the vaunted Republican Guard and other Iraqi forces. Economic growth, however, continued to be slow.

The image of the Democrats, too, was grounded in substance. The Democratic leadership in Congress had argued that economic sanctions imposed on Iraq should be given more time to work. They were reluctant to jeopardize American lives for what many saw to be a fight over oil. But in the eyes of the public, if the Democrats were hesitant to use force against a regime as clearly evil as that of Saddam Hussein's, when, if ever, would they be willing to use force? In the issue area of the economy, Jimmy Carter's administration had been unable to come to grips with the problem of "stagflation." The public had its doubts as to whether any of the new crop of Democratic candidates could do any better.

In the 1992 presidential election, voter reactions to the Gulf War and the state of the economy provide examples of *retrospective* evaluations—one of the primary ways in which issues influence presidential elections. The public does not rigorously examine the competing policy promises of presidential candidates. Instead the public registers its degree of satisfaction or dissatisfaction with past performance, especially the performance of the incumbent administration.

Public reaction to the Gulf War provides some insight as to how retrospective evaluations take shape. Before the war, voters did not have a clear and strong opinion as to what course of action the United States should follow. It was not clear how long and how costly—in terms of lives lost and money spent—a military intervention Americans would support. Before the fighting began, the Pentagon had placed an order for 40,000 body pouches for potential fatalities! Americans did not prospectively choose among competing promised courses of action in the Gulf region. Such a choice was too difficult. The American public as a whole did not live up to the model of the classic, well-informed democratic citizen who chooses among candidates on the basis of their policy promises.

After the war, however, American opinion was crystal clear. In the wake of victory, President Bush consistently received approval ratings from more than 80 percent of those polled. The public retrospectively approved Bush's successful handling of the war. Post hoc evaluations of performance colored Americans' perceptions of the President and the political parties.

Later, in Chapter 3 we will discuss more fully the role issues play in presidential elections. *Retrospective voting,* choosing a candidate based on past performance, is a prominent means by which issue evaluations affect voter choice. In recent years, voters' retrospective evaluations have focused to a great extent on the nation's economic well-being and the President's handling of foreign policy.

But retrospective voting is not the only means by which issues influence presidential elections. As we shall see, voters are also capable of making broad choices between the general policy directions or action orientations offered by competing presidential candidates. Voters are also more prone to vote on "easy" rather than conceptually difficult issues.

The exact influence of issues in presidential elections is a matter of much debate. The argument of this book is that issues count, that they have a greater influence on how Americans vote for president than the general public and political commentators often allege. Presidential campaigns are far from the image-making spectacles devoid of issues that they are so often portrayed to be in the popular culture.

Yet, this argument can be made only by examining the evidence in the issue voting debate and by looking at the role played by issues—as opposed to candidate images and partisanship—in individual presidential elections. This is a task we shall begin in Chapter 2.

Chapter 2 reviews the changing context of American presidential elections. We observe the influence of television and the rise of professionally mediated campaigns. We also observe the growing independence of the American voter. One of the clearest trends in electoral politics is the declining importance—though far from the disappearance—of partisanship. The declining significance of partisanship has allowed both personal images and policy issues to play a greater role in presidential voting. Reforms in the presidential nominating system and campaign finance have also led to a new prominence of both issue groups and professional image-makers in the candidate-centered campaign.

In Chapter 3 we examine the evidence in the issue voting debate. For a long time political scientists were of the opinion that party identification and candidates' personality factors were the most important influences on voter choice. Issues appeared to have little, if any, influence on the outcome of presidential elections. Even today, a number of political scientists continue to produce evidence of the continuing lack of sophistication of the American voter. Yet, this view of the seeming unimportance of issues to the voting decision has come under great attack. Political scientists have begun to conceptualize various ways in which issues influence voting behavior.

Beginning in Chapter 4 we examine how Americans have chosen their Presidents from Franklin Roosevelt to George Bush. The relative importance of three factors—issues, personal images, and partisanship—varies from election to election. Chapter 4 describes the New Deal political era, a time when partisanship may have been the dominant influence on the voting decision. But even here the relative impact of issues is still the subject of some debate. Chapter 4 also observes the role of television in its infancy, a role that will change over time as both political elites and the public-at-large grow more accustomed to television as an everyday part of their lives.

Chapter 5 describes the 1964–1972 period during which Americans perceived a fairly distinct directional choice between Democrats and Republicans in each of the presidential elections of this period. As we shall argue beginning with Chapter 5, presidential advertising can be constructed on issue-based images as well as on more personal candidate images. Where issue-based images or even more direct issue appeals are stressed, the televised campaign can actually help voters to distinguish between the competing action orientations of presidential candidates.

Chapters 6 through 8 detail the 1976–1988 "retrospective era," an era during which voters' performance evaluations of the economy and other issues were critical to the outcome of each election.

Chapter 8 devotes special attention to the 1988 contest between George Bush and Michael Dukakis, an election that is often viewed as having turned on well-constructed, professionally mediated images. It is argued here, however, that even in 1988 the voters perceived a basic directional choice between the candidates. Bush's and Dukakis's dispositions on issues mattered to voters! The highly symbol-laden, image-based campaign appeals of 1988 provided citizens with sufficient, although somewhat distorted, information to make an informed choice between the competing broad policy directions offered by the candidates. As in other presidential elections of the 1970s and 1980s, retrospective performance evaluations centering on peace and prosperity mattered as well in 1988.

The concluding chapter of this book looks to the future and seeks to identify those strategies that the Democratic and Republican parties could profitably adopt if, as this book argues, issues count in presidential politics.

THE STAGES OF THE PRESIDENTIAL SELECTION PROCESS

American presidential elections provide a confusing spectacle. We conclude this opening chapter with a brief overview of the stages in the presidential selection process.

We can best understand the process as occurring in two grand parts. The first is a time of intraparty battle through the winter and spring's state-by-state primaries and caucuses, and culminates in party nominations at a national convention. The second, an interparty race between the winning Democratic and Republican nominees, culminates in the fall's general election. Stages One through Five shown in Table 1.1 on page 15 make up the party nomination race, whereas Stage Six determines the winner of the general election and next occupant of the Oval Office.

Stage One: The Preliminary Period

Two or more years before a presidential election, potential presidential candidates begin raising the resources and political support necessary for a presidential race. The race for the presidency is extremely expensive. No candidate can attempt a serious presidential campaign effort without first establishing a broad base of funding. Even in advance of declaring for the presidency, candidates must set up exploratory committees to begin raising funds

Table 1.1 Overview of the Presidential Nomination and General Election

NOMINATION POLITICS

stage	what the candidate does	what the media does
1. **The Preliminary Period** **Begins 18–24 months before November general election**	All potential Democratic and Republican candidates form exploratory committees and begin fundraising and issue development. Candidates attempt to secure the support of important political leaders and groups, especially in key primary and caucus states.	The press plays the part of the "Great Mentioner," speculating as to which candidates will enter the race and which are the true "heavyweights."
2. **The Early Rounds** **January–February of election year**	Iowa's party caucuses and New Hampshire's primary are the first tests of voter response to the candidates; candidates begin advertising blitzes in states with upcoming primaries.	Media focus heavy attention on the candidates who do well or better than expected.
3. **The Long Haul** **March–May of election year**	Serious contenders emerge in both parties as more states hold primaries or caucuses to select delegates to the upcoming national conventions.	Media scrutinize all aspects of front-running candidates; attention turns away from weaker candidates further depleting their ability to raise money and support.
4. **The Final Races** **May–June of election year**	If the race within a party is close, the final states' primaries can be very decisive. Most often, races are decided before the final primaries, e.g., California.	Media begin comparisons of leading Democratic and Republican candidates and speculations on potential vice-presidential nominees.
5. **The National Party Conventions** **July of election year**	In separate national conventions, the Democratic and Republican delegates chosen in preceding state races meet to cast ballots for the party's presidential nominee. The chosen nominee's first duty at the convention is selecting a vice-presidential running mate to complete the party's ticket.	The conventions are media events carefully orchestrated to appeal to a national viewing audience. The media analysts scrutinize the acceptance speech, which usually contains some hints about the candidate's issues and positions as reflected in the party platform adopted at the convention.

ELECTION POLITICS

6. **The General Election Campaigns** **August through national election day, first Tuesday after the first Monday in November**	The two presidential tickets now tour the country in media-oriented stops. The official campaigns are paid by public funds. Both campaigns use "tracking polls" to adjust their message daily. Especially during the final days of the race, campaign resources are devoted to winning pivotal states in the Electoral College. Independent groups also sponsor ads, both negative and positive, on behalf of the candidates.	The media give scrutiny to each member of the ticket. More often than not, media coverage focuses on candidates' gaffes and errors, on polling results, and on other "horserace" aspects of the race rather than on the details of the candidates' policy promises. The media bore in on the candidates' performances in televised debates.

and identifying the key traits voters like. This fundraising is especially necessary for candidates who are not members of Congress
and who have no other source of funds to pay for their preliminary
campaign activities.

Early financial contributions are important for three reasons.
First, a candidate and his organization need a large base of financial support to adequately plan a nationwide campaign. Second,
early contributions that meet the eligibility requirements set by
federal law help the candidate to qualify for federal matching
funds. Federal matching funds, in effect, multiply the impact of
small money contributions during the nominating season. Third,
early contributions serve as evidence of a candidate's political viability. During the early stages of a presidential race, the press will
look at a candidate's financial backing as one indicator of a campaign's political viability.

During the preliminary period of a presidential race, would-be
candidates visit local party leaders and activists in an effort to gain
their support. Better-known presidential aspirants will speak at
fundraising dinners for state and congressional candidates to win
their gratitude. A candidate and his supporters usually establish a
political action committee (PAC) to pay for the candidate's expenses as he travels around the country to attend various political
functions. This presidential PAC will even make campaign donations to favored congressional candidates.

During this period, the press plays the role of what *Washington
Post* columnist David Broder once called "the Great Mentioner."
In deciding which candidates in a large field are prominently
mentioned in the news, the press virtually tells the public which
candidates merit serious consideration. Candidates who are not
mentioned prominently need a good showing in an early political
contest to break into the elite circle. Candidates will stack state
conventions with their supporters in an attempt to win otherwise
meaningless straw polls and influence press and public perceptions.

Candidates who are short on resources will concentrate their
efforts in the states with the initial nominating contests. A good
early showing in these early races will bring a candidate new publicity and financial contributions, resources that can be used in the
races that immediately follow. In recent years, the initial Iowa
caucuses and New Hampshire primaries have attracted media coverage grossly disproportionate to the small number of national
party convention delegates that are actually chosen in these states.

During much of the preliminary stages, potential contenders
will refrain from officially announcing their candidacies. As

Edward "Ted" Kennedy found out much to his chagrin in 1980, once a candidate formally declares for the race, he receives a much greater level of scrutiny from the press. As Kennedy moved to announce his candidacy, the press raised new questions of Kennedy's preparedness for the presidency and revived old questions regarding the Senator's actions at Chappaquiddick.

Stage Two: The Early Rounds

In the early stages of the race, especially in Iowa and New Hampshire, candidates engage in *retail politics*. They attend coffee-klatches and meet small groups of voters. A candidate may even stay in the homes of local supporters. Much of this highly personalized campaign activity is done in the absence of intensive media coverage.

Once the initial nominating contests approach, one-on-one retail politics is no longer enough. The emphasis of presidential campaigns is switched to the mass media, particularly to television. Those who can afford it will blitz strategic early caucus and primary states with television ads. Usually these are positive ads that seek to build a relatively unknown candidate's leadership image in the eyes of the voters. However, negative ads are also used to diminish a front-runner's political standing.

The early primaries serve to winnow the presidential field, setting the table for the nominating races that follow. Candidates who do poorly in these early races have trouble raising money and support and soon drop out of the presidential race. The early races can also establish the seriousness of a contender whom the press did not mention prominently in its early handicapping of the presidential field. In 1984 Colorado Senator Gary Hart catapulted into the Democratic race because of his strong showing in Iowa and his victory in New Hampshire.

"Winning" or "losing" early races sometimes has less to do with the actual vote cast than with the media's interpretations of the results. In 1972 Maine Senator Edmund Muskie won 46 percent of the vote in New Hampshire; South Dakotan George McGovern finished second with 37 percent. But according to the press's general interpretations at the time, Muskie as the front-runner "lost" New Hampshire as he had done less well than expected. In more recent years, the media has been wary of overinterpreting the results of any one particular nominating race. Nonetheless, the risks of overinterpretation remain as the media attempt to find the story in a day's political events.

Stage Three: The Long Haul

Jimmy Carter used the Iowa caucuses and the New Hampshire primary as the path to the presidency. Yet, an early victory provides no guarantee that a candidate will go on to win the party's nomination. In 1984 former Vice-President Walter Mondale came back to win the Democratic nomination despite Gary Hart's victory in New Hampshire. In 1988 the winners of the Democratic and Republican caucuses in Iowa, respectively, were Richard Gephardt and Robert Dole. Neither went on to win his party's presidential nomination.

An early victory is not enough in a race of fifty or so primaries and caucuses. A candidate must demonstrate staying power. Here is where a candidate's fundraising and organizational work during the preliminary stages of the presidential race can prove to be an important advantage. The *frontloading* of the system, where more and more states have scheduled primaries and caucuses in the early part of the nominating year, has placed an additional premium on campaign resources and organization. In 1984 Mondale's superior financial base and ties to state and local party leaders allowed him to eventually put down the Hart brushfire after New Hampshire. Hart, in contrast, lacked the money and staff to campaign effectively in a large number of states at the same time. Hart further suffered when, as the new front-runner, the press began to subject his candidacy to more critical scrutiny.

The long haul can at times be a political slugfest. Now that the field has been narrowed, candidates will often resort to attack advertising to undermine the support of a rival.

Stage Four: The Final Races

If the race is close, the battle for the nomination can come down to final primaries. In 1964 Barry Goldwater may have clinched the Republican nomination with his closing primary victory over Nelson Rockefeller in California.

In recent years, however, the final state races have not always been that decisive to the nomination. Instead, the more usual pattern is for one candidate to build a clear lead with delegates won in the early and mid-primary season states. The leading candidate then wins enough delegates in the nominating season's closing contests to hold on to the nomination.

As a result, California and other states that traditionally mark the close of the primary season do not seem to possess the importance they once did. There has been some talk in California of moving its primary to an earlier time in the year in order for the state to regain some of its lost influence in presidential selection.

Stage Five: The National Party Conventions

The role of national party conventions has changed greatly over time. Earlier in the century, party conventions acted as independent vehicles at which party leaders gathered to choose a presidential nominee. Today, however, the selection of a presidential nominee by party elites would be considered an undermining of democracy, a devaluation of the people's ballots cast in the caucuses and primaries. The decline of party organizations and the reform of presidential selection rules further ensure that national party conventions can no longer play the roles they once did.[4] Instead, contemporary national party conventions tend to reflect and reaffirm the choice made by voters during the nominating season.

The national conventions also give some hints as to the political orientations and style of a candidate and his supporters. Will the new nominee compromise on certain policy planks in an effort to promote unity? Or will the winning candidate and his supporters insist on maintaining their ideological purity? The nominee's televised acceptance speech also reveals his action orientations and the themes he will repeat throughout the fall campaign.

The selection of the vice-presidential nominee is almost always made by the party's presidential nominee. Presidential candidates have usually looked for running mates who can balance or otherwise add politically to the ticket. In 1988, Michael Dukakis chose Texan Lloyd Bentsen as his running mate with the hope that he could pull Texas into the Democratic column. George Bush chose Dan Quayle, whose youth and vote-winning ability among women were seen as political assets.

The function of national party conventions has clearly been transformed over time. While great fights can still take place between various party factions at a convention, the national convention has increasingly become a televised spectacle that provides a candidate's media handlers one more opportunity to craft a carefully sculpted message for the viewing public. In some recent conventions, the presidential candidate has been introduced by a film, a retrospective piece designed for the viewing audience at home, not the delegates on the convention floor.

An incumbent President likely will gain renomination without being scarred by brutal inner-party battles. This, however, is not always the case. Jimmy Carter earned renomination in 1980 only after putting down a challenge by liberal forces committed to Ted Kennedy, an insurgency that lasted through the Democratic convention.

Stage Six: The General Election Campaign

Traditionally, candidates pause after the summer conventions and recoup after the exhaustion of the nominating race. Nowadays, however, the fall campaign begins well in advance of its traditional Labor Day kickoff. Political strategists have come to recognize the potential importance of establishing and reinforcing campaign themes during this summer lull period. It was during this period that George Bush continued to hit at the symbolic themes that turned around the 1988 election.

The fall campaign is increasingly geared to television. Often campaign stops do little more than serve as backdrops for *free media* televised messages—news clips that will reach the viewing audience at home. Predictably, the candidate who trails in the polls will challenge an opponent to a series of televised debates, hoping that citizens will change their voting intentions after having viewed the candidates in the debate. The leading candidate, in contrast, will seek to limit the number of debates and structure his format to minimize the chance of making a politically damaging gaffe or error. Both major party candidates usually declare their willingness to debate; but the debates are not easily arranged because each camp's advisers seek to negotiate debate terms that will be to their candidate's advantage.

The fall campaign schedule is also dictated to some extent by the unique demands of the Electoral College. Largely, the Electoral College is an antiquated institution. Technically, Americans do not vote directly for their President; instead they vote for electors who meet in December to choose the President. But electors do not act as an independent voice in the presidential selection as the founding fathers had anticipated. Except for the problem caused by an occasional faithless elector, the Electoral College merely confirms the popular vote cast in each state in November. It is the November election that decides who wins.

Hence, political campaigns gear their schedules to producing the majority of Electoral College votes required to win the presidency. They will use tracking polls to find out how they are doing in each stage and, especially in the closing days of the campaign, will concentrate their efforts in those winnable states whose votes are needed to produce an Electoral College majority. It is important for a presidential candidate to win middle-sized and large states, even if such states are carried by very small numbers. Under the Electoral College's *unit rule,* the entire electoral vote of a state goes to whichever candidate gets the popular vote plurality in that state.

Presidential campaigns are a mix of paid and free media. Despite the new prominence of negative advertising, presidential campaigning is not predominantly negative. Candidates need to establish both their personal warmth and their presidential stature in the eyes of the public. Candidates also will stress those positive images that can help compensate for weaknesses in their records and thereby inoculate themselves against an opponent's likely attacks. Presidential campaigns almost always finish with a positive, upbeat message.

THE CHANGED SETTING OF PRESIDENTIAL ELECTIONS

Do issues or images win presidential elections? This book's argument is quite simple: In the race for the presidency issues count!

The popular stereotype of presidential elections sees imagemaking and television as the keys to winning office. New cadres of public relations, fundraising, and advertising personnel have come to occupy prominent positions in the modern presidential campaign. Largely, public opinion pollsters, media consultants, computerization experts, direct-mail specialists, and other practitioners of these new campaign technologies have displaced an older generation of party politicians from positions of authority in campaign hierarchies.

Campaign consultants study voter demographics to selectively market a candidate to the different segments of the electorate. Public opinion experts take daily soundings called *tracking polls* to monitor a campaign's progress. A candidate who is not doing well in the polls can manufacture new spot advertisements and buy additional blocks of air time virtually overnight. Such flexibility gives a candidate the ability to deal quickly with an unexpected turn of events or to respond immediately to charges that are made by an opponent.

The cost of campaigning in the television age is expensive. The public funding of presidential elections has ameliorated but not eliminated the problems posed by the quest for money in the presidential race. During the primary season, when various candidates compete to gain their party's presidential nomination, campaigns are only partially publicly funded. Each candidate still must be able to raise sufficient sums of money to qualify for federal matching funds. The more money a candidate raises, the more federal funds he receives, and the more he has to spend. Taxpayer money pays the full costs of the official campaigns only after the two major parties have selected their presidential nominees.

But even this brief description understates the role played by money in the presidential election. During both the primary and general election campaigns, independent political action committees (PACs) and various state and local party committees raise and spend money beyond the ceilings imposed on the official campaign. Independent spending can be substantial. According to one estimate, independent committees spent $17.5 million in 1984; $16.3 million or 93.4 percent of this total went to benefit Republican candidates.[1] The Democrats, in contrast, enjoyed a large edge in spending by organized labor.

As we shall see in this chapter, other trends in recent years, not only the maturation of television and the rise of a professional consultant industry, have changed the nature of the presidential race. The decline of political parties, the rise of voter independence, and changes in party nominating and finance reform rules have all acted to increase the potential influence of both issues and images in presidential elections.

Most significant was the decline of partisanship. An American electorate more independent of party affiliation could be moved by issues or images. Which would it be? Some political scientists observed the increasing power of issues in presidential elections. Yet others disputed the apparent rise of issue voting. They see images and partisanship as more important influences on voting behavior.

CAMPAIGNING IN A TELEVISION AGE

According to popular wisdom, professional image merchants package candidates who are then sold to the public in thirty- and sixty-second "spot ads," much as a laundry soap or sports car is marketed. Television is a visual media that encourages viewers to judge candidates on the basis of their personal image. Consequently, media consultants advise candidates on what to say and how to behave on live television. Speech coaches work to make a candidate's speech pacing and hand gestures more effective. They even advise prospective presidents on how to dress for the television camera; the dark-blue suit and red tie have become the uniform of the presidential candidate campaigning in the media age.

According to this view, issues play only a secondary, relatively minor role in presidential elections. Candidates avoid many issues, perhaps the most important issues of the day, as they have no easy, winning answers. Candidates avoid taking clear stands on such issues as the economy and the budget, as they find it difficult to clearly communicate an effective and coherent strategy in policy areas so complex. Candidates similarly fear taking a strong stand on an issue when they fear doing so will offend an important block of voters.

As a consequence, according to many critics, the presidential campaign is too often reduced to a battle of "sound bites" in which candidates attempt to articulate an attractive phrase that the media will pick up for its evening newscasts and the next morning's papers. Even in candidate debates and forums, candidates avoid the serious discussion of many issues and instead search for the witticism that shapes the next day's news coverage. Slogans and sound bites seldom present voters with well-thought-out and workable solutions to difficult national problems.

The 1988 race for the presidency, perhaps more so than any other contemporary presidential election, has been reviled as a contest in which personal images and the influence of professional campaign handlers determined the outcome. Well into the presidential race, George Bush, the incumbent Vice-President, trailed Michael Dukakis, Governor of Massachusetts, by 17 points in the polls. Bush campaign advisers—campaign manager Lee Atwater, media adviser Roger Ailes, pollster Bob Teeter, chief of staff Craig Fuller, and long-time friend Nicholas Brady—advised the Vice-President to get more aggressive. They and other Republican consultants tested potential campaign themes and issues before focus groups of "Reagan Democrats"—those swing voters whose support Bush would have to gain to win the election. Bush eventually won the presidency only by seizing the powerful media visages of the escaped convict Willie Horton, the Pledge of Allegiance, pollution in Boston Harbor, and a Clint Eastwood-type vow of "Read my lips; no new taxes!"

Negative advertising was the dominant hallmark of the 1988 race. The Bush campaign charged Dukakis with having run a "revolving door" prison program as governor. An advertisement sponsored by an independent PAC went even further by showing the picture of one criminal, Willie Horton, a black man, and detailing the heinous crimes that Horton committed when he had escaped while on furlough. The Bush campaign further denied Dukakis's claim to having led an economic revival in the "Massachusetts miracle"; instead, they portrayed the state under Dukakis's leadership as "Taxachusetts." They also charged Dukakis with being soft on national defense and being an incompetent manager who presided over the pollution of Boston Harbor.

Dukakis eventually, and belatedly, responded with negative ads of his own. Each campaign accused the other of lying. Neither candidate discussed important issues of the day in depth. Neither laid out a detailed strategy for dealing with such important problems as the nation's escalating budgetary deficit, declining productivity, the savings and loan failures, or the need to forge a new diplomatic and military strategy in the wake of the monumental changes taking place in the Soviet Union and the Eastern bloc.

Instead of outlining detailed positions on issues, a well-organized presidential effort, like Bush's 1988 campaign, selects a "theme of the day" and a "theme of the week" and coordinates all public appearances and statements to maximize the effective presentation of a predetermined candidate image. Bush's campaign had such coordination; Dukakis's did not. A candidate seeking to impress farmers, for instance, would stage a visit to a family farm to share a meal with the family and bale some hay. Such an event provides the wonderful pictures or visuals that constitute a media opportunity. If the candidate and his advisers closely guard what they say and speak of nothing other than the farm problem, the media will have little alternative but to cover the campaign pseudo-event on its evening news broadcasts. The campaign has succeeded in portraying its candidate as the champion of the family farmer. But little substance has been revealed as to how the candidate hopes to resolve farm problems.

The techniques of the modern media campaign have become increasingly sophisticated. No longer does a campaign seek to present a single candidate image to the entire American public. Instead, different candidate images are marketed to different segments of the American polity. A candidate's campaign advisers, for instance, may choose to emphasize different themes and concerns when seeking the support of Hispanic voters as opposed to Anglo voters. Such concerns can be marketed through television commercials aired only in predominantly Hispanic communities.

More specialized messages are placed on Spanish-speaking television and radio and in Spanish-language newspapers. A sophisticated campaign will also realize that Mexican-Americans,
Cuban-Americans, and Americans of Puerto Rican ancestry all
have somewhat different opinions and concerns. The sophisticated
campaign will use polling to uncover these concerns and then target different messages to the different audiences.

The Image Merchants: Just How Powerful?

If the public's voting intentions in presidential elections are as
malleable as the description above implies, then American democracy is in trouble. Elections are the most significant device through
which citizens articulate their concerns and hold government accountable. If campaigns offer citizens little more than concocted
media images, then voters are given no meaningful choice at the
polls. Such manipulated appeals also border on demagoguery and
often have little relevance to the task of governing the nation.

Journalists who cover the presidential race often inadvertently
contribute to the perception that presidential elections are determined by behind-the-scenes strategizing and brilliant campaign
moves. Formerly, these stories told of the machinations of the old-
party professionals. Now they more often than not describe the sophisticated wizardry of the new image merchants.

To a great extent this tradition of reporting has its roots in the
works of Theodore White whose landmark book, *The Making of the
President 1960,* captured the drive, energy, and tactical moves of
John Kennedy and his staff as his campaign maneuvered to victory in the spring primaries, the national party convention, and
the fall election.[2] White wrote similar epics that detailed the strategic elements of the 1964 and 1968 contests. His style of reporting
was quickly emulated by other writers.

Efforts to capture and expose the inner workings of the modern political campaign have not been confined to the written word.
Television and the movies, too, have tried to reveal the nature of
modern campaigning.

There is perhaps no more searing indictment of the conduct of
contemporary American elections than Jeremy Larner's 1972
movie *The Candidate.* Robert Redford plays a young idealist, the
public interest advocate J. J. McKay, who is recruited by a professional campaign consultant to run for the United States Senate.
The unnamed state is clearly California. In his search for victory
McKay loses both his ideals and his morality. Following the advice

of his campaign consultants, he retreats from the clear stands on issues he took earlier in the campaign. His commercials are all personal-image puffery. After he wins, he asks his campaign manager, "What do we do now?" McKay can no longer act without a script.

The movie is at its best in portraying the techniques of modern campaigning and the heightened role played by the new campaign consultants. A media consultant tests possible advertisements and shows McKay which spot ad ideas effectively come across on the tube. On the command of his advisers, McKay switches neckties before participating in a televised debate. In his public appearances, he is reduced to uttering stock phrases of a set campaign speech. His campaign uses tracking polls to gauge its daily progress. When McKay expresses his resentment at being yoked back on too many issues, his campaign manager shows him the improvement in his poll ratings as evidence that their present strategy is working.

The campaign is geared to television. McKay's campaign handlers change the candidate's schedule at the last minute to take advantage of new media opportunities. McKay flies to the scene of a forest fire to use the dramatic backdrop for an attack on his opponent's record on watershed protection. However, the incumbent Senator, Crocker Jarmin, turns the tables on McKay when he, too, flies to the scene of the fire to announce the Jarmin Watershed Protection Bill. As chair of a key congressional committee, Jarmin says that he can guarantee speedy passage of the legislation. Jarmin demonstrates the power of incumbency; McKay as the challenger can only harp and criticize. Whether the bill will actually accomplish much, which seems unlikely given Jarmin's interest-group ties and past record in the environmental protection arena, matters little in the election. Jarmin can win votes merely by taking a popular position on an issue and by claiming credit for having authored a new bill.[3]

The movie also shows the torture-trail aspects of electioneering in major state and national races. In what are essentially *tarmac campaigns,* candidates make brief speeches at airports as they attempt to hit as many media markets as possible in a single day. A candidate suffers not only from exhaustion but also from the personal slings and insults from citizens and commentators alike. The demands and rigors of public life can draw a candidate away from family. Especially when it comes to presidential campaigns that often begin in earnest two or more years before the actual election, the rigors of the campaign trail can serve to weed out good candidates. In 1976 Walter Mondale dropped out of the presidential race as he could no longer tolerate a life of rubber-chicken dinners and empty hotel rooms away from his home and the people he loved. New York Governor Mario Cuomo may have chosen to forego the 1988 presidential race for similar reasons.

For all its accuracy in describing the conduct of modern elections, *The Candidate* exaggerates the power held by the new campaign elite. On one end of the spectrum are candidates so spineless they will alter their beliefs in response to the shifting winds of public opinion. At the other extreme are zealots who do not compromise, who act from a set of uncompromising issue beliefs. Politicians are persons of issue conviction to a greater degree than we often suspect. Most politicians probably fit somewhere between the extremes. Studies of Congress, for instance, have reported the rise of a new breed of issue-oriented politician, a politician who comes to Congress anxious to make his or her mark on a policy area of importance.[4]

The Candidate presents an overly generous portrait of the power of media consultants in the modern campaign. Media consultants play an important role in political campaigns, but they are not all-powerful. Media consultants can only control or manipulate a candidate who is willing to be manipulated. A candidate listens to consultants where their expertise is of value; but ultimately it is the candidate, not the handlers, who decides what happens in a campaign. While it is true that it is a poor candidate who attempts to be his own campaign manager, it is still the candidate who hires and fires his top campaign staff and sets the parameters that delimit their action. A candidate may easily defer to advice on how to dress for a televised debate. Candidates will not so easily give in to requests that they alter entrenched patterns of behavior or deeply held positions on issues.

The history of presidential elections is filled with candidates who ignored the advice of their consultants. In 1984 Walter Mondale refused to restyle his hair in a way that his handlers thought would enhance his appeal to younger voters. Similarly, in a televised debate during the 1988 Democratic primaries, Democrat Paul Simon refused to go along with his handler's instructions that he suddenly remove his fabled bowtie and clip on a necktie to illustrate how easily his opponent, Richard Gephardt, had changed his position on the issues.[5] Throughout the 1988 election Michael Dukakis resisted his consultant's advice on what to say and how to say it.[6] The Willie Horton ad had hurt Dukakis's political standing badly. Yet Dukakis resisted his handler's advice that he respond by personalizing the crime issue. Dukakis would not exploit his family's personal tragedies. Only late in the campaign, with his presidential effort in dire straits, did Dukakis reluctantly tell the nation how his father had been robbed at gunpoint and how his brother had been killed by a hit-and-run driver.[7]

The point of *The Candidate* most worth debating, however, is its portrayal of the American election process as devoid of issue content. McKay runs on the vacuous slogan, "McKay. The Better Way." He wins on the basis of his dynamic image and good looks. The film has found an easy Hollywood theme: American democracy does not work. Elections have been stolen by professional image merchants and consultants. And the voters fail to fulfill their obligations as democratic citizens.

The only problem with the film's point of view is that it is not totally true. In presidential elections, at least, issues play a larger role in the campaign and in voters' decisions than the portrayal in *The Candidate* would have us believe.[8]

Personal imagemaking, of course, is a very important part of presidential elections. But issues, too, have played an important role in modern presidential elections. New nominating reforms have allowed issue activists to influence the process of presidential selection. When political parties offer more issue-oriented or ideologically disposed candidates, the American voter responds in kind.

Campaign finance reform, too, has made it easier for more ideologically disposed candidates to enter the presidential race. In 1988 the short-lived Republican presidential efforts by conservatives New York Congressman Jack Kemp, Delaware Governor Pierre DuPont, and Christian talk-show host Pat Robertson were all facilitated by public funding.

In addition, numerous political science studies have pointed to the rise of a more independent American voter who is capable of taking issues and performance evaluations into account when going to the polls. Televised campaign commercials that seek solely to define a presidential candidate's personal qualities do not effectively appeal to the new independents. The most persuasive advertising in recent presidential elections has fused issues and images, using powerful symbols to give voters enough information to differentiate between the general policy directions of the major candidates.

Even in 1988—the year of the Willie Horton ads and George Bush's vow on the Pledge of Allegiance—much of the campaign advertising and rhetoric succeeded in distinguishing between the

Table 2.1   Party Identification, 1952–1988 (percent)

	1952	1956	1960	1964	1968	1972	1976	1980	1984	1988
Democrats	47.2	43.6	45.3	51.7	45.4	40.4	39.7	40.8	37.0	35.2
Independents	22.6	23.4	22.8	22.8	29.1	34.7	36.1	34.5	34.2	35.7
Republicans	27.2	29.1	29.4	24.5	24.2	23.4	23.2	22.4	27.1	27.5
Apoliticals	3.1	3.8	2.5	0.9	1.4	1.4	0.9	2.2	1.7	1.6
Democratic plurality	20.0	14.5	15.9	27.2	21.2	17.0	16.5	18.4	9.9	7.7
Democrats plus										
Democratic leaners	56.8	49.9	51.6	61.0	55.2	51.5	51.5	52.3	47.8	47.0
Pure Independents	5.8	8.8	9.8	7.8	10.5	13.1	14.6	12.9	11.0	10.6
Republicans plus										
Republican leaners	34.3	37.4	36.1	30.2	32.9	33.9	32.9	32.6	39.5	40.8
Apoliticals	3.1	3.8	2.5	0.9	1.4	1.4	0.9	2.2	1.7	1.6
Democratic plurality	22.5	12.5	15.5	31.1	22.3	17.6	18.6	19.7	8.3	6.2

Source: Martin P. Wattenberg, *The Decline of American Political Parties, 1952–1988* (Cambridge, Mass.: Harvard Press, 1990), p. 140.

different value orientations and policy dispositions of the Republican and Democratic nominees.[9] As Jean Bethke Elshtain observes:

> Issues are what actually take root as preoccupations and themes. Thus, whether the symbolic meaning of the Pledge of Allegiance *is* an issue becomes an issue; the outcome of the 1988 election turned partly on who had best made his case. Voters and candidates are co-constructors of issues. Candidates speak and act in response to their perceptions of the concerns of the electorate.[10]

The presidential landscape has changed. Issues count.

TRENDS IN PARTISANSHIP

Eroding Partisanship

One of the clearest trends in American politics in recent years has been the rise of voter independence. The surveys of the National Election Studies taken since the 1950s reveal the declining hold of political parties on the American electorate, although the decline has leveled off in recent years (see Table 2.1). In 1988 for the first time the number of self-identified independents exceeded the number of self-identified Democrats.

A second trend apparent in Table 2.1 is the narrowing of the Democratic partisan advantage over the Republicans. Since the New Deal of the 1930s, the Democrats have been the majority party. But by the 1980s, fewer voters saw the relevance of political parties formed along the cleavage lines of the New Deal era. Furthermore, the slippage in Republican identification, apparent in the 1960s and 1970s, was reversed by the Reagan years. The Democratic advantage of twenty or so points in party identification in 1952 was reduced to just six or seven points by 1988.

The Democratic advantage virtually disappears when differential voter turnout rates are considered. As a whole, Republican voters tend to be better educated, of higher income, and nonminority status—factors all associated in the United States with higher rates of voting.[11] Because of the greater tendency of self-identified Republicans to go to the polls, the Democrats enjoyed only a very narrow 47.2-to-46.1 percent edge in partisan identification among persons who said that they voted in 1988.[12]

Eroding partisanship is also apparent in the increased number of self-identified partisans who cast their votes as if they were "behavioral independents."[13] *Switchers* vote for the presidential candidate of one political party in one election and the candidate of another party in the next election. *Ticket splitters* fail to cast a straight party ballot in a single election; instead they vote for candidates of different parties for different offices (see Figure 2.1).

Who are these ticket splitters, these new independents? According to Walter DeVries and V. Lance Tarrance, the ticket splitter tends to be better educated, professional, suburban, and of high or middle income. The ticket splitter is also inclined to be both politically active and an avid consumer of the mass media, a person who decides how to vote on the basis of what she has learned about the candidates in an election.[14]

The ticket splitter described by DeVries and Tarrance is a far cry from the self-identified independent observed in the classic voting study *The American Voter*. Using survey data from the 1950s, *The American Voter* found voters who identified themselves as independent seemingly because they did not care enough to follow political campaigns or identify with a party.[15] The increased number of ticket splitters, in contrast, represents a new force in American politics, the rise of a more informed and aware independent voter.

Causes of the New Independence

The move away from political parties in this country has been of long duration. As Walter Dean Burnham has observed, the "onward march of party decomposition" has been happening since the turn of the century. It was interrupted briefly during the

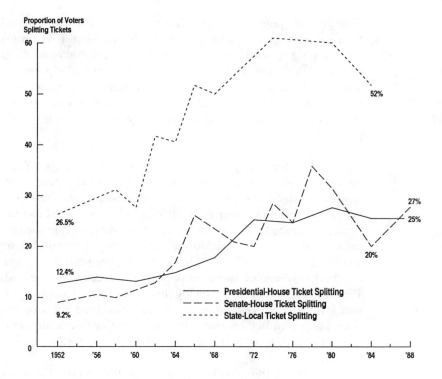

Proportion of Voters Splitting Tickets

Figure 2.1   Ticket splitting, 1952–1988
Source: Michael M. Gant and Norman R. Luttbeg, *American Electoral Behavior* (Itasca, Ill.: F. E. Peacock, 1991), p. 37; Martin P. Wattenberg, *The Decline of American Political Parties, 1952–1988* (Cambridge, Mass.: Harvard Press, 1990), p. 97.

New Deal when the Democratic party became a Depression-era advocate of Americans in need. According to Burnham, voters have tended to see parties as increasingly irrelevant.[16]

What are the reasons that underlie the more recent decline of parties and rise of the new independence? They can be summarized as follows:

Education.   In part, voters are better educated today; they can decide how to vote without depending on a party label for guidance. Yet, according to Martin Wattenberg, the rise in education alone does not explain the new independence. Independence has increased even among voters of low education.[17]

The Pervasiveness of Television.   The rise of television also helps to explain the new voter independence. Americans report that they get most of their political information from television. In a presidential race, even viewers who do not watch television news programs will see paid spot ads or hear references to political candidates on celebrity talk shows. Television viewers cannot help but learn something about the candidates. Inundated with political messages from television and other media, citizens fashion their own views regarding issues and candidates without having to rely on party labels.

Candidate-Centered Campaigns and Changing Media Coverage. The way the mass media covers elections also reinforces the public's perception of the decreasing relevance of political parties. Newspapers, magazines, and television have all adapted to the rise of candidate-centered campaigns. Election stories have increasingly focused on the candidate, to the exclusion of mentioning partisan philosophy or even political party ties. Martin Wattenberg has examined the electoral coverage of two newspapers (the *Chicago Tribune* and the *Washington Post*) and three weekly news magazines (*Newsweek, Time,* and *U.S. News and World Report*). His analysis clearly documents the decreasing number of times that presidential candidates were in some way linked to their political parties in news stories (see Figure 2.2).[18]

Reforms in the presidential selection process have also helped yield the perception that parties are irrelevant. The nominating rules were changed after 1968 to create a more open and democratic presidential selection process. But those changes also transformed the nature of political parties in a presidential year. Candidate-centered organizations have displaced political parties as the most important vehicles in presidential elections. The candidate who wins the nomination dictates the party platform and the fall campaign themes. The nominee's loyal advisers—not senior party officials—determine general election strategy. In a presidential year, the political party becomes little more than an extension of the candidate-centered campaign.

Nominating and Finance Reform. Post-Watergate changes in campaign finance rules have also decreased the importance of political party organizations in presidential elections. As a result of public funding, presidential candidates are now less dependent than ever on a party's fundraising capacity. Even during the primaries, partial public funding has made it easier for candidates to raise the money without having to rely on ties to party leaders and fundraisers. Finance reform helped make it possible for party outsid-

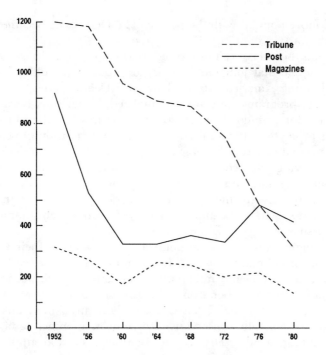

Figure 2.2   The role of the media: Number of substantive linkages between parties and candidates in news stories, 1952–1980

Source: Martin P. Wattenberg, *The Decline of American Political Parties, 1952–1988* (Cambridge, Mass.: Harvard Press, 1990), p. 97.

ers such as Jimmy Carter and Gary Hart to become incipient presidential candidates while at the same time attacking the insularity of established party elites.

The Fading Relevance of the New Deal Party Alignment.   As we have seen, the basic divisions between the Democratic and Republican parties were forged during the New Deal. The Democrats stood for a more activist approach to government. The Democrats sought to defend labor's right to organize. The Democrats also sought to smooth out the ups and downs of economic cycles and provide health and income protection to the aged, the infirm, and others in need. The Democrats sought to ensure a fairer distribution of America's industrial wealth. The Republicans, in contrast, stood for a less interventionist, more laissez-faire approach to government. Given the vast social insecurity that existed in the absence of government social programs, it was the Democratic approach that proved more popular with the people. The Democrats became the majority party.

But as the old issues were solved, new issues arose. In the post-industrial age that followed, new issues crosscut the older cleavages, dividing Americans from their New Deal loyalties.[19] As the New Deal programs were institutionalized, Americans began to take them for granted. Further, Americans expressed their unwillingness to see their taxes raised to pay for the extension of benefit programs to a new set of recipients, especially to beneficiaries seen as undeserving. New concerns for the cost and effectiveness of government programs and rising inflation competed with the older preoccupations with unemployment and job creation. At times, social issues such as law and order proved more salient than economic issues.

For many Americans, no political party captures their views across the broad range of issues. Large numbers of Americans, for instance, find the Democratic party acceptable on basic economic protections, but too liberal on welfarism and affirmative action, and too soft on national defense. Similarly, many Americans approve of the generally conservative Republican approach to taxing and spending; yet they also see the Republicans as too supportive of the rich, too conservative on personal morality issues, too willing to cut the safety net of programs provided to people in need, and too unwilling to enforce strong regulations to protect the environment.[20] For these voters, neither of the parties of the New Deal party alignment represents a meaningful choice. These are the new independents who vote in a presidential race in response to particular candidate, issue, and performance evaluations.

Generational Replacement. Younger citizens are among the most independent in the nation. They are, however, the age group least likely to vote. In part, younger citizens have yet to build up the habit of voting, a habit that reinforces party identification. The electorate as a whole becomes more independent as the older generation of partisans dies off and is replaced by a new generation of more independent voters.

According to Paul Allen Beck, today's younger voters have not been well-socialized in the affiliations of the New Deal era. For the nation's senior citizens—voters who lived through the New Deal era—the choice between Democrats and Republicans is meaningful. Their children, in turn, were socialized across the dinner table about the virtues of one political party over another. They learned from their parents just who were the good guys and bad guys of

American electoral politics. Today's younger voters, in contrast, have not been taught with equal passion the importance of partisanship. Unless a partisan realignment occurs that will raise the salience of new issues and generate a new and meaningful sense of partisanship, younger voters are likely to continue to be independent.[21]

Yet, as Wattenberg warns, the generational theory of voter *dealignment* (the move away from parties) should not be overstated. The decline of partisan attachments is evident among voting groups of all ages.[22]

Consequences of the New Independence

The rise of voter independence has led to a two-tier system of American elections—a system of split results where the outcome of presidential races is different from the outcome of congressional races (see Figure 2.3).[23]

In presidential races citizens are able to make up their own minds. Salient issues of the day and voter evaluations of candidates and their past performance records are likely to dominate presidential races.

In contrast, elections for the U.S. House of Representatives and other lower visibility offices are less likely to turn on issue-oriented and broad-based performance evaluations. In these latter races, voters know relatively little about the candidates and issues involved. Hence, name recognition, constituency service, and voter partisanship prove more influential on the voting decision. Unless a member of Congress makes a grievous error that converts a low-visibility race into a high-visibility one, an incumbent enjoys considerable reelection advantages. These include name recognition, credit for having performed effective casework and constituent service, the ability to raise substantial financial contributions from individuals and PACs that want access to the member, the ability to convert these donations into paid commercials, the favorable drawing of district lines as a result of reapportionment, and the franking privilege that allows for free mass mailings to district residents for "official business." It is little wonder that approximately 95 percent of House incumbents who choose to stand for reelection are successful.

In presidential contests, Republicans have seized upon visible issues—the social issue in 1968 and 1972, and the issues of big government and tax relief in the 1980s—to win five of the six presidential elections from 1968 to 1988. Yet, during the same time

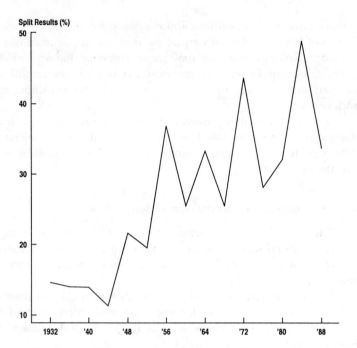

Figure 2.3   District-level split results of House and presidential
elections, 1932–1988

Source: Gary C. Jacobson, *The Electoral Origins of Divided Government* (Boulder,
Colo.: Westview Press, 1990), p. 11.

period, Democrats have used the advantages afforded by incumbency and partisanship to maintain solid control of the House of Representatives.

In the Senate, the results are more mixed. Senate races are more visible than House races. Being statewide, Senate districts are more heterogeneous; district boundaries cannot be sculptured or gerrymandered during reapportionment to provide a safe district for an incumbent's reelection. Yet, incumbent Senators still possess the advantages of name recognition, the credit for having performed casework and constituency service, and greater access to campaign funds. As a result, the fight for control in the Senate has been more competitive. In 1980 elections the Republicans regained control of the Senate for the first time since 1953. In recent years neither political party has been able to establish dominant control over the Senate.

The advantages of incumbency and partisanship have helped to separate congressional elections from the presidential race. Yet, despite these buffers, congressional elections have not been insulated totally from mood swings resulting from citizens' evaluations of the nation's economic performance. Economic conditions do influence the exact balance of seats in any election.[24]

The result of the separation of presidential from House elections is divided government. Republicans have controlled the presidency, but they have failed to control the Congress. The result is often deadlock and frustration.[25] Voter confidence in government continues to fall as partisan sniping emerges when divided government proves unable to undertake a clear and consistent course of programmatic action.

The rise of voter independence has also changed the conduct of elections. Each campaign must set out ad hoc to build a candidate's ties to voters. Candidates no longer depend on partisanship for votes. In fact, presidential candidates rarely even mention their partisan affiliations in their advertisements. Instead, each candidate's organization seeks to establish the personal appeal of a candidate—his warmth, sincerity, integrity, and leadership capacity—with voters. When deemed necessary, campaign managers have also resorted to negative advertising to win votes. In presidential races, issue-based images—both positive and negative—have proved effective in winning the votes of the new independents.

Despite the growth in independence, partisanship is not dead. Large numbers of voters still cast their ballots for the candidate of their traditional party. Partisanship also continues to influence how Americans perceive candidates and issues. Partisanship is still an important influence on the voting decision; but it is much less an influential factor in presidential races now than it was in the 1940s and 1950s.

THE REFORMED PRESIDENTIAL NOMINATING PROCESS

Nominating Reform and the Primaries

The shape of the presidential nominating process was changed forever as a result of the turbulence that surrounded the 1968 Democratic convention. In 1968 a badly divided Democratic party gave its presidential nomination to Hubert Humphrey. Humphrey had not won a single primary that year; he had not even entered the primaries. The vast majority of Democratic convention delegates were not chosen by voters in primaries, but by party leaders in closed party meetings or caucuses. As a prominent Democrat of long standing and as Lyndon Johnson's loyal Vice-President, Humphrey was able to use his ties to the Democratic party establishment to win the nomination.

Antiwar Democrats claimed that the presidential selection system was undemocratic and unfair. The Democratic national convention turned into a riot as police and antiwar activists clashed in the streets of Chicago and angry exchanges marred the convention's proceedings. All the ill events were duly recorded on television. Badly divided, the Democrats went down to a narrow defeat in 1968. The Republican Richard Nixon became President.

Reforms were needed to bring the Democratic party together in order to avoid a repeat disastrous performance in the next election. Indeed, it was widely recognized that the existing procedures for nominating the President were undemocratic and in need of change.

Four years previously, party rule changes had involved civil rights. At the party's 1964 convention, a slate from the Mississippi Freedom Democratic Party challenged the seating of the all-white regular Mississippi delegation. In a compromise, the convention voted to seat two of the Freedom Democrats and treat the rest as "honored guests." The convention also passed resolutions banning discrimination in the delegate selection process and asserting the party's right to require compliance. The national party had begun to expand its control over the delegate selection process, control that it would assert more strongly after the events of 1968.[26]

The initial post-1968 Democratic party rules changes were popularly referred to as the McGovern-Fraser reforms, after South Dakota Senator George McGovern and Minnesota Congressman Donald Fraser, who co-chaired the party's commission on reform. In succeeding years, other party commissions would add to and refine the basic rules adopted under McGovern-Fraser.

The McGovern-Fraser reforms emphasized the values of timeliness, openness, and demographic representativeness. Under the old delegate selection system, state and local party leaders often chose national convention delegates in caucuses and conventions that barred the participation of all but a few loyal party regulars. In some states, these delegate selection meetings took place well in advance of the presidential calendar year, before the major contenders for the nomination were known.

The new rules required that the public be given adequate advance notice of any meetings involved in delegate selection and that the process of delegate selection take place in the same calendar year as the presidential convention. All persons who declared themselves to be Democrats were entitled to participate in these meetings.

The new rules also required that delegates to the national convention be picked in such a way as to ensure the fair representation of minorities, women, and youth. These were the constituencies that had been severely underrepresented in past party conventions dominated by elderly, white, male party leaders. The rule changes here were attacked for constituting population quotas. They were later modified by the Mikulski Commission, which set out strict requirements for affirmative action but explicitly barred the use of quotas. Eventually, the Democrats did adopt one quota. The Winograd Commission mandated the equal division of convention delegates by gender for 1980.

States could meet the party's various new delegate selection rules by reforming their caucus and convention processes or by switching to a primary in which all Democrats could vote. As Table 2.2 shows, states immediately began to switch to primaries. Beginning in 1972, the majority of convention delegates in both parties were chosen in primaries. No longer could a candidate win a first-ballot convention victory, as Humphrey had in 1968, without entering and winning state primaries. Starting with the 1972 election, the race for the presidency would be more open to outsiders.

As a result of the McGovern-Fraser rule changes, the number of Democratic office-holders who attended the party's national conventions dropped sharply. Elected officials represent important constituencies. Yet, leaders who supported losing presidential contenders during the primaries were no longer entitled to a seat at the convention. Many more would not even consider running for convention delegate under the reformed rules; they did not wish to declare a candidate preference and thereby alienate constituents loyal to other presidential hopefuls.

Critics of the McGovern-Fraser rules charged that these party professionals represented a voice of reason and balance that needed to be restored to a party convention increasingly vulnerable to capture by party outsiders.

Because of these concerns the Winograd Commission set aside an add-on of up to 10 percent in additional seats for party leaders for 1980. Four years later, the Hunt Commission increased the number of *superdelegates*—office-holders and party leaders entitled to attend the national convention without having to run in the primaries—to 566, or 14.4 percent of the convention total. The feeling among many Democrats was that the earlier reforms had

Table 2.2   Proliferation of Primaries and the Growing Importance of Presidential Primaries to National Convention Votes, 1968–1984

year	Democrats			Republicans		
	no. of primaries	no. of delegate votes	% of all votes	no. of primaries	no. of delegate votes	% of all votes
1968	17	983	37.5	16	458	34.3
1972	23	1,862	60.5	22	710	52.7
1976	29	2,183	72.6	28[a]	1,533	67.9
1980	35	2,378	71.8	34[b]	1,516	76.0
1984	25[c]	2,431	62.1	30[c]	1,551	71.0

[a]Does not include Vermont, which held a nonbinding preference primary but chose delegates by caucus/convention.

[b]Includes Puerto Rico and D.C. Does not include Vermont.

[c]Includes Puerto Rico and D.C. Does not include five states that held nonbinding primaries but chose delegates by caucus/convention.

Source: William Crotty and John S. Jackson III, *Presidential Primaries and Nominations* (Washington, D.C.: CQ Press, 1985), p. 63.

gone too far in totally stripping the party's national leaders, including its top elected officials, of any role in determining the party's presidential nominee.[27]

The Republicans had been less aggressive in the pursuit of delegate selection reform. A more homogeneous party, they were less torn apart than the Democrats by the Vietnam War and the social polarizations of the 1960s and 1970s. Further, having won five of the six presidential elections from 1968 to 1988, the Republicans saw no great urgency to reform a presidential selection system that was apparently working so well.

Yet, the Republican presidential selection process was modified.[28] In part, the new Democratic spirit of openness led the Republicans to revise their rules to make their conventions more open to participation by rank-and-file party members. These changes helped Ronald Reagan in his 1976 and 1980 bids for the Republican nomination. Also, changes in state law resulting from Democratic reforms affected the Republican selection process as well. When a number of states switched their delegate selection system from caucuses to primaries, they did so for the Republicans as well as for the Democrats.

The Republicans, however, did not pursue demographic representativeness to the extent that the Democrats did. The Democrats banned winner-take-all primaries and in their place instituted modified proportional representation (PR) in an effort to fairly represent the diverse candidate factions at the national convention. Under PR, a candidate who lost a state nominating contest but whose vote was above a certain minimum threshold would still win delegates to the national convention in rough proportion to the vote received. The shift to modified proportional representation made it difficult for a front-runner to assemble the large blocks of delegates needed to assure the nomination.

Polarization in the Nominating Process

The new Democratic reforms assured a more open delegate selection process and produced national conventions that were more demographically representative of rank-and-file Democrats. Yet, according to critics, the reformed nominating process in both the Democratic and Republican parties alike also helped produce presidential conventions vulnerable to more ideological factions. The democratic nature of the national conventions was still very much a matter of debate. Openness was no guarantee of policy representativeness.

Two studies that compare the policy views of Democratic presidential convention delegates with the opinions of rank-and-file Democrats underscore the unrepresentative nature of the party's 1972 convention. One study was conducted by Denis Sullivan and his associates; the other was conducted by Jeane Kirkpatrick, then a leader of the party's more conservative wing and later ambassador to the United Nations under the Republican administration of Ronald Reagan.[29] The results show a serious difference of policy views between convention delegates and the party's mass base of support. Democratic convention delegates were vastly more liberal than rank-and-file Democrats when it came to such issues as welfare, school busing, amnesty for draft evaders, law and order, protecting the rights of the accused, and attitudes toward the military (see Tables 2.3 and 2.4).

The Democratic convention was so unrepresentative of the American people that it nominated a candidate, George McGovern, who was seen to be too extreme by the American public and was rejected in the November election by a landslide margin.

How could the 1972 convention be so unrepresentative of the party's mass base? According to Kirkpatrick, the new delegate selection rules helped to facilitate the seizure of the party by a

Table 2.3   Differences Between Delegates and Democratic Rank and File on Issue Opinions, 1972

	delegates	rank and file
Busing		
Favor busing with no qualifications	25%	30%
Favor busing if only means to racial balance and educational equality	54	not available
Oppose	21	70
Amnesty		
Favor without punishment	46	31
Favor with punishment	36	not available
Oppose	18	69
Guaranteed Annual Income		
Favor	74	43
Oppose	26	57

Source: Denis G. Sullivan, et al., *The Politics of Representation: The Democratic Convention, 1972* (New York: St. Martin's Press, 1974), p. 32.

"new presidential elite," a new breed of issue activists loyal only to their candidate and their cause-of-the-moment.[30] McGovern's avid supporters showed up and dominated the new open caucuses and district conventions—at times quite lengthy and drawn-out affairs—while less issue-intense and more moderate Democrats remained at home.[31] McGovern's followers were even able to stack caucuses and conventions in such conservative states as Oklahoma and Virginia, states where rank-and-file Democrats were not part of McGovern's natural constituency.

Low-turnout caucuses and primaries tend to produce nominating electorates that are unrepresentative of the nation or party as a whole. Sometimes the resulting bias is classist. Low-turnout affairs tend to be dominated by better educated, higher status voters. Yet this is not always the case. In 1988 relatively high turnouts in poor and black sections of Detroit helped Jesse Jackson to win Michigan's otherwise low-turnout presidential caucuses. Once again, open caucuses proved vulnerable to capture by a candidate with an intensely motivated group of supporters.

Not all political scientists accept the view that the open presidential selection system is as biased as Kirkpatrick and other critics charge. Thomas Marshall, for instance, has examined the 1972 caucuses in Minnesota. While he found the overrepresentation of upper-status groups in the caucuses, he did not find the policy views of caucus participants to be greatly out of line with those of party supporters.[32]

Table 2.4   Differences Between Delegates and Democratic Rank and File on Issue Opinions, 1972

(a) Welfare Policy (percent)

		identifiers	all delegates
Abolish poverty	1	12 ⎫	28 ⎫
	2	6 ⎬ 22	17 ⎬ 57
	3	4 ⎭	12 ⎭
	4	9	15
	5	7 ⎫	6 ⎫
	6	12 ⎬ 69	7 ⎬ 28
Obligation to work	7	50 ⎭	15 ⎭
Weighted N=		1040	2532

(b) Busing Policy (percent)

		identifiers	all delegates
Bus to integrate	1	8 ⎫	34 ⎫
	2	4 ⎬ 15	20 ⎬ 66
	3	3 ⎭	12 ⎭
	4	6	9
	5	4 ⎫	4 ⎫
	6	7 ⎫	4 ⎫
Keep children in neighborhood schools	7	71 ⎬ 82	17 ⎬ 25
N=		1275	1492

(c) Get Tough vs. Protect the Accused (percent)

		identifiers	all delegates
Protect the accused	1	19 ⎫	53 ⎫
	2	10 ⎬ 36	18 ⎬ 78
	3	7 ⎭	7 ⎭
	4	14	9
	5	10 ⎫	5 ⎫
	6	11 ⎫	3 ⎫
Stop crime regardless of rights of accused	7	29 ⎬ 50	5 ⎬ 13
N=		1013	1493

(d) Attitudes Toward Political Demonstrators (percent)

	feeling thermometer score	identifiers	all delegates
Unfavorable	0	35 ⎫	7 ⎫
	10	12 ⎫	3 ⎫
	20	8 ⎬ 67	3 ⎬ 22
	30	6 ⎭	4 ⎭
	40	6 ⎭	5 ⎭
Neutral	50	18	19
	60	4 ⎫	12 ⎫
	70	4 ⎫	13 ⎫
	80	3 ⎬ 14	14 ⎬ 59
	90	1 ⎭	10 ⎭
Favorable	100	2 ⎭	10 ⎭
Weighted N=		1058	2582

(e) Attitudes Toward the Military (percent)

	feeling thermometer score	identifiers	all delegates
Unfavorable	0	4 ⎫	4 ⎫
	10	2 ⎫	8 ⎫
	20	1 ⎬ 16	7 ⎬ 43
	30	5 ⎭	11 ⎭
	40	4 ⎭	13 ⎭
Neutral	50	16	14
	60	8 ⎫	7 ⎫
	70	12 ⎫	10 ⎫
	80	13 ⎬ 67	9 ⎬ 42
	90	13 ⎭	7 ⎭
Favorable	100	21 ⎭	9 ⎭
Weighted N=		1058	2619

Source: Jeane Kirkpatrick, *The New Presidential Elite: Men and Women in National Politics* (New York: Russell Sage Foundation, Twentieth Century Fund, 1976), information extracted from Tables 10-1, 10-2, 10-3, 10-5, and 10-7, pp. 299–308.

Table 2.5   Self-Identified Ideology of National Convention Delegates, Party Members, and Mass Public, 1972–1980

self-identified ideology	1972		1976		1980		party members (1980)		mass public (1980)
	D	**R**	**D**	**R**	**D**	**R**	**D**	**R**	
Liberal	79%	10%	40%	3%	46%	2%	21%	13%	19%
Moderate	13	35	47	45	42	36	44	40	49
Conservative	8	57	8	48	6	58	26	41	31

Source: William Crotty and John S. Jackson III, *Presidential Primaries and Nominations* (Washington, D.C.: CQ Press, 1985), p. 118.

Similarly, Herbert Kritzer found Democratic primary voters in 1972 to be fairly representative of Democrats as a whole.[33] A study by William Crotty and John Jackson of voting in the 1980 primaries essentially reinforces Kritzer's point of view. While ideologically extreme voters tended to be disproportionately active in participating in primaries, primary voters on the whole were not all that different from nonvoters regarding issue preferences.[34] Primaries, it seems, have larger turnouts than caucuses and are less prone to capture by unrepresentative bands of candidate and issue activists.

The nominating system reforms were not entirely to blame for the unrepresentative nature of the 1972 convention. As Herbert McClosky's classic study of the 1956 Democratic and Republican conventions showed, national convention delegates in both parties tend to be more to the extreme than rank-and-file party members. National party delegates, like other political elites, are more interested in politics and aware of issues than the average citizen.[35]

The more extreme nature of the 1972 convention was also a result of the anti-Vietnam War insurgency that captured the Democratic party. McGovern rode the crest of antiwar sentiment to the nomination. As Crotty and Jackson observe, once the Vietnam issue and the McGovern insurgency passed, Democratic national conventions lost some of their extreme left-wing flavor. The 1976 and 1980 Democratic conventions were less liberal than was the 1972 convention, although delegates to these conventions were still more liberal than rank-and-file Democrats and the mass public as a whole (see Table 2.5).

The work of Warren Miller and M. Kent Jennings reinforces Crotty and Jackson's findings. Delegates at the 1976 and 1980 conventions were more liberal than Democratic followers; yet these

delegates showed new concern for winning and an increased willingness to compromise as compared to Democrats who attended
the McGovernite-dominated 1972 convention.[36]

Poll data from 1984 continues to confirm the overall picture.
Delegates to the 1984 Democratic convention continued to be
more liberal than the public-at-large on such issues as support for
the Equal Rights Amendment, decreasing the military budget,
and in seeing blacks as continued victims of discrimination. Delegates to the San Francisco convention were also less willing than
the general public to use force to stop Communism.[37]

Democratic conventions are not the only ones that have been
ideologically out of line with party followers and the mass public.
Delegates to the 1976 and 1980 Republican conventions were more
conservative than Republican identifiers and the public-at-large
(see Table 2.5). In fact, elite polarizations heightened in 1976 and
1980 as activists committed to Ronald Reagan's candidacy helped
give the 1980 Republican convention a more ideological flavor
than if these conventions had been dominated by the more moderate supporters of Gerald Ford and George Bush.

Overall, elites at national party conventions show continuing
evidence of policy polarization. Democratic and Republican conventions are populated by delegates of competing ideologies and
competing visions of America. Even the superdelegates to the 1984
and 1988 Democratic conventions showed a distinct preference for
nominating the more liberal candidates, Walter Mondale and Michael Dukakis, over Democrats who offered more moderate policy
alternatives.

National convention elites are increasingly prone to nominate
candidates who offer voters a choice on the issues.[38] As Crotty and
Jackson observe:

> It is no longer accurate, if it ever was, to say the parties are alike as
> Tweedledum and Tweedledee. In fact, the parties may now offer
> more systematic philosophical differences at the elite level than ever
> before in their history.[39]

FINANCE REFORM

The Federal Election Campaign Act (FECA) amendments of 1974
(hereafter referred to as the Act) provide a very complex set of
rules for the financing of presidential elections. Put simply, the Act
seeks to limit the potential of private money in the presidential

race. The Act provides for full public funding of the major-party fall presidential campaigns, the partial public funding of primary campaigns, and the imposition of certain limits on donations and on spending by candidates who choose to accept public funds.

Presidential candidates almost universally choose to accept public funds. For many candidates government funds represent more than the candidate can hope to raise on his or her own. Other candidates accept public funding and its accompanying spending restrictions because they do not wish to be branded as the captive of "special interests."

To receive matching funds during the primaries, a candidate must raise a total of $100,000 in donations from individuals, of which $5,000 must be raised in each of twenty or more states. The government matches only the first $250 of each individual contribution; no match is given to money received from political action committees (PACs). The purpose of the Act is to have candidates seek a broad base of support from individuals and small-money donors. A candidate who fails to win 20 percent or more of the vote in each of two consecutive primaries loses his or her eligibility for matching funds. Eligibility can later be restored if the candidate receives 20 percent of the vote in a primary contest.

The donation and spending limits imposed by the Act are even more complex. No individual can give more than $1,000 to a candidate's primary and general election campaigns. Nor can an individual's donations in any year exceed a maximum of $25,000 to all federal candidates. An organization can give a candidate donations up to a ceiling of $5,000. Each candidate is then subject to limitations placed on overall spending and on spending in each primary and caucus state.

The Act is filled with loopholes. The various members of a family can each give $1,000 to a presidential candidate. While each PAC is limited to $5,000 in the donations it gives to a candidate, there is no limit as to how many PACs may form. Affected interests in a policy area may form multiple PACs, and, within certain limitations, each may contribute up to the allowable ceiling. As a result, the 1974 amendments have led to a rise in the number of PACs involved in the presidential race.

Another important loophole is the result of the 1976 United States Supreme Court decision *Buckley v. Valeo.* The *Buckley* decision overturned part of the FECA amendments, ruling that some of the spending limitations imposed on independent organizations amounted to an undue restriction on free speech.[40] Individuals and PACs possess the free-speech right to spend money to advocate the election of the candidate of their choice. These independent expenditures cannot be counted against a candidate's allowable ceiling so long as the actions of the independent committee are not coordinated with those of the official campaign. As a consequence of the Supreme Court's decision, independent expenditures represent a growing proportion of spending in a presidential year.

Presidential candidates also found various ways to circumvent some of the limitations imposed by the Act. In advance of making a formal announcement for the presidency, a candidate may be aided by a PAC organized exclusively for the benefit of the presidential candidate. This PAC can pay a candidate's expenses as he or she travels around the country as the "spokesperson" for the group, as it aids friendly Senate, House, and state and local candidates. In essence the PAC pays for the predeclaration expenses of the presidential candidate, expenses that are not later charged against the candidate's permissible spending ceiling. Notable candidate PACs have included Edward Kennedy's Fund for a Democratic Majority and Walter Mondale's Committee for the Future of America, each of which spent over $2 million in the 1981–1982 election cycle.[41] By October 1986, two years in advance of his presidential election, George Bush's Fund for America's Future had already raised over $9 million.[42]

The state-by-state spending limits imposed on public funding recipients during the primary season are particularly difficult to enforce. Candidates spend more than the allowed amounts in key states such as Iowa and New Hampshire. They know that any Federal Election Commission ordered fine will be imposed well after the election is over. Campaigns also circumvent state spending limits by creatively shifting expenses to other states, for instance, by renting cars in neighboring states for staff use in Iowa and New Hampshire.

Walter Mondale's 1984 campaign also took advantage of a loophole designed to encourage grass-roots activity by delegate committees formed in the various states to support the selection of national convention delegates. These committees could receive donations from persons who had maxed out to the Mondale campaign. Spending by these committees did not count against the official campaign's allowed ceiling.[43]

In 1979 new FECA amendments allowed for the greater activity of state and local party organizations to promote grass-roots campaign activity. No limitations were placed on state and local party funds spent to register voters, print literature and sample ballots, pay for bumper stickers and yard signs, and organize get-

Table 2.6   Sources of Funds, Major-Party Presidential Candidates, 1984 General Election

		(millions)	
	sources of funds	Reagan	Mondale
Limited Campaign			
Candidate controlled	Federal grant	$40.4	$40.4
	National party	6.9	2.7
Unlimited Campaigns			
Candidate may coordinate	State and local party	15.6[a]	6.0[b]
	Labor[c]	2.0	20.0
	Corporate/Association[c]	1.5	0.1
	Compliance	2.4	1.2
Independent of candidate	Independent expenditures[d]	8.5	0.7
Total		$77.3	$71.1

[a]Includes both money raised by the national party committee and channeled to state and local party committees and money raised by state and local party committees from their own sources.

[b]Includes only money raised by the national party committee and channeled to state and local party committees; an estimate of money raised for presidential campaign purposes by state and local party committees from their own sources is not available.

[c]Includes internal communication costs (both those in excess of $2,000, which are reported, as required by law, and those less than $2,000, which are not required to be reported), registration and voter turnout expenditures, overhead, and other related costs.

[d]Does not include amounts spent to oppose the candidates.

Source: Herbert E. Alexander and Brian A. Haggerty, *Financing the 1984 Election* (Lexington, Mass.: Lexington Books/D.C. Heath, 1987), p. 331.

out-the-vote drives. Only a portion, at most, of the costs incurred would be allocated as presidential expenditures.[44] Virtually unlimited by law, these donations to state and local political parties are often referred to as *soft money*.

According to campaign finance expert Herbert Alexander, it is useful to think of the presidential campaign as three parallel campaigns conducted simultaneously.[45] The official or *controlled campaign* is mostly subsidized by federal funds and is legally limited. The second or *unlimited campaigns* are conducted by state and local party committees and various PACs. This second campaign has no legal spending limits. Although it lies partly outside the control of the candidate and his or her organization, the activities of the second campaign frequently are coordinated with those of the first campaign. Finally, the third campaign comprises *independent expenditures* undertaken without consultation and collaboration with the candidate or his or her campaign.

The relative size of these three campaigns is seen in Table 2.6. In 1984 Republicans enjoyed an edge in spending by state and local parties, corporate PACs, and independent PACs. Democrats enjoyed the advantage in spending by labor organizations.

In 1988 Dukakis campaign operatives aggressively raised "soft money" from large contributors to finance state and local party campaign activities. The Republicans responded by tapping big donors of their own. The result was an increase in soft money in 1988 with Democratic soft money expenditures ($23.0 million) narrowly exceeding equivalent Republican expenditures ($22.0 million). As a result of these efforts and the continued Democratic edge in labor contributions, total Democratic presidential spending in 1988 exceeded Republican spending—a sharp reversal of the pattern in previous elections.[46]

By helping to pay for the costs of a presidential race, public funding has also at times encouraged the candidacy of outsiders. In 1976 Ellen McCormack, running solely to publicize right-to-life's opposition to abortion, received over $244,000 in public funding.[47]

The availability of public funding may also have been a factor in the decision of Louisianan David Duke, once a self-proclaimed Nazi and Ku Klux Klan leader, to challenge President Bush in the 1992 Republican primaries and caucuses.

Campaign finance reform and the resulting loopholes also have led to a new prominence of PACs in the presidential race. The growth of activity by ideological PACs, especially independent expenditure campaigns by conservative PACs such as NCPAC (National Conservative Political Action Committee) has provided a stimulus for issues in the presidential race. PACs can bring up issues that a presidential candidate may find too politically troublesome to push. In 1988, for instance, the more aggressive and controversial commercials exploiting the Willie Horton issue were aired not by the Bush campaign but by independent PACs.

SUMMARY

The United States has entered an era of candidate-centered campaigns. Political party leaders no longer play the role they once did in selecting presidential candidates and in running presidential campaigns. Nor do presidential candidates depend on the pull of party loyalty to win votes in the fall election. Instead, each presidential hopeful is supported by his own personal campaign organization. Each candidate uses the mass media to appeal directly to an increasingly independent electorate.

Often, these appeals focus on a candidate's personal attributes and leadership qualities. But issues too have played a role in presidential campaigns more than is commonly realized. Changes in nominating system and campaign finance rules have helped to facilitate the rise of candidate-centered campaigns. Reforms in the nominating process, in particular, have opened the door to new influence by issue groups. Delegates to recent Democratic and Republican conventions have differed sharply ideologically.

As the context of presidential elections changed, so has voting behavior. Studies of voting behavior completed in the 1940s and 1950s refuted any idea that Americans were issue-oriented. Few citizens were knowledgeable on the issues; few could capably distinguish one party or candidate from another on the basis of the issues.[48] Issues had little to do with election outcomes.

But this was about to change. In the 1960s, television brought into citizens' living rooms dramatic footage of the civil rights movement, urban riots, the Vietnam War, massive demonstrations at home against the war, and the new life-styles of hippies and the 1960s counterculture. Issue activists would seize control of the nominating process and present voters with candidates who offered a choice on the issues. Americans became more aware of issues. Issues were increasingly related to the voting decision.

Yet this revisionist portrait of the American electorate is not universally accepted. While a number of studies observed the increased issue orientation of American voters, studies by other political scientists pointed out that American voters failed to meet the requisites of issue voting.

The next chapter examines the continuing debate over issue voting.

THE DEBATE OVER ISSUE VOTING

N umerous academic studies have attempted to determine what role issues have played in American elections. A number of studies point to a prominent role played by issues; other studies point to the continuing influence of partisanship and candidate personal images. While no consensus exists, there is a greater recognition of the role played by issues today than there was a decade or two ago.[1]

The debate over issue voting has been framed largely by the standards set down in *The American Voter*, the University of Michigan Survey Research Center's highly influential portrait of voting behavior in the 1952 and 1956 elections.[2] *The American Voter* followed a decade of research on voting behavior by a group of Columbia University sociologists. These two studies revealed new and unflattering insights into the nature of voting in the United States.

SOCIAL SCIENCE DISCOVERS THE AMERICAN VOTER

Not until the late New Deal era were social scientists able to perfect public opinion and survey research instruments that provided for in-depth studies of the American electorate. In the initial studies done in the 1940s, sociologists interviewed and reinterviewed panels of voters in a single community. Although a limited national survey was undertaken in 1948, it was not until the 1950s that political scientists at the University of Michigan were able to complete a series of national surveys with questions directed at gaining better insight into why Americans voted as they did.

Largely, the findings of these studies came as quite a surprise. They dispelled any notion that Americans behaved as classic democratic citizens. *The People's Choice,* which looked at voting behavior in the 1940 election in Erie County, Ohio, found that most Americans did not listen to the promises of the competing candidates before deciding how to vote. Newspaper and radio coverage of the campaign had little effect on the voting decision.[3] Instead, most Americans decided whom to vote for before the campaign even began, before the parties chose their candidates at the national nominating conventions! Voters knew whether they approved of Franklin Roosevelt for a third term or if they wanted a change. Voters were also influenced by their membership in different social groups. Protestant and higher status groups were more likely to vote Republican; Catholics and lower status groups were more likely to vote Democratic.

Bernard Berelson, Paul Lazarsfeld, and William McPhee gave a similar disparaging portrait of Americans in *Voting,* their study of Elmira, New York, during the 1948 presidential election.[4] These researchers found that political preferences are highly self-maintaining, that even voters who admit some dissatisfaction with their party's performance tend to return to their normal party preference as the campaign progresses.

According to Berelson and his colleagues, voters have a psychological need for conformity. Citizens, though, are often subject to the cross-pressure of competing opinions because of their involvement in heterogeneous work and social groups. These citizens are likely to resolve the conflict by lessening their interest in politics and abstaining from voting. They are able to maintain their working and social relationships only by coming to believe that political questions are of no great importance.

The Elmira study was potentially troubling for a country that saw itself as a model democracy. As most voters exhibit long-lasting partisan loyalties, it is the least interested and least informed voters who switch from one party's candidate to the other's and thereby decide the outcome of elections: "Since the bulk of each party's votes move only sluggishly if at all, the short-term change that 'decides' close election is disproportionately located among those closer to the border line of disinterest."[5] Berelson continues, "The classic 'independent voter' of high interest but low partisanship is a deviant case."[6]

How can American democracy survive if the polity fails to meet the requirements of an alert electorate? Berelson can only offer an elitist theory of democracy where he argues that the political system is actually helped by the passivity of so many of its citizens. Continuity and stability in the political system are provided by the many Americans who show enduring party allegiances. Their moderation further helps to mute the intensity of political conflict. Those persons least committed to democratic norms of compromise and respect for the rights of others fortunately are the least likely to participate. The mass base for fanatical and extremist movements is thereby removed from American politics. Passivity and apathy further afford political leaders room for pluralist bargaining and compromise: "The apathetic segment of America probably has helped to hold the system together and cushioned the shock of disagreement, adjustment, and change."[7]

The group theory of politics advanced by the sociologists would soon be found wanting. The political scientists at the University of Michigan would cast it aside in favor of a different theory, one that emphasized the primacy of psychologically based party identification.

THE AMERICAN VOTER MODEL

The Prevalence of Partisanship

The American Voter included results from the 1948 election study but focused on the more extensive data collected during the Eisenhower elections of 1952 and 1956. The second great volume of University of Michigan research, *Elections and the Political Order,* studied voting behavior during the 1960 election and essentially reinforced the interpretations advanced in the earlier work.[8]

The American Voter painted a portrait of an electorate where the partisan decisions of individuals are "profoundly affected by... psychological forces."[9] The great majority of Americans had some sense of affiliation with one party or the other, the roots of which were to be found in social psychology, not in rational decision-making. Individuals did not choose their party affiliations after carefully weighing the competing issue positions of the two major parties. Rather, identification with party was formed quite early in life, before individuals even had the ability to understand politics and issues. There was a close correspondence between the party affiliation of voters and their parents. Party identification was transmitted from parent to child and remained relatively immutable over time.

Party identification served "as a supplier of cues" by which individuals evaluated candidates and political events.[10] Republican and Democratic partisans tended to judge their party's candidate favorably even when they knew little about him other than his party label. If necessary, a voter would even distort his perception of events to be consonant with his partisanship:

> Identification with a party raises a perceptual screen through which the individual tends to see what is favorable to his partisan orientation. The stronger the party bond, the more exaggerated the process of selection and perceptual distortion will be.[11]

Republican identifiers who favored the government provision of health care for the elderly were likely to believe that Eisenhower supported such a program, even though Ike had actually opposed such an initiative as the beginning of socialized medicine.

The Relative Unimportance of Issues

The American Voter found that citizens were for the most part unfamiliar with and disinterested in issues. The public's understanding of issues was poorly developed. For instance, the Democratic party chose to make the antilabor Taft-Hartley Act a major point of attack in its 1948 campaign; yet "almost seven out of every ten adult Americans saw the curtain fall on the presidential election of 1948 without knowing whether Taft-Hartley was the name of a hero or a villain."[12]

Most voters had no strong opinions on key issues of the day. Even when they did, voters could not discern differences between the parties on the issues. The public paid scant attention to politics and the campaign debate. Issue discussion was for the most part confined to political leaders and a thin top strata of the electorate.[13]

The authors of *The American Voter* specified three conditions that had to be fulfilled before an issue could be considered to have influenced an individual's voting decision[14]:

1. "The issue must be cognized in some form." The voter must be familiar with what the government is doing on an issue and have an opinion on the matter.
2. "It must arouse some minimal intensity of feeling." Unless a voter cares about an issue, it cannot influence the voting decision. Issues that arouse only mild sentiments are not politically important.
3. "It must be accompanied by some perception that one party represents the person's own position better than do the other parties." The voter must be able to see a difference between the parties on the issue and discern which party better represents his point of view.

In a survey of citizens' beliefs on sixteen issues, *The American Voter* found that only 22 to 36 percent of the electorate in 1956 were able to meet these three minimal conditions on any specific issue. Yet, even these numbers overstated the extent of issue voting: "[T]hey represent no more than a maximum pool within which the speci-fied issues might have conceivable effect."[15] A voter might have an opinion, care about an issue, and see a difference between the parties on the matter, but still find that other factors outweighed the policy issue in determining the voting decision.

Self-described independents were the least informed and aware of all voters. These citizens seemingly classified themselves as inde-pendents only because they did not care at all about politics.

The Lack of Voter Sophistication

Voters lacked strong opinions on many questions but still an-swered pollsters' questions anyway. Philip Converse labeled these responses, which did not indicate strong convictions or well-thought-out beliefs, "nonattitudes."[16] Voters' opinions on policy questions were quite unstable and varied greatly over time. When posed the same question at different points in time, a respondent would often give different answers.

Converse's evidence is presented in Figure 3.1. A panel of voters interviewed in 1958 was revisited in 1960. The numbers presented on the chart are rank-order correlation (tau-beta) coeffi-cients. If all persons interviewed had exactly the same opinions on an issue in 1960 that they had in 1958, the correlation coefficient for that issue would be 1.00. Roughly put, the greater the stability of opinions over time, the higher the correlation coefficients; the greater the apparent opinion change, the lower the coefficients.

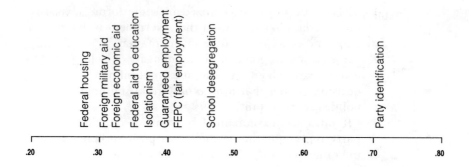

Figure 3.1   Temporal stability of different belief elements for individuals, 1958–1960
Source: Philip E. Converse, "The Nature of Belief Systems in Mass Publics," *Ideology and Discontent,* ed. David Apter (New York: Free Press, 1964).

As Figure 3.1 shows, the public's opinion on most issues showed very little stability; opinions varied widely over the course of only two years. It was almost as if the public had no serious opinions on policy questions. Only on the issue of school desegregation did attitudes remain fairly consistent over time. Converse explains that this in itself does not indicate sophisticated thinking; rather, voters simply held strong attitudes toward a social group, African-Americans, that ordered their opinions.

The strong .78 correlation over time for party identification stands out in marked contrast to the low longitudinal correlations for the various issues. Citizens were consistent in their partisanship over time. Apparently, party identification was more central than issues to the belief systems of the mass public.

The lack of voter sophistication was also apparent in citizens' answers to open-ended questions about what they liked and disliked about the parties and the candidates. *The American Voter* team attempted to explore the degree to which voters had an *ideology*—the degree to which voters were consistent in their opinions and able to understand the general liberal and conservative choices presented to them by the candidates. As Table 3.1 shows, very few Americans—only 3¹/₂ percent of the electorate—had full-blown ideology. Only 15 percent of the electorate can be seen to possess an ideology, even defined in the broadest of terms.

For most American voters the terms *liberal* and *conservative* lacked clear meaning. Voters could not understand the choice offered by the two competing parties, one offering a more conservative and the other a more liberal policy direction.

Table 3.1   Levels of Ideological Thinking and the American Voter, 1956

	proportion of total sample	proportion of voters
Ideology		
Ideology	2½%	3½%
Near-ideology	9	12
Group Benefits		
Perception of conflict	14	16
Single-group interest	17	18
Shallow group benefit responses	11	11
Nature of the Times	24	22
No Issue Content		
Party orientation	4	3½
Candidate orientation	9	7
No content	5	3
Unclassified	4½	4
	100%	100%

Source: Angus Campbell et al., *The American Voter,* abridged ed. (New York: John Wiley & Sons, 1964), p. 144.

Only in the area of domestic policy did the authors find some apparent structure or consistency of beliefs. But in-depth discussion revealed that voters could not explain their issue preferences with any sort of sophistication. Instead, what was apparent was merely "ideology by proxy," where group interest and personal self-interest gave some order to the voter's responses.[17] Voters cast ballots for the party of labor and the little man, or for the party of small business, or for the party of the farmer, or for the party of the South. A fifth of the electorate voted on the basis of "The 'Goodness' and 'Badness' of the Times"; in bad times they voted to oust the incumbent administration. Nearly 20 percent of the electorate was unable to give any issue-based reason whatsoever in answering questions about candidates and parties. Among this group were voters whose responses showed strong candidate and partisan orientations but no issue content whatsoever:

(Like about Democrats?) I'm a Democrat. (Is there anything you like about the Democratic Party?) I don't know.

(Dislike about Democrats?) I'm a Democrat, that's all I know. My husband's dead now—he was a Democrat. (Is there anything you don't like about the party?) I don't know.

(Like about Republicans?) I don't know.

(Dislike about Republicans?) I don't know.

(Like about Stevenson?) Stevenson is a good Democrat. (Is there anything else about him that might make you want to vote for him?) No, nothing.

(Dislike about Stevenson?) I don't know. (Is there anything about him that might make you want to vote against him?) No.

(Like about Eisenhower?) I don't know. (Is there anything about Eisenhower that might make you want to vote for him?) I don't know.

(Dislike about Eisenhower?) I don't know. (Is there anything about him that might make you want to vote against him?) No.[18]

According to the Michigan studies, Eisenhower won the 1952 election on the basis of his strong personal appeal. The public's personal endorsement of Ike proved especially strong in his 1956 reelection. In 1952 the Republicans also gained the public's favor in the area of governmental management, responding to allegations of corruption and irregularities in the Truman administration. The short-term factors of Eisenhower's personal appeal and allegations of Democratic corruption overshadowed the advantages that the Democrats retained in domestic policy and group-related attitudes. These long-term partisan ties would help produce a Kennedy victory in 1960.

ARE THE VOTERS FOOLS?

The American Voter was a seminal work that widely influenced a generation of voting studies and the perspectives of informed observers of American politics. Yet its portrayal of the relative unimportance of issues in presidential voting did not go unchallenged. Harvard political scientist V. O. Key, Jr., reviewed Gallup poll data from the New Deal era and argued that

> voters are not fools...[I]n the large the electorate behaves about as rationally and responsibly as we should expect, given the clarity of the alternatives presented to it and the character of the information available to it. In American presidential campaigns of recent decades the portrait of the American electorate that develops from the data is not one of an electorate straitjacketed by social determinants or moved by subconscious urges triggered by devilishly skillful propagandists. It is rather one of an electorate moved by concern about central and relevant questions of public policy, of governmental performance, and of executive personality.[19]

Key accepted the Michigan Survey Research Center's finding that partisanship was a major influence on voting behavior. Yet Key did not find voters to be as anchored in place by party identification as *The American Voter* had reported them to be. Rather substantial interparty movement by voters takes place between elections even during periods of seeming electoral stability:

> Such evidence as can be mustered suggests that the popular majority does not hold together like a ball of sticky popcorn. Rather, no sooner has a popular majority been constructed than it begins to crumble . . .[T]o govern is to antagonize not only opponents but also at least some supporters; as the loyalty of one group is nourished, another group may be repelled. A series of maintaining elections occurs only in consequence of a complex process of interaction between government and populace in which old friends are sustained, old enemies are converted into new friends, old friends become even bitter opponents, and new voters are attracted to the cause—all in proper proportions to produce repeatedly for the dominant party its apparently stable and continuing majority.[20]

Key divided the electorate into *standpatters*—those voters who remained with the same party in two consecutive elections—and *switchers*—those voters who moved from one party to another in two consecutive elections. Key found that both groups of voters were basically where they should be on the basis of the issues. Those who stayed with their party did so as they approved of their party's record and promises. Those who were dissatisfied switched: "party switchers move towards the party whose standpatters they resemble in their policy views."[21] Switchers, whose movement decides the outcome of elections, were not the "repulsive type of 'independent' " described by *The American Voter.*[22] Switchers were as informed and educated as standpatters.

Key found that the Democratic party majority was based on voter approval of Democratic activist New Deal policies.[23] Even in the then-solidly Democratic South, loyalty to the Democratic party was not a simple reflection of partisan attachments handed down since the Civil War. As the poorest region in the nation, people in the South were the beneficiaries of the many Democratic economic and social welfare programs.[24]

The 1952 and 1956 elections were not simply personal endorsements of Eisenhower; rather, voters rejected the performance of the Truman administration on "Communism, Corruption, Korea." Charges of Communist penetration into the government in Washington, China's entry into and prolongation of the Korean War, and the allegations of corruption in Truman's kitchen cabinet were all important influences on the vote in 1952. According to Key, voters "ousted from power a political party of whose perform-ance they did not approve."[25] In 1956, voters endorsed Eisen-hower's first-term performance; the war in Korea had been brought to an end, and there was a general level of citizen satisfac-tion with things both at home and abroad. Kennedy's narrow 1960 victory represented a vote for change—a rejection of America's sluggishness during the late Eisenhower era.[26]

Issues, Key argued, were important to presidential voting even during the decade that provided the data for the generaliza-tions made by *The American Voter*. Democracy in the United States was not endangered.

But Key's corrective was not universally acclaimed. Political scientists who accepted *The American Voter*'s viewpoint on the unin-formed voter questioned the validity of Key's use of recall data. Voters had been asked why they voted as they did in previous elec-tions, yielding the risk of selective memory and projection in their answers. Standpatters and switchers could have cast their ballots on any number of grounds but still justified their votes to the inter-viewer by claiming satisfaction or dissatisfaction with their party's performance and policies.[27] Furthermore, Key had not attempted to discover whether citizens met the issue-voting criteria set forth in *The American Voter*. He did not demonstrate that voters saw the party they voted for to be in agreement with them on the issues or that voters cared enough about the issues for which Key claimed they voted.[28]

THE DEBATE OVER ISSUE SALIENCE

David RePass was another political scientist who objected to the Michigan school's portrait of a voting decision "not rich with spe-cific issue content."[29] RePass found that different voters were con-cerned with different issues. *The American Voter*'s methodology was flawed. It had asked respondents to agree or disagree with a series of closed-ended, preformulated policy statements. According to RePass, *The American Voter* concluded that issues had little influence on the voting decision only because voters were asked their opin-ions on policy questions that mattered little to them.

When respondents are given the opportunity to identify for themselves which issues are of greatest importance, the results are much different. RePass analyzed voter responses to a new set of questions in the 1964 national survey, which allowed respondents to indicate how important they considered a particular issue to be. RePass found that voters were able to perceive differences between the parties on issues they considered salient. More important, voters' opinions on salient issues were closely linked to party identification and the presidential voting decision.

Defenders of the Michigan model point out that positions on salient issues explain the voting decisions of very few citizens.[30] They further point to the limited political significance of highly individualized issue concerns. In 1964 no single issue was considered salient by more than 12 percent of the respondents.[31] If each voter casts a ballot on the basis of a concern for a different issue, then election results cannot constitute a set of instructions or mandate for any specific policy change. For elections to constitute meaningful instruments of policy control, voters must be able to choose between the general liberal and conservative alternatives offered by the two major parties. Voters who cannot understand the liberal-conservative dialogue do not comprehend the basic programmatic choices before them in a presidential election.

IS THERE A CHANGING AMERICAN VOTER?

Many of the generalizations drawn from the first generation of University of Michigan studies are clearly time-bound, a factor not always made clear in the period's writings on voting behavior:

> The findings, and particularly the overall conclusions, of *The American Voter* were not presented as the results of a given era, but as relatively long-term truths about the characteristic quality and behavior of the United States electorate. The possibilities of change were hardly discussed, and the brief consideration of such possibilities was only in the context of unexpected catastrophes such as civil war or a major depression.[32]

A new generation of Americans was soon to come of voting age. They did not inherit the partisan orientations of their parents to the extent that voters had in the 1950s. The transference of party affiliation from parents to children, so much a part of the psychological model provided by *The American Voter* model, was greatly weakened in the 1970s and 1980s.[33] These younger and more educated voters would become part of a new rootless "no majority" electorate.[34] Unencumbered by strong party identification, these voters would be free to respond to new political cues—racial issues, social issues, and a changed economy marked at times by high rates of both stagnation and inflation.

The American Voter paradigm was challenged by a new set of works that purported to show that voting behavior became more issue-oriented and ideological as a result of the changed nature of the times. RePass's study of voting in 1964 concluded that issues were important, as Barry Goldwater and Lyndon Johnson presented Americans a distinct choice on specific policy matters. A number of major longitudinal studies also concluded that the nature of voting in the United States had changed.

Gerald Pomper: The Times Have Changed

Gerald Pomper found the increased influence of issues on party identification. He saw the new prominence of issues as the result of the "national metamorphosis" that occurred in the 1960s and 1970s.[35] According to Pomper, *The American Voter*'s conclusion as to the low ideological awareness of voters "may have resulted from the generally low level of ideological stimulation" during the Eisenhower years.[36] But television was soon to bring the turbulence associated with the black revolution, the Vietnam War, and the changing social mores into voters' homes. As politics became more pressing and relevant, Americans developed more coherent belief systems.[37] Pomper further theorized that especially among the young, "The brutality of Vietnam, the cruelties of racism, the corruption of a president, the separatism of the youth culture have stimulated new loyalties and new attitudes."[38]

In 1956, as *The American Voter* had reported, issue preferences were only very mildly related to party identification. But starting in the mid-1960s, Pomper found that Democratic and Republican identified partisans were increasingly differentiated by their views on domestic policy.[39] By 1968 the parties had also developed much clearer identities. During the 1950s a great many voters failed to perceive the Democrats as the liberal party. By 1964 and 1968 voters in all partisanship categories correctly saw the Democrats as the liberal alternative (see Table 3.2).

What explains the increase in voter awareness and partisan distinctiveness? According to Pomper:

> The most important electoral event of this period appears to be the 1964 presidential campaign. Senator Barry Goldwater consciously sought to clarify and widen the ideological differences between the parties. The evidence presented here indicates that he accomplished

Table 3.2   Consensus on Positions of Parties on Policy Issues, by Party
Identification*

	consensus on party positions									
	education, taxation					medical care				
group	1956	1960	1964	1968	1972	1956	1960	1964	1968	1972
Strong Democrat	90.5	95.2	96.5	94.1	64.6	93.9	95.8	98.2	98.8	84.0
Weak Democrat	88.5	90.5	93.6	82.6	71.4	84.6	90.4	95.8	88.7	80.6
Independent	66.3	74.6	83.8	64.3	76.1	76.4	87.7	93.5	82.7	90.5
Weak Republican	37.2	60.9	55.8	58.7	77.7	64.3	52.2	77.6	85.0	88.5
Strong Republican	31.6	47.9	55.0	41.2	83.1	57.8	51.3	79.8	63.6	89.7

	fair employment, minority aid					school integration, busing				
group	1956	1960	1964	1968	1972	1956	1960	1964	1968	1972
Strong Democrat	64.6	83.5	96.9	97.3	78.5	39.1	34.7	96.2	95.3	65.6
Weak Democrat	63.6	65.5	93.9	88.3	81.3	51.5	42.5	90.3	87.1	64.6
Independent	49.4	53.4	89.5	75.6	72.4	45.8	46.4	91.8	83.4	68.0
Weak Republican	23.6	18.3	81.0	70.2	79.6	45.1	49.3	83.9	75.4	86.0
Strong Republican	6.0	17.2	67.6	56.4	88.5	59.4	48.5	71.3	69.5	94.0

	job guarantee					foreign aid, defense spending				
group	1956	1960	1964	1968	1972	1956	1960	1964	1968	1972
Strong Democrat	85.5	98.8	98.8	97.0	83.1	57.1	80.9	98.1	93.0	76.4
Weak Democrat	71.8	93.3	93.9	88.5	80.1	53.0	60.2	94.2	89.2	84.6
Independent	61.9	82.3	89.3	71.4	83.0	54.5	46.8	88.1	83.1	84.4
Weak Republican	60.0	67.3	72.5	69.4	91.4	46.2	13.0	67.8	81.5	86.1
Strong Republican	47.0	32.3	63.8	53.9	83.0	29.3	21.4	70.8	61.6	81.0

*Cell entries are percentages of voters that select Democrats as liberal among those voters who perceive party differences.

Source: Gerald Pomper, *Voters' Choice* (New York: Dodd, Mead, 1975), p. 172.

his goal, although this did not benefit the Republican party. Voters, previously unable to see differences between the parties, learned the lesson of "a choice, not an echo." They accepted the senator's characterization of the Republicans as conservative and the Democrats as liberal, and, on the specific issues involved, they preferred the liberal alternative.[40]

But according to Michael Margolis, Pomper's work does not necessarily document an increase in issue voting. Pomper's evidence pointing to the increased association between party identification and voters' issue preferences actually shows little about issue voting. It does not demonstrate that voters cared about specific issues, knew what the government was doing in these policy areas, or saw any differences between the parties on these issues.[41]

Even where Pomper does try to show that voters met some of the conditions of issue voting, Margolis is still critical. The problem is that Pomper's percentages in Table 3.2 are based not on the entire sample but on only those voters who perceive party differences. When Margolis recalculates Pomper's data for the entire sample (Table 3.3), increased voter awareness and recognition of party differences was not as strong as Pomper suggested.[42]

Do Voters Think Ideologically?

Pomper's findings were reinforced by those of a major research effort published under a title, *The Changing American Voter,* that indicated its quite different view of the electorate than the earlier University of Michigan studies. The most important of *The Changing American Voter*'s findings showed a dramatically sharp increase in ideological thinking beginning in 1964.[43] The American voter had changed over time.

The new findings represented a dramatic clash with those of the earlier era reported by Philip Converse.[44] As we have already seen, Converse found voter opinions to be so loosely held that he labeled them "nonattitudes." Converse further found that belief systems in the mass public were not well structured or well ordered. Voters did not hold consistent liberal or conservative opinions. Instead, a citizen who was a liberal on one issue was almost as likely to be a conservative as a liberal on another. Voters generally did not recognize the underlying philosophy or ideological dimension to link their opinion on one issue to their opinion on another.

Converse's original findings are reported in Table 3.4. The low correlation coefficients for the mass public (the cross-section sample) indicate the lack of issue constraint or ideological thinking. Had liberals on one issue been liberals on another, and had conservatives on one issue been conservative on another, the correlation coefficients for each pair of issues would have been much greater. Foreign policy attitudes are not at all linked in conservative-liberal terms with opinions on domestic matters.

It is not that ideological thinking is impossible. Converse contrasted the scores of the mass public with the much higher scores reported for a sample of congressional candidates (again, see Table 3.4). Political elites, but not the mass public, show evidence of consistent, ideological thinking.

Converse further found that only for the political elite was there a strong relationship between domestic policy attitudes and political party preference. For the general public the correlation is

Table 3.3   Issues and Party Positions, 1956–1968

	aid to education				medical care			
	1956[a]	1960	1964	1968	1956[a]	1960	1964	1968
Democrats Favor	17%	32%	37%	31%	15%	35%	55%	46%
Republicans Favor	13	10	8	11	11	8	3	5
No Difference	28	34	25	30[b]	22	31	15	21
Don't Know	10	13	12	9	11	18	9	10
DK Gov't Policy	23	c	c	c	29	c	c	c
No Opinion or No Interest on Issue	10	11	18	19	12	9	16	16
N	1749	1898	1563	1553	1749	1905	1559	1541

	fair employment				school integration			
	1956	1960	1964	1968	1956	1960	1964	1968
Democrats Favor	13%	18%	47%	41%	18%	15%	43%	42%
Republicans Favor	15	17	6	9	16	11	5	7
No Difference	29	44	25	31	30	46	28	32
Don't Know	10	11	9	7	11	14	12	7
DK Gov't Policy	19	c	c	c	13	c	c	c
No Opinion or No Interest on Issue	13	11	13	12	12	15	13	11
N	1742	1910	1553	1550	1740	1913	1568	1542

	job guarantee				foreign aid			
	1956	1960	1964	1968	1956	1960	1964	1968
Democrats Favor	19%	39%	46%	42%	12%	14%	39%	31%
Republicans Favor	14	9	6	10	16	15	5	6
No Difference	25	27	23	27	29	46	36	42
Don't Know	8	15	10	10	10	13	10	8
DK Gov't Policy	23	c	c	c	16	c	c	c
No Opinion or No Interest on Issue	10	10	15	11	16	12	11	13
N	1750	1893	1564	1541	1748	1900	1560	1553

[a]In 1956 question of Aid to Education and Medical Care referred to which party was closer to the respondent's own position.

[b]Includes 1% who said Wallace favored aid.

[c]No question on whether R had information about government policy was asked after 1956.

(Source: Inter-University Consortium for Political Research: SRC/CPS American National Election Studies.)

Source: Michael Margolis, "From Confusion to Confusion: Issues and Voters, 1952–1972," *American Political Science Review* 71 (March 1977), pp. 31-43.

quite weak. Voters do not select a party on the basis of their policy views.

Given the starting point provided by Converse's research, the changes over time reported by *The Changing American Voter* are all the more startling (see Figure 3.2). Beginning in 1968 we find a sharp

Table 3.4   Constraint between Specific Issue Beliefs for an Elite Sample and a Cross-Section Sample, 1958*

	domestic (%)				foreign (%)			
	employ-ment	educa-tion	housing	FEPC	econo-mic	military†	isolation-ism	party preference
Congressional Candidates								
Employment	—	.62	.59	.35	.26	.06	.17	.68
Aid to education		—	.61	.53	.50	.06	.35	.55
Federal housing			—	.47	.41	− .03	.30	.68
FEPC				—	.47	.11	.23	.34
Economic aid					—	.19	.59	.25
Military aid						—	.32	− .18
Isolationism							—	.05
Party preference								—
Cross-Section Sample								
Employment	—	.45	.08	.34	− .04	.10	− .22	.20
Aid to education		—	.12	.29	.06	.14	− .17	.16
Federal housing			—	.08	− .06	.02	.07	.18
FEPC				—	.24	.13	.01	− .04
Economic aid					—	.16	.33	− .07
Soldiers abroad†						—	.21	.12
Isolationism							—	− .03
Party preference								—

*Entries are tau-gamma coefficients, a statistic proposed by Leo A. Goodman and William H. Kruskal in "Measures of Association for Cross Classification," *Journal of the American Statistical Association,* 49 (Dec. 1954), No. 268, 749. The coefficient was chosen because of its sensitivity to constraint of the scalar as well as the correlational type.

†For this category, the cross-section sample was asked a question about keeping American soldiers abroad, rather than about military aid in general.

Source: Philip E. Converse, "The Nature of Belief Systems in Mass Publics," *Ideology and Discontent,* ed. David E. Apter (New York: Free Press, 1964), p. 228.

and relatively lasting increase in attitude consistency scores. The attitudinal consistency scores for the mass public in the late 1960s and early 1970s even surpass those of the 1958 sample of congressional candidates. Like Pomper, *The Changing American Voter* authors find the explanation for the increased coherence of mass belief systems in the changed social and political context of American elections.

The Changing American Voter also found increased issue voting. By 1972 the linkage between policy attitudes and the vote approached that of party identification and the vote (see Figure 3.3). Voters' answers to open-ended questions exhibited more frequent

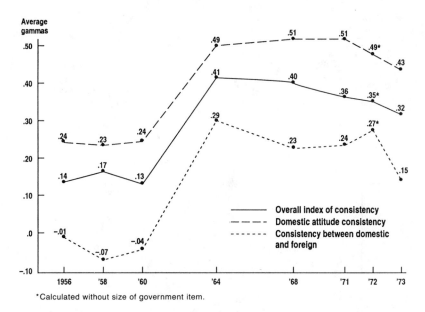

*Calculated without size of government item.

Figure 3.2   Changes in attitude consistency, 1956–1973
Source: Norman H. Nie, Sidney Verba, and John R. Petrocik, *The Changing American Voter* *(Cambridge, Mass.: Harvard Press, 1976), p. 129.*

references to issues, nearly equaling the number of mentions of candidates' personal attributes (see Figure 3.4). References to partisanship fell dramatically.

But the conclusions of *The Changing American Voter* have been hotly debated. Between 1960 and 1964 the Survey Research Center rewrote many questions to rid their surveys of the hidden bias of an acquiescent response set resulting from their old format, which depended on one-sided questions. Critics of *The Changing American Voter* charge that much of the increase in correlation scores is an artifact of changes in question wording, not an indicator of genuine voter behavioral change. They further charge that in collapsing respondents' answers from a five-point scale to a three-point scale, Norman Nie and his colleagues, the authors of *The Changing American Voter,* inadvertently committed another methodological error that caused the rank-order correlation coefficients to increase in size.[45]

Could changes in question wording be responsible for most of the correlation coefficient increases reported by Nie? John L. Sullivan and his colleagues reported that they obtained a similar change in scores in a split-sample study where they submitted the

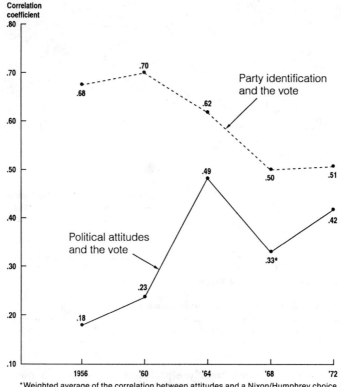

Figure 3.3 shows the correlation coefficient chart with values for "Party identification and the vote" (.68, .70, .62, .50, .51) and "Political attitudes and the vote" (.18, .23, .49, .33*, .42) across years 1956, '60, '64, '68, '72.

*Weighted average of the correlation between attitudes and a Nixon/Humphrey choice, a Nixon/Wallace choice, and a Humphrey/Wallace choice.

Figure 3.3   Pearson correlations between party identification and the presidential vote and between the summary measure of political beliefs and the presidential vote, 1956–1972
Source: Nie et al., *The Changing American Voter,* p. 165.

old-format questionnaire to one-half of the sample and the new-format questionnaire to the other half.[46] Differences in question wording did produce differences in scores.

Norman Nie and James Rabjohn respond that the changes in political attitudes over time are real and are not simply an artifact of question wording. They report the increased consistency of citizens' responses to a set of questions, known as the Stouffer tolerance items, that were asked in both the mid-1950s and early 1970s and were uncontaminated by a change in format. The average association between questions increased in all but one of the thirty-six pairs.[47] Nie's critics respond, however, that the Stouffer items were intended to form a unidimensional scale and do not pose a

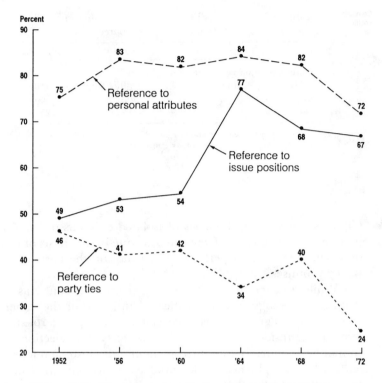

Figure 3.4   Frequency of evaluations of candidates in terms of party ties, personal attributes, and issue positions, 1952–1972
Source: Nie et al., *The Changing American Voter,* p. 167.

valid test of the consistency of the public's beliefs across a broad set of domestic and foreign policy questions.[48]

The Center for Political Studies (formerly the Survey Research Center) repeatedly interviewed a panel of voters throughout the 1972 to 1976 period. The results from this panel study also challenge the notion of a changing American voter. The 1970s sample showed no increased attitudinal stability compared with the 1950s sample studied by Converse in his famous nonattitude study (see Table 3.5). Voter attitudes in the 1970s were no more stable than those of the earlier era.[49]

POLITICAL SCIENCE UNCOVERS THE ROLE OF ISSUES

The debate on voter ideology continues. But voters do not have to think ideologically or sophisticatedly to vote on the basis of issues.

Table 3.5   Attitudinal Stability over Time; the
1950s and 1970s Compared

	1956–60	1972–76
Government job guarantee	.457	.493
School desegregation	.397	.410
U.S. stay home	.347	.309
Foreign aid	.292	.264

Source: Philip E. Converse and Gregory B. Markus, "Plus ça change
. . .: The New CPS Election Study Panel," *American Political Science
Review* 73 (March 1979): pp. 40–41.

Citizens can vote on the basis of isolated opinions or more frag-
mentary belief systems. They can also vote on the basis of results,
on evaluations of past performance, if not on the basis of future
policy promises.

While no consensus exists among political scientists as to the
degree of ideological or sophisticated thinking of the American
voter, there is a greater consensus that issues do play a role in contemporary presidential voting. We now believe that election results
cannot be adequately explained without at least some reference to
issues. Issues influence presidential elections, but in a manner
quite different from that suggested by *The American Voter* in its criteria for issue voting.

The Survey Research Center/Center for Political Studies initially did not recognize the influence of issues; their data showed
that issues were not a major factor in presidential voting. But
V. O. Key's challenge forced the Center to respond. By 1968 the
Center admitted that the voter was capable of voting in response to
issues. Their data pointed to the fact that in the 1968 election supporters of third-party candidate George Wallace, Governor of Alabama, were issue voters. But overall, according to the Center's
major report, issues had little to do with the voter choice between
Nixon and Humphrey. Voters could not discern clear differences
in the policy positions of the major-party candidates, even on the
question of the Vietnam War.[50] By 1972, however, the Center's
data would point to a great change: issues approached partisanship in influencing the choice between McGovern and Nixon.[51]

Yet the conclusions of the Center's interpretation of voting in
1968 are somewhat incongruous. One of the least sophisticated
segments of the American public, Wallace voters, is reported to
engage in issue voting while more educated voters are seen to be

enslaved by partisan identification![52] How can this be? Two possible explanations come to mind.

The first is that voting choices congruent with party identification are influenced by issues, but in a manner that is not easily detected by the Center's methods. It is relatively easy to spot the influence of issues when policy concerns lead an individual to vote against his usual party. It is more difficult to discern the influence of issues independent of partisanship when policy positions reinforce a voter's traditional party loyalty.

The American Voter portrayed political party affiliation as psychologically determined and highly fixed. Once handed down from the parent to the child, it remained stable over the citizen's life. Yet, more recent studies of political behavior have begun to refute this picture of immobile, psychologically determined party identification. Recent findings show that voters' partisan affiliations do change over time, as they are greatly influenced by adult political experiences including policy attitudes.[53] As Morris P. Fiorina put it, "Controversies about issue voting versus party identification miss the point: the 'issues' are *in* party identification."[54]

The second explanation is that voters do not have to be sophisticated to vote in response to issues. Wallace voters were moved by protest and racial backlash concerns. According to Edward Carmines and James Stimson, Wallace voters were responding to "easy" issues.[55] There was nothing complex about the Wallace voters' concerns about the Vietnam War, social change, and law-and-order. It was easy for these voters to have clear-cut opinions on victory through strength and the undesirability of school desegregation or street demonstrations. More complex and difficult issues, however, are less likely to become the basis for the mass public's voting decision.

Citizens, then, do not have to think in an ideological or sophisticated fashion to vote in response to issues. Indeed, voters do not even need to be able to explain the meanings of liberalism and conservatism. Instead, voters need only to perceive and be able to vote on a basic choice before them. For some voters that choice might be along liberal-conservative lines. For other citizens the voting choice might be based on an alternative ideological dimension or a key or salient issue. Still other citizens might cast their ballots on the basis of their degree of satisfaction or dissatisfaction with the times, to choose to continue or change the direction of current policies in Washington. Many voters who fail to meet *The American Voter* criteria for issue voting still know why they voted as they did. As Fiorina explains, a voter need not spend his life watching "Meet the Press" and reading the *New York Times.* He can look at the evening news and observe the coffins being unloaded from Air Force transports, the increasing price of a basket of groceries between this month and last, and the police arresting demonstrators of one stripe or another. What does it matter if this voter is not familiar with the nuances of current government policies or is not aware of the precise alternatives offered by the opposition? He is not the professional policy formulator. He has not devoted a career to pursuit of public office nor sought such office on the basis of his competency to govern. Perhaps he can't "cognize the issue in some form," but can go to the polls and indicate whether or not he likes the way those who can "cognize the issue" are in fact doing so.[56]

The criteria for issue voting set down in *The American Voter* are increasingly irrelevant. "Perhaps," as Fiorina criticizes, "we find the electorate wanting because our tests are wanting."[57] Political scientists should begin to identify the various ways that issues influence presidential voting.

THREE COMMON VARIANTS OF ISSUE VOTING

More recent writings in political science have observed the prominent role played by issues in presidential elections. These writings have attempted to explain just how issues influence the voter's choice—why some issues have a greater effect on elections than do other issues. Three different variants of issue voting are particularly noteworthy: retrospective voting, directional voting, and voting in response to easy and hard issues.

Retrospective Voting

Relatively few Americans engage in prospective issue voting by comparing the policy promises of the two major parties and their candidates across a broad range of issues. Instead, policy concerns in presidential elections are often reflected in *retrospective issue voting* as opposed to prospective voting. Fiorina describes the thought calculus of citizens engaged in retrospective voting:

[T]hey typically have one comparatively hard bit of data: they know what life has been like during the incumbent's administration. They need *not* know the precise economic or foreign policies of the incumbent administration in order to see or feel the *results* of those policies. And is it not reasonable to base voting decisions on results as well as on intentions? In order to ascertain whether the incumbents have performed poorly or well, citizens need only calculate the changes in their own welfare.[58]

Citizens who vote retrospectively look not so much at a candidate's policy promises for future action as they look back at the recent past. If citizens are satisfied with the performance of the incumbent administration, they can vote to continue its tenure in office; if dissatisfied, they can vote for a change.

It can be argued that voting on the basis of retrospective evaluations provides a more reliable basis for voting than does voting in response to a candidate's promises. Candidates for office are too willing to promise citizens anything, no matter how unrealistic or unattainable, in order to get their votes. A party's past record also gives a fairly reliable indication as to the future actions a candidate might undertake.[59]

According to a number of studies, economic issues have played a prominent role in voters' decisions in statehouse and congressional as well as presidential elections. Whether citizens are voting in response to their own pocketbook or to their perceptions of the overall economic well-being of the country is still a matter of some debate.[60]

Retrospective evaluations have been evident in a number of presidential elections. In 1968 the electorate voted to reject a Democratic administration incapable of handling campus demonstrations, ghetto riots, and rising welfarism. The outcome of the extremely close race of 1976 was influenced by the public's dissatisfaction with Watergate and President Ford's pardon of Richard Nixon.[61]

Retrospective evaluations based on the economy have determined more recent presidential elections. In 1980 Jimmy Carter was ousted from office primarily because of his inability to handle the twin issues of recession and inflation.[62] Carter's standing in the polls was amazingly low even before the intrusion of the Iranian hostage crisis. By 1984 the nation's economy had rebounded and the United States was at peace. As a result, the 1984 race was essentially a retrospective endorsement of Ronald Reagan's first four years in office. Even the 1988 George Bush-Michael Dukakis race was influenced by retrospective evaluations as citizens cast their ballots to continue the long period of economic prosperity of the Reagan-Bush administration. Had the country in 1988 been in the midst of an economic downturn or suffering from high rates of inflation, both the rhetoric and the outcome of the election would likely have been quite different than they were.

Directional Voting

Retrospective voting is, in effect, a vote for a choice of direction, to continue or change present policies in Washington. Voters indeed have only one basic choice in a presidential election, a choice of direction, but that choice is not always a retrospective one.

Under *directional voting,* citizens need only to be able to discern a diffuse preference between the competing symbolic themes and broad policy alternatives represented by the two major-party candidates.[63] They do not need to possess great knowledge or well-thought-out opinions on a large number of specific issues. Instead, voters need only to discover which of the two general directions presented before them they prefer. Do they want to continue the general direction offered by the present administration or do they prefer an alternative? Do they prefer the general policy directions advocated by the Republicans or the general policy directions advocated by the Democrats?

Symbolism plays an important role in directional voting. As George Rabinowitz and Stuart Elaine MacDonald explain, "The key tenet of symbolic politics is that for issues (or other political cues) to have impact, they must evoke emotions and sentiments rather than simple objective appraisal of information."[64] In 1968, "law and order" and "welfare" were particularly powerful symbols; "middle America" voted for Nixon's more conservative approach to welfare and social issues as contrasted with the more liberal course of direction represented by the Democrats. In 1988 the Republicans found a particularly potent and visceral symbol in Willie Horton and Michael Dukakis's "revolving door" furlough program.

As Rabinowitz and MacDonald further explain, directional voting is likely to be quite strong in an election when one side fails to take a stand on a symbolically powerful issue:

> The most meaningful policy guidance that results directly from election outcomes occurs when a majority exists for a policy, but that majority is either not obvious to politicians or is not courted by one of the parties for ideological reasons. Under such conditions the election will tend to be won by the candidate espousing the majority direction.[65]

This observation helps to explain the outcome of the 1988 election. George Bush seized the Willie Horton issue. Michael Dukakis failed to respond quickly and strongly; he did not believe that the furlough question could dominate a presidential election. Dukakis was reluctant to compromise his progressive beliefs on penal reform. Furthermore, he also was not willing to take a strong law-and-order stance that could be perceived as racist. Bush courted the national majority on the issue and won; Dukakis did not declare his clear support for law and order until it was too late.

Easy and Hard Issues

Not all issues are capable of moving the American electorate. As the theory of directional voting indicates, issues that can be portrayed with emotive symbolism are more likely to evoke voter response than those which cannot be similarly portrayed. Symbolism plays an important role in another theory of issue voting, that advanced by Edward G. Carmines and James A. Stimson.

According to Carmines and Stimson, there are essentially two different types of issues, each capable of evoking a response from a different group of voters.[66] *Hard issues* present voters with complex and difficult-to-understand policy alternatives. Voters must use intellect and reason in sorting out the policy alternatives on hard issues. Well-educated, better informed, and more active voters—in short, more sophisticated citizens—are more likely to respond to hard issues.

Easy issues, on the other hand, evoke what Carmines and Stimson call "gut responses." Easy issues tend to be symbolic; they can be understood simplistically. They are also likely to be of long duration on the political agenda. As the easy-issue voter need not approach politics with any intellectual sophistication—the easy-issue voter only needs to know if he or she is for or against a particular matter—easy-issue voting in presidential elections is likely fairly commonplace.

The difference between easy and hard issues explains why race and crime were issues in the 1968 election but the Vietnam War was not. As Carmines and Stimson observe, the typical voter sees racial desegregation as a simple issue. White middle America did not want school busing or the quickened pace of racial integration, policy positions associated with the Democrats in 1968. Similarly, middle Americans did not want to understand the social roots of criminal behavior, urban unrest, or campus protests; they wanted law and order. These were easy issues, and in 1968, white middle America knew what it wanted and voted for it. The Vietnam War, in contrast, presented a more complex matter. In 1968 both candidates promised the goal of peace, but neither would state clearly how that goal was to be reached. Further, many voters could not themselves discern what road provided the best route to peace—

accelerated bombing or a bombing halt, increased troop commit-ments or unilateral troop withdrawals, escalation of the military effort or de-escalation to promote peace talks. Vietnam was a hard issue, one that was too difficult to guide less informed, less sophis-ticated voters in casting their ballots.[67]

Similarly, in 1988, easy issues, not hard issues, were again fac-tors in the presidential vote. The Willie Horton/furlough, the Pledge of Allegiance, and no-new-taxes matters were easy issues that evoked a gut response from many citizens. Voters knew where they stood on these issues. Opinions on the tax issue were also quite compartmentalized; voters could declare their strong opposi-tion to new taxes without first resolving the question of how to solve the nation's budget deficit. The deficit itself, much to the Democrats' chagrin, was not an important influence on voting in 1988. Few citizens could discern a workable and desirable solution to the deficit problem. Nor could they discern desirable solutions to such intricate problems as coping with the foreign trade im-balance or the savings and loan crisis.

Race is an easy issue—a fact that helps explain the evolution and staying power of this issue in contemporary elections.[68] Race continued to be an important electoral factor as the United States entered the 1990s. The new race issue, at least for the early 1990s, was quotas and affirmative action. In North Carolina, conserva-tive Republican Senator Jesse Helms withstood a challenge from Harvey Gantt, the black Mayor of Charlotte, in part with the help of an ad that appealed to white resentment of affirmative action programs. The ad showed the hands of a white worker crumbling a rejection notice in frustration as the audio announces that the worker was turned down despite the fact that he was the best quali-fied applicant for the job. Likewise, in Alabama incumbent Re-publican Governor Guy Hunt rode the affirmative action issue to reelection. In California, Pete Wilson gained a narrow victory in the gubernatorial race after Democrat Dianne Feinstein intimated that she would impose virtual racial quotas on hiring by the state government.

SUMMARY

Relatively few voters live up to the model of the ideal democratic citizen who examines the prospective promises of each candidate before voting. Instead, voters are more likely to respond to issues retrospectively by judging the performance of the incumbent administration and the general records of the two major parties. Voters are also capable of choosing between the broad, general policy directions offered by the two major parties. Citizens are also capable of voting in response to issues they find to be of great salience. Easy issues, not hard issues, are more likely to influence the mass public's voting decision in presidential elections.

Of course, not all citizens are issue voters. Many persons continue to vote in response to their party affiliation or a candidate's personal image and qualities. Partisanship and personal images continue to be important influences on American voting behavior. But the influence of issues in the presidential race is more and more evident. The relative importance of each varies with the context of the specific presidential election.

In the following chapters we attempt to trace the changing balance between partisanship, issues, and candidate personal images in presidential elections. In each election—especially those since the mid-1960s—issue-based evaluations can be seen to have played an important role in the election outcome.

THE
NEW DEAL
ERA

We commonly think of the United States as having a more or less class-based party system. The Democrats represent a broad-based coalition of diverse ethnic and working-class constituencies against a Republican party dominated by business groups and upper-status interests.

Yet, this commonplace view provides an accurate picture of the political party alignment only at one point in time—the New Deal era. As we shall see, class-based cleavages did not dominate presidential voting prior to the 1930s. The importance of class-based patterns and partisanship to the presidential vote has also weakened over time.

As we saw in Chapter 3, the first high-quality insights into American voting behavior were gained from studies of presidential elections during the 1940s and 1950s. These studies pointed to the importance of partisanship and presidential candidates' personal images to the voting decision. Few voters were concerned with issues. The findings of these studies helped shape the thinking of political science for the next two decades and longer.[1]

Yet, even at the time, these conclusions were not universally accepted. V. O. Key, Jr., prepared a major work challenging the conclusions of these studies. According to Key, voters were not fools. Instead, substantive evaluations were a part of their voting decision. Many Americans cast their ballots in light of their retrospective evaluations of the performance of the incumbent administration.[2]

The accepted "truths" regarding American voting behavior are quite ephemeral. The American voter changes over time. We start by looking at voter attachments during the System of 1896, the party alignment that preceded the New Deal era.

THE SYSTEM OF 1896

In the early twentieth century, the key voting cleavages in the United States were along regional or sectional lines, not social class lines. Largely, voting behavior during the early part of the century was shaped by the election of 1896. This election is often described as a *critical election* as that year's campaign generated perceptions and loyalties that seemingly influenced presidential elections for the next three decades.[3] William Jennings Bryan, the 1896 Democratic presidential candidate, left the party with the taint of rural populism. It was an association that was not popular in a nation that was speedily becoming industrialized and urbanized.

Bryan appealed to farmers in the South and West who faced difficult times as a result of the Depression of 1893. These farmers resented the power of corporate elites. They further resented the alien cultures of immigrants who resided in the cities of the Northeast and the Midwest. An eloquent orator, Bryan promised to end the gold standard to inflate currency and thereby ease the repayment of their debts: "You shall not crucify mankind upon a cross of gold!" According to Bryan, it was clearly city folk who owed their existence to people in the country: "The great cities rest upon our broad and fertile prairies."

As Walter Dean Burnham describes:

> Bryan's appeal at base was essentially Jacksonian—a call for a return to the simpler and more virtuous economic and political arrangements which he identified with that bygone era. Such nostalgia could evoke a positive response among the native-stock rural elements whose political style and economic expectations had been shaped in the far-away past. But it could hardly seem a realistic political choice for the ethnically pluralist urban populations, large numbers of whom found such nostalgia meaningless since it related to nothing in their past or current experience.[4]

Bryanism was an appeal to the virtues of small-town and rural America that offered little to citizens of the big cities of the Northeast. Samuel Lubell observed that Bryan's "revivalist oratory might inflame the Bible belt—but in the city he was a repellent, even comic figure."[5] The nativist elements of Bryan's support only further alienated voters of immigrant stock. Bryan's fundamentalist following saw themselves, native Protestants, as virtuous; they too often viewed immigrants and Catholics as threatening intruders and the source of "demon rum," filth, disease, sloth, crime, and corruption.

Bryan's agrarian appeal cast the Democrats "in the role of reactionaries" who opposed change.[6] In contrast, Republican presidential candidate William McKinley promised a "full dinner pail," a new era of industrial growth that would provide prosperity for all Americans. Both factory workers and owners alike responded to this Republican appeal. Faced with a choice between Bryan's rejectionism and Republican industrialization, the urban masses voted Republican. The Democratic party was virtually wiped out by the reaction against Bryanism in large areas of the Northeast and the Middle West.[7] In the 1890s "the Republican party alone retained some relevance to the urban setting."[8]

After 1896 the United States was essentially a country divided politically by region. The Republicans gained dominance in national politics because of their popularity in the more populous Northeast. The Democrats dominated the South. White voters in the South also continued to vote solidly Democratic because of their memories of the Civil War and the harsh reconstruction efforts pushed by Radical Republicans. Agrarian protest movements would continue to rise in the West. Republican control over the presidency for the next twenty-six years was interrupted only as a consequence of Theodore Roosevelt's Bull Moose Party revolt, which divided the normal Republican vote. As a result, Democrat Woodrow Wilson won the presidential election in 1912 and was reelected four years later.

THE CHANGING SOCIAL FABRIC

An electoral system that ignored class issues could not last long in a nation that had to deal with the problems posed by a new industrial order. The Republican party could not represent the interests of factory owners while meeting the demands of workers who sought unionization, hours and wage legislation, safe working conditions, and social security. These workers would have to turn to an opposition party not allied with corporate owners—the Democrats.

The Democratic party was bitterly divided by a schism between its agrarian wing and a northern wing of big city voters and political machine leaders. The 1924 Democratic convention lasted 103 ballots. New York Governor Alfred E. Smith, an Irish Catholic and a "wet" on the issue of Prohibition, fought William Gibbs McAdoo, a Protestant and an antialcohol "dry" who also had the support of the Ku Klux Klan. Given the cultural and sectional cleavages that divided the party, neither candidate could gain the two-thirds vote then necessary for the nomination under the party's rules. The convention finally and unhappily settled on a compromise candidate, John W. Davis.

Four years later, Smith gained the nomination, setting off a virtual "Al Smith Revolution" as cities with large foreign-born populations were drawn into the Democratic column.[9] Smith had grown up on the streets of the East Side of New York City; he spoke with a New Yorker's nasal twang. He was the first Catholic to gain a major party nomination for the presidency. Smith's nomination sent a message to America's new arrivals, particularly to Catholics, in the Northeast: the national Democratic party was their party; it was no longer the party of Bryan.

Smith lost the 1928 race badly as the nation was not yet ready to vote for a Catholic for president. The normally solid Democratic South was split by Smith's Catholicism. The Republican candidate, Herbert Hoover, gained unprecedented victories in five states in the rim or outer South. Only in the Deep South, with its Democratic loyalty rooted in its Negrophobia, did white voters swallow their compunctions and vote Democratic.

In 1928 the Democrats lost the battle but began to win the war. The Irish, Italians, and other new-stock citizens voted for Smith in large numbers. They were the beginnings of a soon-to-be Democratic majority, a majority that would be cemented in place as a result of the Great Depression and voter endorsement of Franklin Delano Roosevelt's New Deal recovery programs.[10] The nation's Republican majority was about to give way to a new Democratic era.

THE NEW DEAL REALIGNMENT

The Great Depression and Roosevelt's New Deal response ushered in a new voting alignment that gave shape to the modern voting era—an era that is only now undergoing great change. Roosevelt was swept into office in 1932 as voters blamed the Republicans for the Depression. The Democrats derisively campaigned against Hoovervilles, the tent cities that had sprung up across America. For the next thirty years the Democrats would attempt to campaign against the ghost of Herbert Hoover. They would portray the Republicans as the party of the Depression. The Democrats, in contrast, would promise that "happy days are here again."

The Democrats won office in 1932 simply by blaming the Republicans for the nation's economic collapse. They promised economic recovery and relief, but were not yet wedded to activist government intervention in the economy and the provision of social welfare programs. The 1932 Democratic platform even went along with the prevailing economic philosophy of controlling government spending to ensure a balanced budget and enhanced business confidence.

Once in office, however, Democrat Franklin Delano Roosevelt switched to a more activist government response to the problems of the Depression. By 1935 the Democrats had initiated a number of programs that promised much needed benefits to huge numbers of Americans, including native-stock voters, members of more established immigrant groups, and more recent foreign-stock voters alike. The Works Progress Administration provided work relief for thousands. The National Labor Relations Act (also called the Wagner Act after the Democratic senator from New York who authored it) protected labor's right to organize and forced employers to bargain collectively with unions. The Social Security Act provided cash assistance to the elderly, the unemployed, and the disabled. A soak-the-rich tax bill in 1935 also clearly established the Democrats as the party of the working man fighting against the party of the upper class.

The result was that by 1936, working class, native-stock voters were added to the Democratic party's immigrant base, virtually completing the nation's realignment from a Republican to a Democratic era. Black citizens, among the nation's most deprived groups, were also gradually moving away from the party of Lincoln and shifting their loyalty to the party that was promising them much-needed material assistance in their lives. By 1936 the Democrats had assembled a coalition of labor, new-stock ethnic groups, southern whites, and a growing black vote to become the new national majority party.

The new class pattern to voting helps explain the sudden demise of the *Literary Digest* poll in 1936. The *Literary Digest,* a popular magazine, had accurately predicted the outcome of a number of presidential elections. In 1936 the *Digest* became the laughing stock of the nation when it predicted that the Republican, Alfred Landon, would win the presidency by nearly twenty points. As it turned out, Roosevelt won reelection by a landslide, taking 523 of the 531 electoral votes and 60 percent of the popular vote. The magazine lost credibility and soon went out of business.

What had gone wrong? The *Digest* had failed to poll a representative sample of American voters. Instead the *Digest* had its subscribers fill out and mail back sample ballots to the magazine. The magazine also used phone books, automobile registrations, and lists of club memberships in its polling effort which, not so coincidentally, was aimed at gaining the magazine new subscribers. Over 2 million ballots were returned. Yet, despite its large size, the sample was unscientific. During the Depression only financially better-off citizens were likely to subscribe to magazines or own automobiles and telephones. The magazine had inadvertently overrepresented upper-status citizens, who were likely to vote Republican, and failed to contact a representative number of working-class and unemployed citizens, who were now likely to vote for Roosevelt.

The New Deal realignment took place over a series of elections. Voters did not convert at once to new Democratic loyalties. In 1932 the Democrats gained the crossover vote of Republicans disaffected because of the nation's distressed economic conditions. However, it appears that not as many voters changed their party identification as was once believed. The growth of the new Democratic majority was not simply the result of converting former Republican voters. The new Democratic majority also was forged by winning the loyalty of younger and newer voters, voters who had not built strong Republican identifications over the years and were free to respond to the new political cues created by Roosevelt's New Deal.[11]

Gerald Gamm reports in his study of Boston during this era that only Jewish voters in general seemed to convert from Republican to Democratic loyalties. Jews were attracted to the liberalism of the New Deal Democratic party, a liberalism that matched the teachings of their faith. Changes in the partisan attachments of Italians and black voters, in contrast, were much more gradual. While there were some conversions, it appears that the entrance of new voters explains much of the new Democratic partisanship of these groups. Generational replacement provides a particularly strong explanation of the changed partisan affiliation of black voters. Older blacks committed to the party of Lincoln were dying off and were replaced by younger blacks more responsive to the economic and social programs now being offered by the national Democratic party.[12]

Generational replacement, then, helps explain much of the dynamic for change in the electorate. Older voters die off and are replaced by newer voters less restrained by the older loyalties and habits. In the 1960s and 1970s change would emerge again as new voters not well-socialized into the New Deal loyalties would come of voting age.[13]

But as social change continued, new strains would emerge in the Democratic coalition. One immediate problem for the Democratic party was that of race. The party could not harmoniously accommodate blacks, southern whites, and northern liberals. In 1948 this fissure would begin to divide the Democrats. Hubert Humphrey, then mayor of Minneapolis and the darling of white liberals, had pushed through a civil rights resolution at that year's Democratic national convention. A number of southern whites bolted, forming their own party, the Dixiecrats, or States' Rights party. Its candidate for the presidency, South Carolina Governor Strom Thurmond (later to be a U.S. senator), carried four Deep South states, taking thirty-nine electoral votes. Faced with this revolt, the incumbent President Harry Truman squeaked to a somewhat unexpected and narrow victory, garnering 52 percent of the vote. The Dixiecrat revolt was a precursor as to how the Democratic New Deal coalition would begin to unravel over the years as memories of the Depression were forgotten and new racial and social matters displaced older economic concerns in the minds of the voters. As we shall see, a new invention, television, was also about to become a strong influence on voters.

THE 1950s: THE INFANCY OF TELEVISION

Television first became a factor in presidential elections in 1952. At that time approximately four of every ten American households owned a television set. That year saw the first televised broadcast of national party conventions. Dwight David Eisenhower's use of spot ads would begin to change the character of presidential elections.

At first, politicians schooled in the old ways of campaigning were unable to recognize the power inherent in the new communications medium. In 1948 President Truman still campaigned by a cross-country, whistle-stop train tour. His Republican opponent, Thomas E. Dewey, spurned as "undignified" the suggestion that he run television spots in key states in the closing days of his campaign. Had Dewey heeded this advice, he might well have been elected.[14]

In 1952 the Democrats ineptly responded to the opportunities presented by the new medium. Their national convention was so loosely run that Adlai Stevenson delivered his acceptance speech at 2:10 A.M., a time when most Americans had already gone to bed. During the fall campaign, the party bought time in thirty-minute blocks during which it aired lengthy campaign speeches that bored viewing audiences. The speeches were also aired late in the evening to reduce the costs of air time, so the Democrats missed much of their potential audience.[15] Stevenson's campaign headquarters also initially rejected an offer of free time from NBC for a televised presidential debate, despite the fact that the Democratic candidate, less well known than Eisenhower and trailing in the polls, needed the opportunity provided by the debate. Eisenhower's camp astutely rejected the offer knowing that it had more to lose in a televised showdown.[16]

The Democrats provided for the local broadcast of one of Truman's speeches. Technically, Truman was the first presidential candidate to use paid television advertising. Still, it was Dwight Eisenhower who, in 1952, demonstrated that television could be used as an effective presidential campaign tool.

Eisenhower opened his campaign with a simulcast on sixty-five NBC television stations and 165 radio stations. Radio was still essential for ensuring blanket coverage as less than half of the households in America then had television.[17] The Republicans also brought in the Madison Avenue advertising firm of BBD&O to help prepare their advertising campaign. Rather than buy huge blocks of time in the late evening or pay to preempt popular primetime shows, BBD&O and the party's strategists hit on the idea of presenting Eisenhower's image to the public in short spot ads, twenty seconds or so in length, to be aired during commercial time between television programs.

Eisenhower ran on the highly personalized slogan of "I Like Ike!" Eisenhower was sold to the public on the basis of his personal merits—a World War II hero and a citizen-leader who was above the normal political fray. As the campaign's advertising strategy was based on a personalization of the product, both Eisenhower and his vice-presidential running mate, Richard Nixon, were marketed to television viewers "so that the warmth of their personalities can be felt."[18] A Republican memorandum outlined the basic technique of this strategy:

> The spots themselves would be the height of simplicity. People... would ask the General a question....The General's answer would be his complete comprehension of the problem and his determination to do something about it when elected. Thus he inspires loyalty without prematurely committing himself to any strait-jacketing answer.[19]

By today's standards, the Eisenhower spot ads seem quite amateurish and lacking in production values. Yet at the time they proved quite effective. Eisenhower was brought to a studio where a camera crew filmed his answers to a number of questions. In an early bit of television editing, Eisenhower's remarks were juxtaposed as answers to questions posed at different times by a group of everyday Americans. One typical Eisenhower ad was as follows:

EISENHOWER ANSWERS AMERICA ad

VIDEO: Sign reads EISENHOWER ANSWERS AMERICA next to a picture of Ike.

AUDIO (Announcer): "Eisenhower answers America."

AUDIO AND VIDEO (Elderly woman asks): "You know what things cost today? High prices are just driving me crazy!"

Switch to Eisenhower: "Yes. My [wife] Mamie gets after me about the high cost of living. It's another reason why I say it's time for a change, time to get back to an honest dollar and an honest dollar's work."

In his most famous pronouncement of the campaign, Ike promised to go to Korea if elected to bring the war there to an end. He did not, however, supply any hint as to what steps he would take to bring the war to a conclusion. Ike's election eve hour-long simulcast presented Ike as a man of the people. The program concluded with Ike and Mamie cutting a victory cake.[20]

Television also proved critical in rescuing Richard Nixon on the ticket after press stories reported allegations that the vice-presidential nominee had illegally pocketed money from an expense fund raised by his backers. The sums of money involved seem rather paltry by today's standards but in the 1950s it was a major scandal. In the wake of the charges, Nixon's presence on the Republican ticket was an embarrassment to Eisenhower who had campaigned vigorously against "the mess in Washington," including charges of corruption in the Truman administration. Eisenhower was ready to dump his running mate from the ticket unless Nixon could persuasively present his case to the American public. This Nixon did in his famous Checkers speech.

Nixon met with his advisers and decided to respond in a half-hour paid broadcast.[21] The broadcast drew what at the time was the largest televised audience ever for any campaign speech. It was produced by BBD&O and the Kudner advertising agency. Nixon spoke directly into the camera. He claimed never to have taken any money from the fund for his personal use and never to have profited personally from politics. Nixon talked about how he was not a rich man, how as a boy he had worked in the family grocery store. He had also worked his way through college. Nixon went on to say that "probably the best thing that ever happened to me happened" when "I married Pat." Pat, continued Nixon, "doesn't have a mink coat. But she does have a respectable Republican cloth coat, and I always tell her that she would look good in anything." The only gift Nixon acknowledged receiving was a dog:

> A man down in Texas heard Pat on the radio mention the fact that our two youngsters would like to have a dog, and believe it or not, the day before we left on this campaign trip we got a message from Union Station in Baltimore, saying they had a package for us. We went down to get it. You know what it was? It was a little cocker spaniel dog, in a crate that he had sent all the way from Texas—black and white, spotted, and our little girl Tricia, the six-year old, named it Checkers. And you know, the kids, like all kids, loved the dog, and I just want to say this right now, that regardless of what they say about it, we are going to keep it.

The camera focused on Pat at appropriate moments.

At the end of the broadcast, Nixon asked viewers to wire or write the Republican National Committee stating their feelings about his remaining on the ticket. The response was overwhelming; the public had been moved by the Richard Nixon story. The next day Nixon flew to meet General Eisenhower in Wheeling,

West Virginia. Eisenhower met him and responded by putting his arms around Nixon, saying, "You're my boy."

By today's standards, the Checkers speech was a maudlin exercise. The entire scandal had been reduced to the imagery of his wife's cloth coat and a little girl's love for a puppy. One wonders if such a speech could so easily dispel the public's doubts today. In 1952, in the infancy of television, the American public had not yet built any great familiarity with the televised presentation of an orchestrated event.

Television had enhanced the personalization of politics. Viewers could see the candidates up close and judge them on whether or not they appeared to be warm, caring, and trustworthy human beings. Where radio focused on a candidate's words, television focused on a candidate's visual appearance. Candidates were now increasingly judged as individuals, as television performers, not as the purveyors of a political party's platform on issues.

Eisenhower's 1952 and 1956 victories are regarded by political scientists as *deviating elections* in the New Deal era. The Republicans won the presidency without converting new voters to Republicanism. Partisan affiliations established during the New Deal era remained unchanged despite Ike's victories. The Republicans won because of a short-term factor, Ike's personal appeal as a war hero and a citizen-leader above politics. Eisenhower did make substantial inroads in the South as whites in that region showed increasing dissatisfaction with the national Democratic party's progressive racial attitudes. Great ideological issues were absent from the 1952 and 1956 contests.[22]

1960: KENNEDY'S IMAGE PROBLEM AND THE GREAT DEBATES

By 1960 nearly all American households had a television set. The 1960 presidential race was the closest in American history; John Kennedy won the presidency gaining just a hair over 50 percent of the two-party vote. Television was an important influence on the outcome of the election. Yet, in a race so close, image creation on television was only one of a large number of factors that can be said to have made the difference.

Kennedy confronted two major problems in his race for the presidency. First was his relative youth and inexperience. Kennedy was the relatively unknown forty-two-year-old junior Democratic senator from Massachusetts. In the general election he was up against the Republican Vice-President of the United States,

Richard Nixon, a man whom Americans saw as being much more experienced in the critical arena of foreign affairs.

Second was Kennedy's religion; Kennedy was a Roman Catholic. Al Smith had lost badly in 1928. Was America in 1960 ready to elect a Catholic? Although the presidential candidates themselves refrained from making religion an issue, ugly charges regarding Kennedy's religion and virulent anti-Catholic literature circulated among various groups in the population. Would a Catholic President subordinate his policy decisions to those of the church and Pope?

In 1960 only sixteen states used primaries to select their delegates to the national party conventions. In most states, delegates were chosen in closed caucuses dominated by state party leaders and other party loyalists. Candidates for the presidency did not need to enter or win a large number of state primaries. Instead, presidential candidates strategically picked which races they would contest, avoiding as much as possible those states where a possible setback could do critical damage to their presidential effort.

Kennedy needed key primary victories to show party leaders that his youth and religion were not insurmountable handicaps in his search for the presidency. Kennedy beat Hubert Humphrey in the Wisconsin primary. But the Wisconsin results were fairly close and did not prove that Kennedy could win in overwhelmingly Protestant America. Kennedy won by capturing the votes of Wisconsin's sizable Catholic population; he lost the state's Protestant areas.

West Virginia became the decisive showdown between Kennedy and Humphrey. Humphrey made a critical strategic mistake, that of choosing to meet Kennedy's challenge in this overwhelmingly Protestant state. West Virginia was significant in 1960 even though no presidential delegates were chosen in the state's primary. Kennedy used his victory in West Virginia to demonstrate to party leaders and national convention delegates that he could win even in Protestant-dominated areas of the country.

Kennedy met the question of his religion head-on in West Virginia. In a statewide paid television broadcast and in paid commercials Kennedy explained that his religious faith would not in any way affect his handling of the presidency. "Now," as Kennedy said in one of the ads, "you cannot tell me the day I was born it was said I could never run for president because I wouldn't meet my oath of office."[23]

The West Virginia primary underscored the critical role played by money in elections in the television age. Humphrey lacked the funds to effectively counter Kennedy's ads. A half-hour, election-eve telethon broadcast by Humphrey further illustrated the dangers that could result if a campaign lacked the necessary funds or otherwise failed to take the proper steps to control how a candidate's image would be presented to television viewers. Phone calls from the viewing audience were not screened. Humphrey actually fielded questions live from West Virginia's citizens. On the phone, a woman with a high-pitched West Virginia accent repeatedly berated Humphrey to "git out" of West Virginia. Humphrey was rattled. It was not quite the image that the campaign had hoped to get across.

As the media provided the public with additional information about Kennedy in addition to that of his religion, the initially hostile reaction of many Protestants was muted.[24] Still, a number of Protestants could not bring themselves to vote for a Catholic. Many Republican Catholics, on the other hand, now found themselves voting Democratic for one of their own.

Because of his religious affiliation, Kennedy lost about a million and a half votes more than he gained. Yet, in a curious way, his religion may have helped him win the White House. One study of 1960 concluded that "roughly one out of five Protestant Democrats or Protestant Independents who would otherwise have voted Democratic bolted because of the religious issue."[25] But many of the votes that Kennedy lost due to his religion were in the Protestant South. Although Kennedy lost Florida, Kentucky, Tennessee, and Virginia, defections from the Democratic banner in other southern states only cut into the normally sizable margins of victory usually enjoyed by a Democratic presidential candidate.

Catholic voters, in contrast, were concentrated in large two-party industrial states, key battlegrounds in winning the Electoral College in a close race. Kennedy won Illinois by a mere 9,000 popular votes; he won New Jersey by a similarly slim 22,000-vote margin. The greater-than-normal Democratic totals that Kennedy ran up among Catholics may well have accounted for his margin of victory in these two pivotal states. Overall, it appears that Kennedy's Catholicism helped him win Connecticut, New York, New Jersey, Pennsylvania, Illinois, and New Mexico and their combined total of 132 electoral votes, more than offsetting the 110 electoral votes he lost from the more Protestant states that would otherwise have gone Democratic had it not been for Kennedy's religion.

Race may have played a role similar to religion in 1960. Martin Luther King, Jr., had been jailed and sentenced to hard labor in Georgia because of his role in a civil rights demonstration. As the presidential campaign drew to a close, Kennedy placed a phone call to King's wife, Coretta, to offer his assistance. His brother, Robert Kennedy, intervened to help get King released on bail. The phone call alienated a number of white southerners, but it was widely hailed in the black community. The incident may have helped Kennedy to win Illinois and other key electoral states where black voters made up a sizable portion of the electorate.

In the fall campaign, television ads sought to enhance Kennedy's name recognition. One entirely issueless spot had a chorus repeatedly sing "Kennedy, Kennedy, Ken-ne-dy" as viewers were presented with a rapidly changing montage of campaign signs with the candidate's name. Other ads played up the image of Kennedy as a family man (prominently featuring his attractive and telegenic wife, Jackie), the brilliant author of the Pulitzer-prize-winning *Profiles in Courage,* and the heroic skipper of PT-109—a man who swam five miles to help rescue his shipmates.[26] In other ads Kennedy reviewed the Democratic party's achievements. He talked directly into the camera as if to underscore his maturity and seriousness. The Kennedy media campaign was designed to assuage voters' doubts about his youth and leadership abilities. It was almost as if Kennedy had directly responded to the line from the popular song at the time which said "Johnny, you're too young to run for president."

In the Republican ads, Nixon, too, often talked straight into the camera. These ads underscored the achievements of the Eisenhower years and Nixon's experience in foreign policy. The Republican campaign trumpeted Nixon's "kitchen debate" with Nikita Khrushchev. Nixon made a major strategic mistake, however, by promising to campaign in all fifty states. In the closing days of the campaign he was still scrambling to fulfill his fifty-state pledge instead of concentrating on appearances in media markets in key swing states.

Without doubt the most prominent campaign events of 1960 were the Great Debates. Kennedy, as the lesser-known candidate, needed the publicity the debates would generate. His performance in the debates could also assuage the doubts of wavering Democrats.

Kennedy and his advisers understood that television is essentially a visual medium. They believed that Kennedy's performance in the first debate would be crucial in establishing the public's perception of their candidate. Kennedy was tanned (he used sunlamps) and rested. He switched to a dark-blue business suit and light-blue shirt to show up more favorably against the studio background. He was coached to deliver his answers to reporters' questions by peering directly into the camera and looking at the voter back home, not at the questioner or at Nixon.

Kennedy emphasized the need to get America "moving again" after the lethargic Eisenhower years. His own energetic performance seemed to indicate that he was the man capable of moving America forward with vigor. Kennedy rattled off a series of statistics that made him look knowledgeable, informed, and presidential; the presidency was not too large a job for this man. In later debates he would even seize the vulnerable position of Quemoy and Matsu, two obscure islands off the coast of China, both to show his command of foreign policy and to attack the weakness of America's international position during the Eisenhower era. After the debates were over, the fate of the islands was rarely discussed again. Kennedy also attacked the Republicans for having allowed the United States to be caught on the wrong end of the missile gap.

In contrast, Nixon approached the first debate encounter much as he would any ordinary debate. He did not tailor his strategy to television. When the moderator asked him for a response to one of Kennedy's early statements, Nixon declined, in effect throwing away a very valuable ninety seconds of air time when the viewing audience's attention was at its peak. He also declined to draw sharp differences between Kennedy and himself.

In the first debate Nixon focused on the content of what he said, not on his appearance. An infected knee was causing him pain. He had spent the morning in a contentious appearance before a labor union assembly and he was not rested. He wore a gray suit that did not show up well on television against the studio background. He refused CBS's offer to have professional help apply his make-up for television. Instead, Nixon had a member of his own staff quickly apply pancake make-up, which did not effectively conceal his facial stubble. The mythology that has evolved around the debate greatly overemphasizes the extent to which Nixon's five o'clock shadow was apparent on television and an influence on viewer's reactions. It also exaggerates the degree to which Nixon visibly sweated under the studio's lights.

Polls showed that people who listened to the first debate over radio tended to judge Nixon as the winner. Kennedy, in contrast, did not try to win debating points. Instead, he sought to use the debates to fashion an image that would be presented to the television viewers across America. He would use the panel's questions as starting points from which he could launch into campaign statements that he had rehearsed with his advisers.

Media theorist Marshall McLuhan refers to how visual images dominated viewer reaction to the debates. Kennedy, he said, presented "an image closer to the TV hero...something like the shy young Sheriff" while Nixon "resembled more the railway lawyer who signs leases that are not in the interests of the folks in the little town."[27] Yet, McLuhan's assessment, part of the general mythology surrounding the Great Debates, is too severe. Looking at the tapes of the debate today, Nixon does not appear to do nearly as badly as this commentary would have us believe. But, in the first debate he does look *somewhat* less energetic, in-command, and presidential than does Kennedy.

Nixon, frustrated with the public's response to the first debate, adapted his performance to television for the three remaining exchanges. In the second debate, the temperature of the studio was kept very cool to minimize Nixon's sweating. He also had a professional apply his television make-up.

Nixon did better; but by then it was too late. Kennedy's first debate performance had dispelled Democrats' doubts. His campaign picked up momentum. With the age and religion issues somewhat mitigated by Kennedy's performance, normally Democratic voters could now more easily cast ballots for their party's candidate.

The debates proved important as Kennedy's performance removed the qualms that potential Democratic voters had regarding their candidate. Voters who were leaning Democrat were now more likely to vote Democratic. In effect, the debates helped to crystallize the voting decision. But voters may well have moved in these directions as the campaign progressed even had there been no debates.[28]

Very few voters switched from Nixon to Kennedy because of the debates. Public opinion polls revealed no substantial change in voter preferences even after the first debate, a debate Kennedy was generally acknowledged to have "won." Selective perception was at work; Democrats saw the things they wanted to see in Kennedy, and Republicans saw what they wanted to see in Nixon. Each side tended to believe that its candidate won the encounter.

Despite the closeness of the popular vote outcome, 1960 was essentially a *maintaining election* in the New Deal alignment. Kennedy won by gaining the votes of those constituency groups that over the past two-and-a-half decades had usually voted Democratic. Other than some defections in the Protestant South, the Democratic New Deal coalition for the most part remained intact in 1960. Partisanship and personal image were the keys to the outcome of the 1960 election.

SUMMARY

The presidential elections of the late-New Deal era provided the evidence for the University of Michigan Survey Research Center's model of voting. According to *The American Voter* and succeeding studies, party identification was the most important factor in explaining why people cast their ballots as they did. The personal images of candidates also influenced voters, especially less aware and more independent voters. Issues had little to do with the voting decision. Voters were, for the most part, unfamiliar with and disinterested in issues.

According to *The American Voter*, the Democrats were the nation's majority party because of group-related attitudes formed during the New Deal era. Yet, Republican Dwight David Eisenhower was able to win the 1952 and 1956 elections because of the strong personal evaluations given to him by the American public. The public's personal endorsement of Ike was especially strong in 1956. The Republicans also gained the public's favor in the area of government management.

Still, even during Eisenhower's eight years in the White House, the Democrats retained their advantage among the voters in the areas of domestic policy and group-related attitudes. The Republicans continued to be viewed as the party of Depression and the rich; the Democrats, in contrast, were the party of prosperity and the workingman.

In 1960, with Eisenhower out of the race and his popularity no longer a factor, long-term, group-related attitudes reasserted themselves and carried the Democrats to a narrow victory. Kennedy's debate performance helped reassure wavering Democrats who had doubts related to Kennedy's inexperience and religion. Partisanship, group-related attitudes, and personal image—not issues— were again the determining factors in a presidential election.

But V. O. Key, Jr., and others have disputed this view that issues had little to do with voting during the New Deal era. According to Key, any explanation of Democratic popularity during the New Deal era that failed to draw reference to policy considerations was absurd: "It became ridiculous immediately if one contemplates what the fate of Franklin Delano Roosevelt would have been had he from 1933 to 1936 stood for those policies which were urged upon the country by the reactionaries of the day."[29] The passage of the Social Security Act was a particularly important factor in building the Democratic majority in 1936.

Key and other political scientists have come to view the 1952 and 1956 presidential elections as more than a mere personal vote for Eisenhower. Eisenhower's victories were also the result of retrospective evaluations by the electorate. In 1952 voters rejected the performance of the incumbent Democratic administration on the issues of Korea, corruption, and Communism. China's entry in the Korean War had exacerbated the difficulties of that conflict. As the war dragged on, voter anxieties climbed. Newspaper stories charged Truman's kitchen cabinet with scandal and corruption. Senator Joseph McCarthy and others blamed the Truman administration for the fall of China to the Communists. McCarthy bandied about charges of Communist penetration into the government in Washington. The simplest explanation of the outcome of the 1952 election is that voters "ousted from power a political party of whose performance they did not approve."[30]

By 1956 the Korean War was quite over. Citizens were generally satisfied with the order of things both at home and abroad. Voters gave their approval to Eisenhower and his apparent competence and problem-solving abilities. Voter appraisal was performance-related; it was not simply a response to personal qualities of the President irrelevant to performance in office.[31]

Even the 1960 election can be seen to have been influenced by performance evaluations. Kennedy's promise of "vigor" was more than simple image-merchandising; it was a rejection of America's sluggishness during the late Eisenhower era. Kennedy promised to get the country moving again. He would restart the economy. He would alter the missile gap. Republican Richard Nixon, the incumbent Vice-President, bore the brunt of voter retrospective evaluations.[32]

The overall picture painted by *The American Voter* is that of an electorate in the 1950s and the beginning of the 1960s not very absorbed in the discussion of issues. Citizens had little understanding of ideology and the major alternatives before them. Partisanship and personal imagery were the dominant influences on the voting decision. Yet, as we have also seen, this portrait of the American electorate, once so dominant, has come under challenge. Critics of *The American Voter* have charged that issues and performance evaluations may have played a larger role in the New Deal elections than is commonly credited.

Any generalization regarding voter behavior is time-bound. As we saw at the beginning of this chapter, American voting loyalties changed significantly as the nation industrialized. The New Deal alignment replaced the System of 1896.

It is indeed quite likely that interpretations of American voting behavior based on survey data taken in the 1950s are equally time-bound. The United States was about to pass from the quiescent 1950s to the turbulent 1960s and early 1970s. Would voting behavior change? To the extent that *The American Voter* provided an accurate portrait of American voting behavior in the 1950s, would that portrait continue to be accurate in later years?

THE RISE OF ISSUES IN PRESIDENTIAL ELECTIONS: 1964–1972

$$\left(\,5\,\right)$$

The 1960s and early 1970s would be much different from the 1950s. The civil rights movement, inner-city riots, school busing, the war in Vietnam, the rise of the counterculture, and the "war at home" on college campuses would intrude on the lives of all Americans. Politics was no longer remote and distant. Beginning with the 1964 election, the presidential dialogue became increasingly concerned with issues. The voters responded in kind. Issues as well as candidate images and partisanship determined the outcome of elections during this period.

THE 1964 LANDSLIDE DEFEAT OF BARRY GOLDWATER

Barry Goldwater was a different kind of candidate. A man of strong conservative convictions, he was unwilling to compromise or moderate his beliefs to win office. He ran on issues, offering voters "a choice, not an echo." His campaign slogan, "In your heart, you know he's right," pointed not only to the purity of his beliefs but also to the conservative ideological underpinnings of his candidacy. In his acceptance speech at the Republican convention,

Goldwater reaffirmed his commitment to principles and his disdain for unprincipled compromise. He proclaimed that "extremism in the defense of liberty is no vice!" and that "moderation in the pursuit of justice is no virtue!" Goldwater would be tagged as an extremist; it was an image problem that plagued him throughout the fall election.

In 1964 most national convention delegates were still chosen by party activists not in primaries but in closed party caucuses and state conventions. These party activists tended to be more ideological than the public at large—a factor that greatly worked to Goldwater's advantage.

Goldwater's chief rival for the Republican nomination was New York Governor Nelson Rockefeller. The fight between Goldwater and Rockefeller was essentially a battle between the GOP's conservative and more moderate wings for control of the party. In a close contest, Goldwater rode the fervency of conservative party activists to victory.

Rockefeller was dogged in the race by a serious image problem. He had divorced his first wife to marry his second, Happy. To marry Rocky, Happy had divorced her first husband leaving two children behind. In the early 1960s such behavior was considered almost scandalous. Rockefeller image consultant Gene Wyckoff created a series of new commercials that focused on the governor's personal qualities. Wyckoff sought to develop a fresh image for Rocky and thereby overcome the divorce stain.[1] But days before the crucial California showdown, Happy gave birth to Nelson, Jr. The event was widely reported in news stories and reminded voters of Rockefeller's marital record; it resuscitated the morality issue. Goldwater's last-minute ads in the state not-so-subtly featured pictures of a harmonious, intact Goldwater family.[2] Goldwater won California by just one half of a percentage point.

Goldwaterites controlled the Republican national convention, easily turning back the last-minute candidacy of Pennsylvania Governor William Scranton, who attempted to rally the party's moderates. But even in victory, Goldwater spurned the compromises that would have helped unite the party. He refused to accept three platform planks offered by the moderates. The first would give the President, not military field commanders, ultimate control over the use of nuclear weapons; the second would strengthen the party's commitment to civil rights; and the third condemned extremist groups such as the Ku Klux Klan and the John Birch Society. Goldwater backers believed that the purity of issue beliefs and political style were more important than concerns for winning in November.[3] Goldwater chose an unknown, conservative Congressman William Miller of New York, as his running mate. Miller added little to the ticket.

Goldwater alienated moderate voters and lost the November election to Lyndon Johnson by a landslide. Goldwater carried only five states—his native Arizona and four Deep South states (Louisiana, Mississippi, Alabama, and Georgia) where his conservative philosophy and states' rights emphasis, which would have retarded progress on civil rights, appealed to voters.

Lyndon Johnson had the advantage of inheriting a Democratic party that was fairly well unified in the wake of the Kennedy assassination. To further unite the party and help its more liberal wing overcome its suspicions of Johnson's Texas roots, Johnson chose Hubert Humphrey of Minnesota as his vice-presidential running mate.

The Democrats took advantage of Goldwater's many extreme policy statements to make Goldwater *the* issue of 1964. The Democrats made political capital out of Goldwater's proposal that Social Security be made voluntary, a move that the Democrats said would threaten the financial integrity of the Social Security system. One Democratic ad showed a Social Security card being ripped in half while the announcer informed viewers that "[E]ven his running mate William Miller admits that Senator Goldwater's voluntary plan would destroy your Social Security." Social Security was an overwhelmingly popular program, and the voters did not want it tampered with.

The Democrats also portrayed Goldwater as a reactionary on civil rights. In April 1963 Martin Luther King was jailed in Birmingham, Alabama. As the violence in the South continued, Johnson took to the airwaves in support of much-needed civil rights guarantees. Nowadays it is difficult to remember the astonishment and awe that was felt at the time when the President of the United States—and a Texan at that!—repeated the words of Reverend King: "We shall overcome!" It was an action that had great emotional power and helped cement the loyalties of African-Americans to the Democratic party. Johnson and the Democratic party pushed through the landmark Civil Rights Act of 1964—an Act supported by African-Americans and most northern whites. Goldwater voted against the Act, a fact the Democrats used throughout the campaign. The national Democratic party's support of civil rights, though, did have one cost; it alienated many white southerners, especially in the Deep South.

Overall, the Democratic strategy was to turn Goldwater's rhetoric against him, to use the Republican's own words as evidence that he lacked the sense of balance and proportion to be President. The Democratic ads zeroed in on Goldwater's extremism:

 EASTERN SEABOARD ad

VIDEO: A wood model of the United States is floating in a pool of water. The blade of a saw appears and cuts through Ohio and then down through the United States.

AUDIO (Announcer): "In a *Saturday Evening Post* article dated August 31, 1963, Barry Goldwater said, 'Sometimes I think this country would be better off if we could just saw off the eastern seaboard and let it float out to sea.' Can a man who makes statements like this be expected to serve all the people justly and fairly?"

AUDIO AND VIDEO: Saw cuts through the model. Sound of a crashing splash as the eastern seaboard is cut loose and floats out to sea.

The "Eastern Seaboard" ad was also specifically designed to push northeastern "Rockefeller Republicans" disenchanted with Goldwater toward voting for Johnson.

The most severe Democratic attacks against Goldwater concerned the Republican's allegedly relaxed attitude toward the use of nuclear weapons. The "Daisy Girl" ad is perhaps the most famous political spot in history. Although Goldwater's name is not mentioned in the ad, there is no doubt against whom the attack is directed:

 DAISY GIRL ad

VIDEO: A young girl picks petals from a daisy and begins to count.

AUDIO (Little girl): "One, two, three, four, five, seven, six, six, eight, eight, nine, nine."

AUDIO (Technician's voice in background begins a countdown as if for the launch of a rocket): "Ten, nine, eight, seven, six, five, four, three, two, one, zero."

VIDEO: Freeze frame of the girl's face. Move in to a close-up of her face. Camera continues to move in and look into her eye which serves as a screen against which we see the mushroom-cloud blast of an atomic bomb explosion.

AUDIO: Sounds of the blast.

AUDIO (Voice of Lyndon Johnson): "These are the stakes: to make a world in which all God's children can live, or go into the dark. We must either love each other or we must die."

VIDEO (Closing sign): VOTE FOR PRESIDENT JOHNSON ON NOVEMBER 3

AUDIO (Announcer): "Vote for President Johnson on November 3. The stakes are too high for you to stay home."

The attack was so hard-hitting that Republicans cried foul and demanded that the ad be withdrawn. In fact, the "Daisy Girl" ad was shown only once, on *CBS's Monday Night at the Movies.* The spot was too hot for the Democrats to repeatedly use as it risked drawing an adverse public reaction against mudslinging. Yet, the free media continued to convey the message in the ad for the Democrats. The national news networks aired the spot in their coverage of the controversy surrounding the ad. Print commentators, too, wrote about the spot and questioned whether or not Goldwater had demonstrated sufficient responsibility on the use of nuclear weapons. Daisy Girl had accomplished its mission; it probed a weak spot in Goldwater's record and kept the question of Goldwater-and-the-bomb before the American public.

The Democrats hammered away on the nuclear weapons issue in other fear-arousing commercials.[4] One ad, aired only a few days after Daisy Girl, featured a little girl eating an ice cream cone while the narrator informed viewers about the dangers of strontium 90, cesium 137, and radiation poisoning. The narrator pointedly reminded viewers that Barry Goldwater voted against the nuclear test ban treaty. It, too, like Daisy Girl, was aired only once. Still another Democratic commercial featured the visual of a flashing red light on the White House hot line while the announcer cautions, "This particular phone only rings in a serious crisis. Leave it in the hands of a man who has proven himself responsible."

Goldwater complained of the demagoguery in the Democratic ads. He claimed that his position on the use of nuclear weapons had been distorted, that he never proposed that battlefield control of nuclear weapons be given to NATO commanders but only to the NATO commander, who for years already had possessed such authority.[5]

Yet, despite these protestations, the nuclear weapons issue was a legitimate one. Goldwater had indicated a greater willingness to use nuclear weapons than had Johnson. Goldwater refused to rule out the use of tactical nuclear weapons in Vietnam. His off-the-cuff remark that he would "lob one into the men's room of the Kremlin" only heightened the public's fears of putting Barry's finger on the button.

Johnson in his second term did in fact prove reliable when it came to the use of nuclear arms. He escalated the war in Vietnam but did not introduce nuclear weapons into the conflict. Even when faced with the prospects of losing both the war and his hold on the presidency, Johnson did not resort to the use of nuclear weapons, even low-yield tactical or field devices. On the nuclear weapons issue, voters saw a meaningful difference between Johnson, the more moderate incumbent, and Goldwater, the hard-line challenger.

The Republicans tried to seize the offensive on the issue of military preparedness, arguing that the United States was not vigilant enough in the face of an aggressive Communist menace:

 KHRUSHCHEV ad

VIDEO (Film clip of Soviet leader Nikita Khrushchev making a thumping speech. As he points his finger, his words are translated across the bottom of the screen): "WE WILL BURY YOU."

AUDIO: Khrushchev's speech in Russian.

VIDEO: Shift to a classroom in the United States where a group of students is being led in reciting the Pledge of Allegiance by their teacher.

AUDIO: "One nation, under God..."

VIDEO (Shift back to Khrushchev's thumping speech; he continues to point his finger. The translation reads): "YOUR CHILDREN WILL BE COMMUNIST."

AUDIO: Khrushchev's speech in Russian.

VIDEO: Shift back to the American classroom as the Pledge of Allegiance continues.

AUDIO: Children reciting the Pledge.

VIDEO: Goldwater appears on camera and speaks directly to the audience.

AUDIO (Goldwater): "I want American kids to grow up as Americans, and they will if we have the guts to make our intentions clear--so clear that they don't need translation or interpretation, just respect for a country prepared as no country in all history ever was."

VIDEO (Closing sign) Voice of an announcer reads the words:

"IN YOUR HEART YOU KNOW HE'S RIGHT.

VOTE FOR BARRY GOLDWATER."

In another commercial Goldwater attacked the Democrats for having allowed the Communists to gain control of Cuba.

But the Republicans could not gain the initiative. Goldwater's more flamboyant statements had already dictated the course of the 1964 election. The Republicans were on the defensive; they had to try to dispel the public's perception of Goldwater as a dangerous extremist. A number of Goldwater's commercials even featured the candidate talking calmly and directly to the viewing audience as if to demonstrate that he was a calm, thoughtful, and responsible leader, not the dangerous monster the Democrats had made him out to be.[6]

As we saw in Chapter 3, a number of analyses of voting behavior have observed the importance of issues in the 1964 presidential election. David RePass reported that citizens in 1964 cast their ballots in response to salient issues.[7] Norman H. Nie, Sidney Verba, and John R. Petrocik in *The Changing American Voter* report sharp increases in voter ideology beginning in 1964. They also report that beginning in 1964 domestic policy and cold war attitudes were both increasingly linked to the voters' choice.[8] Furthermore, that ideology was related to the vote in 1964 is evident in that defections to Johnson were concentrated among liberal and moderate, not conservative, Republicans. An amazing 63 percent of Republicans who called themselves liberal crossed party lines and voted Democratic for President in 1964![9]

Perhaps the strongest statement regarding the role of issues in 1964 comes from political scientist Gerald Pomper, who sees the Goldwater candidacy as crucial in clarifying the public's perceptions of the differences between the parties. After reviewing attitudes and voting behavior during the years from 1956 to 1972, Pomper concludes:

> The most important electoral event of this period appears to be the 1964 presidential campaign. Senator Barry Goldwater consciously sought to clarify and widen the ideological differences between the parties. The evidence presented here indicates that he accomplished his goal, although this did not benefit the Republican party. Voters, previously unable to see differences between the parties, learned the lesson of "a choice, not an echo." They accepted the senator's characterization of the Republicans as conservative and the Democrats as liberal, and, on the specific issues involved, they preferred the liberal alternative."[10]

But not all voting studies have pointed to the clear-cut importance of issues in 1964. As we saw in Chapter 3, a number of political scientists dispute the methods and findings of both *The Changing American Voter* and the Pomper studies. Furthermore, Donald Stokes' highly influential study using data from the University of Michigan's Survey Research Center concluded that personal factors were more important than issues and partisanship in the 1964 election.[11]

Yet the Survey Research Center's major report on the election finds that "the mass public had some sense that 'important differences' between the two major parties were heightened in 1964."[12] The Center goes on:

> Throughout, the data suggest that Johnson was carried along to an image nearly as positive as Eisenhower's best, less by personal characteristics than by the policies with which he was associated (many of them identified by respondents as continuations from the Kennedy Administration). For Goldwater, if anything, the reverse was true.[13]

The candidates' images as perceived by the public were not the result of idiosyncratic personal evaluations. Rather, they were largely the product of the policies with which each was associated. Johnson was viewed positively despite the public's negative perception of him personally as wheeler-dealer. Likewise, Goldwater was viewed negatively despite the high marks given to him for his personal "integrity" and "sincerity."[14] Voter assessments of the personal attributes of the candidates reflected concerns relevant to presidential performance. They were not mere affective responses to a candate's smile, charisma, or personal appearance.[15]

In 1964 the public's perception of candidate images largely reflected the candidates' competing positions on the issues. Campaign advertising helped to mold and heighten the public's awareness of the differences between the candidates.

While Goldwater lost the 1964 election by a landslide, his candidacy had two long-term effects that proved advantageous to the Republicans in the future. First, the Goldwater campaign showed that substantial sums of money could be raised through direct mail. The campaign maintained a list of highly motivated donors, variously estimated between 221,000 and 410,000, who gave an average donation of $14 to Goldwater. This list was used as the basis for future Republican fundraising efforts and helped give the GOP its initial edge in the direct-mail field.[16]

Second, Goldwater's candidacy effectively realigned the support of the South in presidential elections. The Republicans, the more conservative of the major parties, were becoming the voice of the white South in presidential elections. The third-party candidacy of Alabama Governor George Wallace would complicate matters somewhat in 1968, but the new Republican appeal in presidential elections would be clearly apparent soon thereafter. This new base of support for the Republican party would help produce Republican victories in five of the six presidential elections during the 1968-1988 period. The era of the solid Democratic South was long gone. In fact, the Democrats would lose the votes of a majority of white southerners even in the two post-Goldwater elections, 1976 and 1980, in which they nominated a native southerner, Jimmy Carter.

IMAGES, PARTISANSHIP, AND ISSUES IN 1968

The 1968 election was the end of an era. The nominating rules changes enacted in response to the riotous 1968 Democratic convention would soon reshape presidential politics, paving the way for even greater influence by new issue-oriented elites and candidate-centered campaign organizations.

But all that would come later. In 1968 Richard Nixon and Hubert Humphrey both won their parties' nominations the old-fashioned way, by establishing ties to the elected officeholders and party officials who at that time dominated the selection of delegates to the national party conventions.

Personal images and candidate styles were important factors in the 1968 primaries. But contrary to the conventional wisdom, issues—not simply personal imagery—proved decisive to the outcome of the general election.

The Republican Race: The Unmaking of George Romney

After the Goldwater debacle in 1964, the Republican party was in disarray. Goldwater was discredited. Rockefeller could not command the respect of conservative Republican activists. Into the breach stepped Richard Nixon. In 1966 alone former Vice-President Nixon traveled 30,000 miles and visited eighty-two congressional districts to raise money for Republican candidates; he also maintained control of a fund that he could use to distribute money to candidates of his choosing.[17] Nixon did yeoman's work for the party and earned the debts and gratitude of Republican officials nationwide. He would cash in on these IOUs in his 1968 race for the Republican nomination.

Another early front-runner for the Republican nomination was Michigan Governor George Romney, the former chairman of the board at American Motors. Romney's candidacy was propelled to a great extent by rising public dissatisfaction with the United States' prolonged involvement in Vietnam. The all-out Tet, or Lunar New Year, offensive by the Viet Cong in January 1968 had convinced Americans that no end to the war was in sight.[18] Although Romney did not take a crystal-clear position against the war, he was the first major presidential candidate to lean to the "dove" side and express grave reservations concerning the war effort.

But Romney's candidacy was all but destroyed when, in response to an interviewer's query, he explained his earlier position in support of the Vietnam War by observing that he had been the victim of Pentagon brainwashing:

> Well, you know when I came back from Vietnam, I just had the greatest brainwashing that anybody can get when you go over to Vietnam. Not only by the Generals, but also by the diplomatic corps over there, and they do a very thorough job. And since returning from Vietnam, I've gone into the history of Vietnam, all the way back into World War II and before. And, as a result, I have changed my mind. . . . I no longer believe that it was necessary for us to get involved in South Vietnam to stop Communist aggression.[19]

The substance of Romney's remarks is not that extraordinary. Romney was merely describing the process that the American military used to sell touring VIPs on the U.S. war effort in Vietnam. Like millions of other Americans, Romney had come to question a war effort he initially supported.

But the press focused on questions of Romney's personal abilities, not on the substantive basis of his comments, in the furor that surrounded his remarks. Press reports focused almost solely on Romney's unfortunate spur-of-the-moment use of the word *brainwashing*. The *New York Times* account of the interview ran under the title "Romney Asserts He Underwent 'Brainwashing' on Vietnam Trip."[20] Pack journalism guaranteed that the networks and the rest of the press would follow the *Times'* lead and pick up this "big" story. Romney's presidential image was destroyed. In the eyes of the public, a man who could be so easily brainwashed lacked the strength and judgment to be president.

Why did the press so unmercifully tear apart Romney's credibility and stature? In part, Romney was the subject of undue media scrutiny as he was the only active candidate then on the campaign trail. The press placed him under their microscope and found him shallow, ill-prepared, and wanting. As media commentator and reporter Timothy Crouse observes, "The press likes to demonstrate its power by destroying lightweights, and pack journalism is never more doughty than when the pack has tacitly agreed that a candidate is a joke."[21] Romney also suffered from the attention he received as the race's early front-runner. The media searches for dramatic news; and the fall of a front-runner is dramatic news—even if the press has to shake the wire under the candidate in order to see him fall.

Of course, Romney's withdrawal did not mark the end of the Republican nominating contest. After a great deal of hesitation, Nelson Rockefeller belatedly entered the Republican race on April 30. But by then it was far too late; the deadline for entering most delegate selection contests had already passed, and Nixon was well on the way to garnering a majority of GOP convention delegates. Rockefeller was also hurt by his much-publicized vacillation. The public would not vote for a man who did not seem to know if he really wanted to be President. Even newly elected Governor of California Ronald Reagan's last-minute entrance into the race could not deny Nixon the votes he needed for the nomination.

Nixon sought to balance the ticket by reaching out to the Rockefeller wing of the party; he selected Maryland Governor Spiro Agnew as his running mate. Agnew had the reputation of being a moderate. Largely, this reputation had less to do with Agnew's policy positions and more to do with the fact that he had won a substantial portion of Maryland's black vote in his 1966 contest against a Democrat who opposed fair housing laws and campaigned on the not-so-subtle racist slogan: "Your Home Is Your Castle, Defend It!" Agnew's misstatements and gaffes (such as his blooper, "When you see one slum, you've seen them all") made him the object of ridicule during the fall campaign.

The Unmaking of President Johnson and the Democratic Race

On the Democratic side, President Lyndon Johnson was looking forward to what he assumed to be certain renomination and likely reelection. Peace activists, however, were searching for a candidate to challenge Johnson in the primaries. They approached New York Senator Robert Kennedy and others who spurned their invitations because they saw an intraparty battle with Johnson as doomed to failure. Only Eugene McCarthy, the relatively unknown junior Senator from Minnesota, took up the quixotic quest. McCarthy saw the Vietnam War as immoral. He also was not your usual politician. A former English professor, he would often take time out during the campaign, wandering from his advisers to read poetry.

The McCarthy campaign, too, was quite new and different. The campaign sent a virtual army of student volunteers, motivated by their antiwar convictions, to go house-to-house in New Hampshire to explain the McCarthy candidacy to the voters. "Clean for Gene" was the motto of these grass-roots canvassers.

Johnson underrated the seriousness of the McCarthy challenge. He decided to stay out of the New Hampshire race. He would be the President who remained above the political fray. As a consequence, his name did not even appear on the ballot in New Hampshire, and a write-in campaign had to be organized by supporters on his behalf.

The results from the Granite State were stunning, McCarthy did much better than anyone had expected. In the nonbinding presidential preference portion of the ballot, Johnson won with 50 percent of the vote. But the fact that Johnson, running only as a write-in, had beat McCarthy meant little. It is the press, not the raw-vote totals, that determines who is the winner and the loser of a nominating race. The press virtually declared that McCarthy, in garnering an amazing 42 percent of the vote against a sitting President, was the winner.

A strategic error by the Johnson camp also helped to shape the press's perception of a McCarthy victory. The Johnson camp had allowed too many local candidates to run for national convention delegate on the second part of the ballot. The result was the Johnson vote was split so many ways that McCarthy won almost all of the New Hampshire delegates.[22] McCarthy had won a great media-declared victory. Johnson suddenly was in political trouble.

The McCarthy miracle in New Hampshire cannot be interpreted as a public mandate to de-escalate the war in Vietnam. Certainly the war issue motivated the great portion of the army of grass-roots volunteers who canvassed the state for McCarthy. But not all voters who cast their ballots for McCarthy were doves. According to a survey conducted by the University of Michigan Survey Research Center, nearly 60 percent of McCarthy's votes came not from doves advocating withdrawal from Vietnam but from persons who wanted the Johnson administration to push a *harder* line against Hanoi! As the only real alternative to Johnson on the ballot, McCarthy was the sole vehicle through which these more hawkish Democrats could register their protest against Johnson's handling of the war.[23]

Robert Kennedy entered the presidential race just four days after the surprising New Hampshire results. Kennedy, it can be argued, was more electable than McCarthy. He was better known, he had charisma, and he was acceptable to mainstream party leaders such as Chicago Mayor Richard J. Daley.

But it was a matter of personal image and style that divided the peace movement. McCarthy's supporters argued that their man had shown guts. McCarthy, they argued, had earned the right to the presidential nomination by taking on and slaying the presidential dragon in New Hampshire. Bobby, in contrast, was seen only as a Johnny-come-lately who presumed to be the successor to the throne only after McCarthy's victory made Johnson's weakness apparent. McCarthy's supporters vilified Kennedy as ruthless. They further charged that Kennedy was late in opposing the Vietnam War.

Kennedy was also unacceptable to many McCarthy supporters, as his candidacy did not represent a challenge to old-style politics. The McCarthy movement was more than just an antiwar campaign, it was also a populist effort that sought to change the established way of doing things—to open up party affairs and take party decision making out of the back rooms. McCarthy's campaign posters captured the spirit of this challenge. They showed a picture of the wind blowing through the candidate's white hair over the slogan "Like a Breath of Fresh Air."

After New Hampshire, the McCarthy campaign picked up momentum. President Johnson's campaign polls showed that McCarthy was certain to win the Wisconsin primary by a large margin. Rather than face such ignominy, Johnson withdrew from the presidential race. In his unprecedented televised address, the President said that he was withdrawing to facilitate peace talks with the North Vietnamese. No one would be able to interpret any new American peace initiatives as a cynical effort by the President to revive his sagging political fortunes back home.

With Johnson out of the race, the way was cleared for Vice-President Hubert Humphrey to enter. The deadline for entering most primaries had already passed, and Humphrey chose not to enter or actively contest the few still open to him. Instead he would rely on Johnson's support and his own ties to party officials to garner the number of delegates necessary for the nomination.

The remainder of the primaries became essentially a two-candidate affair. Kennedy won the Indiana and Nebraska races but lost Oregon to McCarthy, thereby ending the Kennedy family record of thirty straight primary and election victories. Kennedy recovered to win the tough slugfest in California by four points. But after delivering his victory speech at the Ambassador Hotel, he was assassinated as he exited through the kitchen.

There is a widely held myth that had Kennedy not been shot he would have gone on to win the nomination. Of course, no one can say for sure what would have happened had Kennedy lived. But, in all likelihood, the nomination would still have gone to Humphrey, not Kennedy.

Even the most optimistic estimates of delegates in the Kennedy camp showed Kennedy coming up short of the nomination. The Kennedy people planned to conduct a guerrilla operation to persuade delegates committed to other candidates to switch to Kennedy. Kennedy was to campaign in major media markets. Scenes of enthusiastic crowds swarming Kennedy were to convince convention delegates that Kennedy was a winner. The Kennedy campaign also planned intensive advertising in those markets in an effort to produce poll results that would show Kennedy to have the best chance of leading the party to victory in November.[24]

But such a strategy was a long shot. Delegates committed to Humphrey were not likely to be easily swayed by poll results. Furthermore, poll results may not have unambiguously indicated

Kennedy to be the stronger candidate. At the time of Kennedy's
murder, polls showed Humphrey, not Kennedy, to be the preferred
candidate.[25] Also, it would have been difficult for Kennedy to unite
the badly divided peace forces. The animosities between the Kennedy and McCarthy camps, already quite deep, were only heightened by the bruising battle in California. In the wake of Kennedy's
death, his delegates would not merge ranks with the McCarthy
forces. It was not McCarthy who got their votes but South Dakota
Senator George McGovern who entered the race at the convention
in an attempt to rally Kennedy delegates.

Issues were important in the primary season to the extent that
they motivated the grass-roots, antiwar McCarthy organization
and divided the party at its Chicago convention. Yet, as our summary of the 1968 nominating race has shown, questions of the candidates' personal qualities and styles, not issues, dominated the
1968 nominating season. George Romney was destroyed and Nelson Rockefeller was severely handicapped as the public saw these
candidates to be lacking desirable leadership attributes. Bobby
Kennedy possessed charisma and turned on the crowds. But he
was hindered by public perceptions of his being ruthless. Questions of personal style further divided the McCarthy and Kennedy
camps. Kennedy was seen as a politician; McCarthy was anti-
politics. McCarthy gained the support of advocates of a "new politics." The television images generated from the tumultuous
convention at Chicago only served to further divide an already
badly divided Democratic party.

The Selling of the President?

According to Joe McGinniss's *The Selling of the President 1968,*
the 1968 election was a triumph of personal imagemaking. Richard Nixon was repackaged and sold to the American public
much like a package of detergent, a brand of cigarettes, or any
commercial product. According to McGinniss, "the citizen does
not so much vote for a candidate as make a psychological purchase
of him."[26] Issues have nothing to do with the selling of a politician:
"On television it matters less that he (the candidate) does not have
ideas. His personality is what the viewers want to share."[27]

As McGinniss portrays the campaign, the Nixon media team,
under the guidance of creative director Harry Treleavan, developed a new image for Nixon. They sold Nixon as a warm, sincere,
informal, humorous, spontaneous, and compassionate person.
The old embittered Nixon, whom the voters had seen and rejected

for the presidency in 1960 and two years later for governor of California, was to be deeply buried.

A series of paid one-hour television programs utilizing the man-in-the-arena format were a central element in constructing the new Nixon image. These shows were produced by Roger Ailes, then the twenty-eight-year-old executive producer of the Mike Douglas Show. Nixon answered questions live from a panel of citizen interviewers. The programs had suspense. Television viewers felt a rush of sympathy for Nixon as he fended off one attack after another. Nixon looked vulnerable and human. He also appeared informed, in-charge, and presidential.

To viewers at home, Nixon appeared to risk all in live television. In fact, Nixon risked very little as the setting was controlled in ways not readily apparent to television viewers. A relaxed conversational tone was established as Nixon exchanged opening pleasantries with University of Oklahoma football coach Bud Wilkinson. The panel of questioners was screened to exclude persons likely to ask tough questions. The studio audience was stacked with persons recruited by local Republican clubs. During the warm-up directly preceding the show the audience was instructed to applaud Nixon's answers and swarm the candidate at the program's conclusion to show their affection. The applause of the studio audience cued viewers at home that Nixon's answers, no matter how general, were winners.

The Republican media campaign also utilized still photography in many of its forty- and sixty-second commercials that attempted to associate Nixon with a series of quickly flashing positive images of America:

> The flashing pictures would be carefully selected to create the impression that somehow Nixon represented competence, respect for tradition, serenity, faith that the American people were better than people anywhere else, and that all these problems others shouted about meant nothing in a land blessed with the tallest buildings, strongest armies, biggest factories, cutest children, and rosiest sunsets in the world. Even better: through association with the pictures, Richard Nixon could *become* these very things.[28]

The ads further associated the incumbent Democratic administration with such problems as the Vietnam War, crime, unemployment, central city slums, urban and rural decay, rioting, and public disorder.

Nixon took no explicit stand on the Vietnam War. He blamed the Democrats for mishandling the conflict and promised to bring the war to an "honorable" end. He did not indicate if he would do so through hawkish escalation or dovish de-escalation of the United States's military involvement:

VIETNAM ad

VIDEO: Fast-paced scenes of a helicopter assault in Vietnam. Wounded Americans and Vietnamese. Montage of facial close-ups of American servicemen and Vietnamese natives with questioning, anxious, perplexed attitude.

AUDIO (Voice of Richard Nixon): "Never has so much military, economic, and diplomatic power been used as ineffectively as in Vietnam. And if after all of this time and all of this sacrifice and all of this support there is still no end in sight, then I say the time has come for the American people to turn to new leadership not tied to the policies and mistakes of the past."

VIDEO: Proud faces of Vietnamese peasants. Close-up of the word LOVE scrawled on the helmet of an American G.I.; camera pulls back to reveal his face.

AUDIO (Nixon): "I pledge to you: we will have an honorable end to the war in Vietnam."

McGinniss, though, is guilty of overstating the power of the Nixon advertising effort. The Gallup poll showed Nixon with a lead of 16 points in mid-August and 15 points in late September. The Harris poll put the Nixon lead at 6 to 8 points during this same time period. Yet, running against a severely underfunded and divided Democratic party, Nixon wound up winning the November election by less than one percentage point. How can the disappearance of a 15-point lead in such a contest be seen as evidence of the success of the Nixon advertising effort? Of course, it cannot.

McGinniss's mistake is that the omits consideration of other factors that influenced the voting decision in 1968. Party identification was a strong determinant of voting behavior in 1968. Blue-collar Democrats were pulled back into the party as a result of the party's traditions of economic, social welfare, and trade union protections. Antiwar Democrats, too, found that they liked the Democratic record in such areas as civil rights, expanding support for education, aid to cities, and the war on poverty. As election day approached, they found it increasingly difficult to cast a ballot for Nixon, a long-time object of liberal scorn. Humphrey tried to make it easy for antiwar Democrats to return to the party. In a September 30 nationally broadcast speech from Salt Lake City, Utah, he promised a bombing halt as a risk for peace. Richard M. Scammon and Ben J. Wattenberg sum up the influence that partisanship had on Humphrey's rebound:

> Essentially, it was this pattern of party voting that enabled Humphrey to make his stretch run such a powerful one. He and his supporters raised the old banner of the Democratic Party, and most of the people who had saluted it in the past found they could not easily abandon it or the political overview that it had for so long represented.[29]

The statistical work of the Survey Research Center confirms the dominant influence of partisanship on the Nixon and Humphrey vote: "it is *party* that towers over all other predictors, and the central 1968 issues tend to give rather diminutive relationships."[30]

But why did Nixon win? Issues played a greater role in the election than McGinniss's theory and the Survey Research Center's data analysis would seemingly indicate. According to Scammon and Wattenberg the *social issue*—America's concerns over crime, riots, civil disorder, too-fast racial integration, welfarism, and a changed social fabric as seen in the challenge of hippies, drugs, and the counterculture—was at the base of the Nixon vote in 1968. Nixon was the "man in the middle" who stood between excessive Democratic liberalism and the extreme racial reactionism of third-party presidential candidate Alabama Governor George Wallace.[31] Nixon stood for the centrist course of action preferred by white middle America, the portion of the electorate that the news media popularly referred to as the Silent Majority.[32]

Nixon's ads effectively tapped voter resentment on social issues, especially on crime and welfare. Nixon campaigned on the slogan of "Law and Order." He retrospectively attacked the inability of the Democratic administration to deal with rising crime rates and public demonstrations; citizens who did not like the Democratic record could vote for a change. Nixon also offered voters a clear policy direction. He was no soft-headed liberal who preached that society must understand the reasons underlying crime, violent dissent, and urban riots:

ORDER ad

VIDEO: Rapidly moving sequence of rioting. Crowds taunting police authorities. Flaming apartment house. Police patrolling deserted streets in aftermath of violence.

AUDIO: Sound effects of rioting.

AUDIO (Voice of Richard Nixon): "It is time for some honest talk about the problem of order in the United States."

VIDEO: Perplexed faces of Americans. Sequences of people moving through battered streets and by destroyed shops and homes. Eloquent faces of Americans who have lived through such experiences, climaxed by a single shot of charred crossbeams framing a riot ruin. In the center of the picture is a battered machine on which can still be seen in red letters the word CHANGE.

AUDIO (Nixon): "Dissent is a necessary ingredient of change. But in a system of government that provides for peaceful change there is no cause that justifies resort to violence. There is no cause that justifies rule by mob instead of by reason."

VIDEO (Closing titles): THIS TIME VOTE LIKE YOUR WHOLE WORLD DEPENDED ON IT.

NIXON.

CRIME ad

VIDEO: A lonely policeman at a call box. Move suddenly to a series of shots of explosive criminal actions with police response-- ending on image of a bullet-shattered automobile window. Pan upon a row of weapons; then continue tilt up "Kennedy rifle." Huge close-up of a hand holding an open jackknife. Montage of faces of Americans; they are anxious, perplexed, frightened.

AUDIO (Voice of Richard Nixon): "In recent years crime in this country has grown nine times as fast as the population. At the current rate, the crimes of violence in America will be double by 1972. We cannot accept that kind of future. We owe it to the decent and law-abiding citizens of America to take the offensive against the criminal forces that threaten their peace and security, and to rebuild respect for law across this country."

VIDEO: Line of hand-cuffed criminals standing by a brick wall, their faces concealed by their hands or coats.

AUDIO (Nixon): "I pledge to you that the wave of crime is not going
to be the wave of the future in America."

VIDEO (Closing titles): THIS TIME VOTE LIKE YOUR WHOLE WORLD
DEPENDED ON IT.

NIXON.

One extremely effective spot, the "Woman" ad, presented a
tension-building little melodrama that captured middle America's
fear of crime:

 WOMAN ad

VIDEO: Fade-up on a diagonal view down on a sidewalk. It is a wet
night. Feet of a woman come into view.

AUDIO: Sound of the city. Sounds of clicking heels.

VIDEO: She is dressed in a cloth coat and looks to be about age 45.
She is apparently coming home late from shopping or work. The
camera begins to travel with her. Behind her a moving figure flows
by the metal-gate covering of a locked storefront. It begins to
get darker as the camera moves in for a medium close-up, and then
a close-up as we continue to travel with her.

AUDIO (Announcer): "Crimes of violence in the United States have
almost doubled in recent years. Today a violent crime is committed every sixty seconds. A robbery every two-and-a-half minutes.
A mugging every six minutes. A murder every forty-three minutes.
And it will get worse unless we take the offensive."

VIDEO: We are in close-up. The camera holds. The woman walks off
down the sidewalk. Hold on this view as her figure grows smaller
against the dark night.

AUDIO (Announcer): "Freedom from fear is a basic right of every
American. We must restore it."

AUDIO: Distant heel clicks.

VIDEO (Closing titles): THIS TIME VOTE LIKE YOUR WHOLE WORLD
DEPENDED ON IT.

NIXON.

The "Woman" ad plays to film conventions that the viewing audience has learned from watching movies and television crime series. Viewers know that the woman will not make it home; they are expecting her to be mugged at any moment.

The Nixon ads similarly assigned retrospective blame and offered voters a choice of directions on the issue of welfarism. Nixon's antiwelfare stance is presented in juxtaposition to the activist government approach of Lyndon Johnson's Great Society and Hubert Humphrey's liberalism. The ads effectively tapped middle America's resentment of expanding, big-spending social programs. In one ad, Nixon narrates as voters are shown scenes of urban and rural decay and a sign on the street that reads "Government checks cashed here":

> For the past five years we've been deluged by programs for the unemployed, programs for the cities, programs for the poor. And we have reaped from these programs an ugly harvest of frustrations, violence, and failure across the land. Now our opponents will be offering more of the same. But I say we are on the wrong road. It is time to quit pouring billions of dollars into programs that have failed.

Issue-based images, not just personal-based images, were the hallmark of Nixon's advertising. To the extent that the Nixon media campaign worked, it did because it employed both issue-based and personal-based appeals. The campaign used different spots and different messages to reach different voters. Nixon offered voters a choice on the highly salient issues of the day.

The Vietnam issue, however, was not a strong influence on voting in the 1968 general election. The ability of voters to use issues to distinguish between the two major-party candidates in this area was diminished by the failure of both Nixon and Humphrey to identify a path of action one way or the other on Vietnam.[33] Citizens could not know for sure which candidate would continue, or which would draw down, the American military presence in Southeast Asia.

As we previously noted, the Survey Research Center found partisanship to be a much stronger influence than issues on voting in 1968. According to the Center, voter "evaluations of both Humphrey and Nixon show a strong factor of traditional party allegiance suffocating most issue concerns into relative obscurity."[34] Yet, even given the strength of partisanship, the findings of the Center point out that issues were important in determining the outcome of an election as close as that of 1968. The Center found that issues were a prominent motivation for George Wallace's voters. More important yet was the Center's discovery that while most citizens voted their usual party allegiance in 1968, "switchers" nearly always moved in the right direction according to the issue preferences.[35] These switchers provided the margin of victory in 1968.

1972: THE REJECTION OF McGOVERN OR McGOVERNISM?

In 1972 Richard Nixon won reelection by a landslide, beating George McGovern by 61 to 38 percent, virtually matching the scale of Lyndon Johnson's victory in 1964. McGovern even lost his home state, South Dakota, and carried only a single state, Massachusetts (leading Bay Staters to proudly sport bumper stickers after the election that read, "Don't Blame Me, I'm from Massachusetts!") and the District of Columbia.

The McGovern campaign was plagued by a series of candidate errors that undermined McGovern's image. Yet, postelection studies showed that it was not just personal image alone that hurt McGovern; issues were also an important influence on the outcome of the 1972 election. Mounting antiwar sentiment coupled with a reformed delegate selection process had led the Democrats to select an extreme liberal as their standard bearer—a candidate who was out-of-step with middle Americans on key issues.

The Democratic Race: Muskie Cries and the Politics of Momentum

At the beginning of 1972 it was not George McGovern but Maine Senator Edmund Muskie who appeared to have a virtual lock on the Democratic nomination. The story of Muskie's demise is an interesting tale that points to the power of the mass media to make and break a candidate's image.

Muskie's front-running position going into 1972 was the result of the favorable publicity he had received as Humphrey's running mate four years earlier. It was also the result of his performance in a single media event, a national broadcast he made on behalf of

Democratic candidates on the eve of the 1970 midterm elections. In this broadcast, Muskie appeared cool, relaxed, personable, and self-assured as he spoke to Americans from his Maine home. His image contrasted quite favorably with that of the more strident Richard Nixon that the Republicans had presented in a film clip in their broadcast that evening. Jeb Stuart Magruder, a member of Nixon's public relations team, would later remark, "It was like watching Grandma Moses debate the Boston strangler."[36]

But the front-runner's position actually worked to Muskie's disadvantage. When Muskie could not live up to the expectations that the media had set for him, press reports virtually destroyed his candidacy. Muskie's advisers had erred in contributing to the over-expectations of success by predicting outright victory; they had sought to create a bandwagon effect which would induce party leaders and followers to line up behind the Muskie effort. Muskie's own behavior also led reporters to question his presidential capabilities.

The key event in the demise of Edmund Muskie was the New Hampshire primary, a state where Muskie was expected to win big. *Washington Post* national politics reporter David Broder was not alone when he wrote in a January 9, 1972, story, "As the acknowledged front runner and a resident of the neighboring state, Muskie will have to win the support of at least half the New Hampshire Democrats in order to claim a victory."[37]

Muskie defeated George McGovern by a 46-to-37-percent margin in New Hampshire. But as Muskie had not met expectations, the media story that emerged was that of a Muskie "loss," not a victory. Because of this media-declared defeat, the Muskie campaign suffered reverse momentum and began its unstoppable slide.

Why did reporters go after Muskie in New Hampshire? In part, the demise of a front-runner provides a dramatic, big story that meets the requirements of horserace journalism. Also, as Timothy Crouse details, reporters covering Muskie had seen the candidate's fits of temper and were eager to expose his shortcoming.[38] Reporters seized on campaign incidents that allowed them to reveal their doubts of Muskie's personal abilities. As a result, the Muskie campaign in New Hampshire was dogged by a series of vicious rumors that found their way into print.

One rumor reported that Muskie had used the derogatory term "Canucks" in reference to the state's Canadian-American population. Another story portrayed Muskie's wife as a foul-mouthed woman with a fondness for drink. These and other such stories were gleefully repeated in the front-page, partisan-style reporting of William Loeb's *Manchester Union-Leader*, the most widely circulated newspaper in the state. After the election, the Watergate hearings would reveal that a number of these stories had their origins in the dirty-tricks unit of the Nixon campaign. Nixon's zealots sought to plant newspaper stories that would undermine the candidacy of the President's strongest potential November opponent.

Muskie personally resented these stories. He was especially taken aback by the slanderous attacks on his wife's character. In an emotional speech, he faced reporters in front of Loeb's offices to decry the smears. Tears filled his eyes as he hoarsely denounced the innuendo. Television cameras rolled as the tears flowed from Muskie's eyes and the snowflakes fell on his hair. This image was repeatedly shown on news broadcasts. For reporters, the outburst only confirmed that Muskie lacked the emotional stability to be president. The public, too, reacted to Muskie in highly personal terms. If he could not hold up under the pressure of the campaign in New Hampshire, how could he be expected to stand up to the Russians and the crushing burden of decision-making in the White House?

In a tailspin from New Hampshire, Muskie finished fourth in the next primary, Florida, behind George Wallace, Hubert Humphrey, and Henry "Scoop" Jackson. The loss brought his candidacy to a virtual end. Interestingly, George McGovern finished even further down the line in sixth place, yet was not harmed by his poor finish. His managers had opined that as a dark horse McGovern lacked the time and money to campaign everywhere; he could only give one full day of campaigning to Florida. They downplayed McGovern's expectations in the state, and the press, to a great extent, bought the line.

When the initial nominating contests were over, Muskie had beaten McGovern four out of four times. He won the Iowa caucuses and the New Hampshire and Illinois primaries. Although he did poorly in Florida, he still outpolled McGovern in that state. Yet, because of press reports, Muskie was out of the race while McGovern remained not only a viable but an increasingly strong contender.

National opinion polls showed that until he sewed up the nomination, McGovern was not the first choice of Democratic voters. Yet, as a result of the intensity of conviction that motivated antiwar forces to turn out and dominate a fair number of delegate selection contests, McGovern was able to win the nomination. McGovern's grass-roots organization had helped to propel him to a strong 22-percent showing in the multicandidate field in Iowa, separating him from the rest of the crowded Democratic pack and providing the momentum that led to his dramatic showing in New Hampshire. He would then win Wisconsin. McGovern's organization also was very effective in packing caucuses and conventions. McGovern eventually gained delegates in such unlikely conservative states as Oklahoma and Virginia.

The McGovern insurgency produced a national party convention that was vastly more liberal than rank-and-file Democrats on such new cultural and social issues as welfare, busing, law and order, and the conduct of the war.[39] The party chose a presidential nominee who represented the views of the new issue activists but not those of the larger party-in-the-electorate.

McGovern sought to unify the party. He sought to have his delegates accept the seating of the challenged Illinois delegation, headed by Chicago Mayor Richard Daley. Daley could prove to be a valuable ally in November. The Illinois delegation had been selected according to state law but in clear violation of the party's new rules for openness. But McGovern could not control his supporters. It was their chance to take revenge against Daley for his taunts at the 1968 convention and his police department's brutal handling of demonstrators outside the convention hall. Viewers watching the 1972 convention on television saw delegates break out in spontaneous applause and cheers as the Daley delegation was unseated and was replaced by an alternative, unelected but demographically balanced delegation headed by Jesse Jackson and the then-liberal Alderman William Singer.[40] More centrist Democrats were left to wonder just whom this new Democratic party represented.

The Fall Campaign

McGovern faced a substantial problem in the general election: how to shift his appeal to a more centrist electorate than the one he mobilized during the nominating season. His handlers changed his campaign slogan from one that emphasized his issue purity—his primary season "McGovern, Right from the Start"—to the more general "McGovern, Democrat, for the People," which emphasized both party loyalty and broader populist appeal.

But McGovern could not pull off the transition. He could not shake the general public's perception of him as an extreme liberal, the candidate who stood for the three A's—acid, amnesty, and abortion. That perception had also been shaped by the controversial proposals that McGovern had staked out early in the primary campaign. In one controversial proposal, McGovern discussed the possibility of giving each American a welfare "demogrant" of $1,000.

Immediately after the convention, the Eagleton affair destroyed whatever presidential stature McGovern had remaining. McGovern had not looked very presidential at the convention in virtually begging Edward Kennedy and other prominent Democrats to join him on the Democratic ticket. McGovern finally settled on Missouri Senator Thomas Eagleton as his running mate. But the McGovern team did not adequately screen the Senator's past. Press reports soon revealed that Eagleton had been under a psychiatrist's care and had undergone electroshock therapy to fight depression.

McGovern assured reporters that he had no intention of dropping the Missourian from the ticket. His staff then issued a notice stating that McGovern was "1,000 percent for Tom Eagleton." But only days later, in the face of the continued public clamour over his presence on the ticket, Eagleton—clearly with McGovern's assent—withdrew. He was replaced by Kennedy clan member Sargent Shriver.[41] In changing his mind after publicly declaring his support for Eagleton, McGovern once again looked wishy-washy. Already he had backed off his earlier $1,000 welfare demogrant and amnesty proposals. McGovern hardly looked presidential.

In an attempt to soften the public's view of McGovern as an extreme liberal, the McGovern commercials in the fall campaign were less specific than his spring ads in their discussion of issues.[42] In both spring and fall, the commercials used cinema verité footage to portray McGovern as a caring man of the people. These commercials typically pictured McGovern listening to groups of Americans—disabled Vietnam veterans, the elderly, blue-collar workers—and then responding to their concerns. McGovern expressed his own concern and his hopes to reestablish the kind of leadership that can help people. But he did not discuss program specifics, as the advocacy of new programs would have given the Republicans further ammunition in their charges against McGovern as a big-spending social liberal.

The ads failed because they did not adequately address voter concerns regarding race and welfare, issues that had led middle Americans and disaffected Democrats to view McGovern as too liberal. The ads further failed as they presented McGovern as a passive listener, not a dynamic leader.[43]

By the end of the campaign the cinema verité ads were withdrawn in favor of a new set of spots that utilized a somewhat unorthodox approach in an attempt to convey to voters the seriousness of the issues in the race. These ads presented no visuals other than the printed word on the television screen. An announcer read the words as they scrolled up from the bottom.

When it came to issues, though, it was the Republicans who enjoyed the clear advantage in the paid media campaign of 1972. The Nixon ads attacked McGovern's past campaign promises on welfare, defense spending, amnesty for draft evaders, and school busing. Probably the most effective ad of the entire campaign was a spot which visually dramatized the potential impact of McGovern's earlier defense proposal:

DEFENSE CUTS ad

VIDEO: A group of toy soldiers. A hand dramatically sweeps about a third of them off the table.

AUDIO (Announcer): "The McGovern defense plan. He would cut the marines by a third..."

VIDEO: Switch to another group of toy military figures. A hand sweeps a sizable number of them off the table.

AUDIO (Announcer): "...the Air Force by one-third."

VIDEO: Cut to other sets of toy soldiers, airplanes, ships, and carriers. In turn, a large portion of each group is similarly swept off the table. The camera than pans the destruction.

AUDIO (Announcer): "He would cut Navy personnel by one-fourth. He would cut interception planes by one-half, the Navy fleet by one-half, and carriers from sixteen to six. Senator Humphrey has this to say about the McGovern proposal: 'It isn't just cutting into the fat. It isn't just cutting into manpower. It is cutting into the very security of this country.' "

VIDEO: Picture of President Nixon standing with a naval officer aboard a ship.

AUDIO: Drum roll followed by the playing of "Hail to the Chief." (Announcer): "President Nixon doesn't believe we should play

games with our national security. He believes in a strong America
to negotiate for people from strength."

VIDEO (Closing sign): DEMOCRATS FOR NIXON

Another Republican ad charged McGovern with having submitted a welfare bill to Congress that "would make 47 percent of
the people in the United States eligible for welfare," an "incredible
proposal" that would cost 64 billion dollars in its the first years:
"That's six times what we're spending now."

Critics charged that the Nixon ads presented such gross distortions of McGovern's proposals that they provided no basis for the
serious discussion of public issues. The visual of toy ships being
swept off the table, for instance, failed to address the question of
what size American defense forces should be and how much fat
could be cut from the military budget. The welfare ad attacks a
proposal that McGovern claimed to have submitted to Congress
only as a courtesy to the National Welfare Rights Organization.[44]

Still, whatever their distortions and incompletenesses, the ads
quite clearly communicate the choice of policy directions offered
by the candidates. McGovern was more disposed to welfare expan-
sionism and was less tolerant of defense spending; Nixon took a
tougher stance toward welfare and was more willing to spend on
defense. The ads met the test of directional voting.

McGovern tried to make the break-in at the Democratic headquarters at the Watergate complex a campaign issue, but no one
was listening. His charges were seen as little more than last-ditch
desperation effort to turn around his much-troubled candidacy. It
would not be until well after the election that voters would begin to
see Watergate as anything more significant than a second-rate bur-
glary.

Issue Voting in 1972

Postelection analyses point to the importance of issues in explaining the 1972 decision. The newer cultural issues represented
in the McGovern insurgency destroyed the traditional class-based
pattern of the vote; McGovern did no better among lower status
voters than he did among higher status voters (see Table 5.1). The
lowest status groups, those most in need of government social welfare programs, continued to support the Democrats. But blue-

Table 5.1   Democratic Percentage of the Presidential Ballots, White
Voters by Socioeconomic Position, 1948–1972

	1948	1960	1968	1972
All				
High SES	30	38	36	32
Middle SES	43	53	39	26
Low SES	57	61	38	32
Women				
High SES	29	35	42	34
Middle SES	42	52	40	25
Low SES	61	60	39	33
Under 30 years of age				
High SES	31	42	50	46
Middle SES	47	49	39	32
Low SES	64	52	32	36
College-educated	36	45	47	45
Noncollege	56	49	33	30

Source: Everett Carll Ladd, Jr., with Charles D. Hadley, *Transformations of the American Party System,* 2nd ed. (New York: W.W. Norton, 1978), p. 240.

collar and middle-class citizens voted less Democratic than normal
as they were alienated by the welfarism, school busing, life-style
liberalism, and the challenge to patriotism they perceived to be associated with McGovernism. On the other hand, better-educated,
new elite voters—the intelligentsia—tended to be more sympa-
thetic to the agenda of the McGovern movement. In 1972 there
was no Republican upper-class versus Democratic lower-class pattern to the vote; instead, McGovern led a narrow "top-bottom coalition" against "the great middle."[45]

In contrast to 1968, the Vietnam War was a factor in the 1972
vote. Despite Nixon's ambiguous pledge of "peace with honor"
and his administration's last-minute announcement that peace was
at hand, voters were still able to see a distinct difference between
the candidates on the war; McGovern was clearly the dove.[46]

But policy voting was not focused solely on the war. Racial integration was another area of policy voting in 1972. The candidates did not discuss race as much as they did Vietnam, but they
did not have to. The different views of the candidates were easy to
observe. McGovern professed a moral commitment to school inte-
gartion, including the use of school busing. Nixon represented a
more "go slow" approach to civil rights. In 1972, then, the "hard"
issue of Vietnam—where voters could not easily identify a work-

able peace plan—and the "easy" issue of racial integration both yielded to policy voting.[47]

Policy voting was so apparent in 1972 that even the studies from the University of Michigan's Center for Political Studies (formerly the Survey Research Center) concluded that issues were an important influence on the outcome of the election. According to the Center, both personal images and issues were important determinants of the vote. One study observes that the 1972 election "was more heavily influenced by issue voting or voting on the basis of policy preferences than any election in the preceding two decades."[48] McGovern suffered his greatest loss of expected support among voters of the Center and the Silent Minority; he maintained the support of believers in the "New Politics."[49] Vietnam, economic, social, and cultural issues were all related to the vote independent of party identification.[50] Still another Center article concludes that voters met the requirements of issue voting; the preferred policy position of defecting Democrats was often to the right of Nixon.[51] The Center's article in the highly influential *American Political Science Review* argued that "a new issue politics" had emerged, as "policy disagreements strong enough to cause massive defections among rank and file Party supporters" became a new characteristic of American national politics.[52]

The evidence pointing to the importance of issues in the 1972 election seems overwhelming. Yet not all liberal activists and political scientists are willing to accept the conclusion that McGovern lost as a result of his extreme liberalism. Samuel Popkin and his colleagues argue that McGovern's policy positions, especially on economic policy and the war, were consistent with those of the majority of the public. Rather, according to Popkin, McGovern lost as a result of his perceived incompetence, not because of his stands on the issues. Even a large number of people who agreed with his policy positions did not vote for McGovern, for they doubted his capacity to deliver what he promised.[53] One of every ten voters mentioned the Eagleton fiasco in pointing to what they most disliked about McGovern. This ratio was higher than the ratio of those who disliked McGovern because of his positions on Vietnam and welfare.[54]

Popkin also suggests that McGovern "may have been hurt by voters' perceptions of the people standing by him: too many young people, too many blacks, too many welfare mothers."[55] But what Popkin fails to realize is that citizens who cast their ballots in response to such perceptions are engaging in a form of issue voting. McGovern, not Nixon, is the candidate most likely to be influenced by these people and their causes. Voters who disliked these causes did well to reject McGovern; it was the rational choice before them.

SUMMARY: IMAGES AND ISSUES

Personal images were important factors in the presidential races of the 1964-1972 period. Goldwater and McGovern were rejected as extremists. McGovern further suffered from a perceived lack of presidential stature; he was viewed as indecisive and incompetent. In 1964 Nelson Rockefeller was hurt by the appearance of immorality; in 1968 he suffered from the image of vacillation. In 1968 George Romney's candidacy was destroyed by the "brainwashing" incident. In the Democratic nominating race, the followers of Eugene McCarthy and Robert Kennedy were divided more by concerns for candidate style and courage than by any great policy disagreements over the war in Vietnam. In 1972 Edmund Muskie learned that voters would not accept a presidential candidate who cries. Richard Nixon earned reelection as "the President."

Yet, purely personal images alone did not dictate the outcome of any of the elections of this period. As we have seen, partisanship continued to be a strong influence on voting in the elections of this period, particularly in 1968. The explanatory power of partisanship was on the wane, but it had not disappeared.

Issues, too, proved to be an important factor in the elections of this period. During the nominating race, the failure to establish and control a candidate's image could quickly lead to the death of a campaign. But issues also affected the nominating process. The conservative ideologues of 1964 and the antiwar activists of 1968 and 1972 were all motivated by issues.

In the general election, there is even less ambiguity. Issues, not just personal images and partisanship, were important in each of the elections of this period. While voters did not always have the specific knowledge necessary for prospective issue voting, they did possess sufficient information and capacity to engage in directional and retrospective voting. The electorate was unwilling to make the sharp changes of direction advocated by Goldwater and McGovern. In 1968 racial and social issues were also an important influence on the vote, just as the Vietnam War and school busing proved to be the most prominent of the issues that affected the vote in 1972.

The election year 1968 can also be interpreted as a retrospective rejection of the Democratic liberalism, especially the Democratic administration's perceived excesses in the area of welfarism and its failure to quell riots and demonstrations. Similarly, 1972 can be seen as a retrospective endorsement for Nixon. Despite the continuing war in Vietnam, a relative quiet returned to the nation as the major inner-city and campus riots had for the most part faded into the past.

By 1972 political scientists had clearly come to recognize the role played by issues in presidential elections. Even the University of Michigan's Center for Political Studies, which had previously disparaged the level of issue voting in the United States, began to recognize the potential importance of issues. It reported that issues were related to the George Wallace vote and party switching in 1968. Issues were even more clearly related to the vote in 1972.

THE POLITICS OF RETROSPECTIVE REJECTION: 1976–1980

B y 1976 the great polarizations of the 1960s and early 1970s had receded into the past. The Vietnam War was over, and demonstrations on college campuses were relatively muted. Inner-city ghettos, too, were relatively quiescent. Richard Nixon had resigned in the midst of the Watergate scandal and was replaced by Gerald Ford, who characterized his term in office as "A Time to Heal."[1]

Issues had been important factors in presidential elections during the turbulent 1964–1972 period. Would they continue to be so as the United States entered a more calm political era?

Jimmy Carter's success in the 1976 Democratic primaries was the result of a campaign that emphasized personal imagery. Yet, as we shall see, candidate factors alone do not explain voting in the general election. In 1976 partisanship was once again an important influence on the presidential vote. Retrospective voting, too, was at work. The public ousted Gerald Ford because of his inability to handle the economy—one that was suffering from both high inflation and a prolonged recession. The public also held the Republicans accountable for Watergate. Four years later, retrospective evaluations would be even more closely related to the vote. Jimmy Carter was ousted from office because of his inability to handle both the economy and foreign policy.

133

1976: PERSONAL IMAGERY, PARTISANSHIP, AND RETROSPECTIVE VOTING

The Selling of Jimmy (not James Earl) Carter

Jimmy Carter and his campaign manager Hamilton Jordan were among the first to appreciate how greatly the reformed delegate selection rules and the proliferation of primaries had altered the nominating process. They adapted their campaign to the new delegate selection terrain. Carter, a party outsider, was marketed directly to caucus and primary voters without the benefit of working through party intermediaries.

Jordan's script for Carter was clear. As a dark horse, Carter had to enter and concentrate his limited resources on the early nominating contests. A win or even just a good showing in these early races was needed to establish Carter's viability, separate him from the rest of the Democratic pack, and attract media interest and new financial contributions.

Television was a key element in Carter's success. Carter won the first-in-the-nation Iowa caucuses by campaigning in the state as if it had a primary. His campaign did more than simply attempt to mobilize a small band of caucus participants, whom Carter met one-on-one in coffee-klatches and small group get-togethers. The Carter campaign also aired a relatively large volume of televised commercials that sought to sell the candidate to voters who had never before participated in the caucus process. No other candidate in 1976 made such extensive use of television in Iowa.

Jordan and other Carter advisers felt that the Watergate scandal had led to a renewed public focus on the personal qualities of a candidate. Carter sought to embody trustworthiness, competence, and integrity. He promised that he would never lie to the American people.

Carter, the relatively obscure former governor of Georgia, was not widely known. Gerald Rafshoon, the campaign's media specialist, saw his first task as establishing Carter's personal image.[2] In the campaign's early ads, Rafshoon presented Carter as a former naval commander, a nuclear engineer, a family man, a businessman, and a peanut farmer. The most famous of these early Carter ads showed the candidate clad in blue jeans and plaid shirt walking through his family's peanut fields in Plains, Georgia.

The Carter strategy worked even better than Jordan had dared hope. The surge of participation in the Iowa caucuses produced a Carter victory. Carter finished far ahead of any of the other candidates, although he still finished behind the number of delegates listed as "undecided." Carter had received very little national media attention while campaigning in Iowa. But his victory changed all that. The day after the Iowa victory, Carter was surrounded by news reporters as he continued his efforts in New Hampshire. The Iowa victory gave Carter the name recognition and momentum that led to a four-point victory in New Hampshire over the second-place finisher, self-styled progressive Arizona Congressman Morris Udall. The New Hampshire victory brought still greater sums of money and publicity to the campaign. Carter was now the front runner.

The primary season shifted to Florida. Carter's newfound national reputation allowed him to run as the more respectable voice of the South and thereby defeat George Wallace. It was a victory he could not have achieved without the momentum and stature provided by his earlier victories.[3] Wallace was further handicapped by doubts about his health. He had to campaign from a wheelchair, the legacy of a 1972 assassination attempt that left him partially paralyzed.

Carter enjoyed the great advantage of winning those initial contests when election story coverage was at its peak. Victories in later primaries and caucuses, even in larger states, did not always translate into equivalent coverage. Washington Senator Henry "Scoop" Jackson beat Carter in Massachusetts, just one week after New Hampshire, but Jackson did not receive the extensive publicity that Carter had received earlier. As Jackson adviser Ben Wattenberg complained:

> After the Massachusetts primary, Jackson, unlike Carter, was not on the cover of *Time*. He was not on the cover of *Newsweek*. We did not get articles about his cousin who has a worm farm. And that was the story of the Jackson campaign for the next six weeks, and that was what I think killed that campaign. Jackson had won a totally unanticipated victory, beyond what the press had expected, in a state with ten times as many delegates as New Hampshire, and the effect was barely visible. We were dismayed.[4]

Scoop Jackson was a centrist Democrat and a strong friend of both organized labor and Israel. He chose to bypass Iowa and New Hampshire, hoping to establish momentum by winning contests in the nation's larger and more industrial states. Jackson beat Carter in New York, a state where Jackson enjoyed great strength in the organized labor and Jewish communities. But he was never able to overcome Carter's early lead. A Carter victory over Jackson in

Pennsylvania destroyed any notion of an unstoppable Jackson bandwagon and put the Washington senator out of the race.

Late entrants in the race—Idaho Senator Frank Church and the California Governor Edmund G. "Jerry" Brown—beat Carter in five of the last twelve nominating contests. But by then it was too late; the race for the nomination was effectively over. By running everywhere, Carter had continued to amass national convention delegates. Even in the states he lost, Carter won much-needed national convention votes as a result of the Democratic party's reformed rules requiring virtual proportional representation. By the end of the nominating season, Carter was far ahead of any other candidate in delegates won. Though he still lacked the majority needed at the convention to become the Democratic nominee, even old-line party leaders, such as Chicago Mayor Richard J. Daley, realized that they could do little but reaffirm the choice the voters had declared in the primaries.

The Republican Race: Ideological Challenge

On the Republican side, President Gerald Ford faced a stiff challenge from Ronald Reagan and the conservative wing of the GOP. President Nixon had named Ford as his Vice-President when Spiro Agnew resigned because of evidence that pointed to his involvement in scandals during his years as Governor of Maryland. When Nixon, in turn, resigned in the wake of Watergate, Ford became President.

Ford enjoyed certain advantages of incumbency, but he was not in an especially strong political position. Having never run for national office, he lacked a national constituency. He also suffered from the image of being little more than an ordinary congressman who had risen above his abilities and who had done little as President. As he self-deprecatingly said in accepting the presidential office, "I'm a Ford, not a Lincoln."

Ford beat Reagan in New Hampshire by the narrowest of margins, one percentage point. New Hampshire would likely have been a media-declared victory for Reagan had it not been for the Reagan camp's strategic blunder of predicting outright victory. Reagan's advisers should have been hard at work in lowering the media's expectations of Reagan, pointing to the advantages that Ford possessed in being able to wrap himself up in the majesty of the presidential office and in being able to steer federal aid projects to key constituencies in New Hampshire. Instead, Reagan's camp had been carried away by favorable news coverage and poll ratings just prior to New Hampshire that pointed to Reagan's emerging strength. As a consequence, when the results of the New Hampshire contest came in, the front-page story nationwide was not that of Reagan's strength but of Ford's victory in fending off the Reagan challenge.

The momentum Ford gained from New Hampshire led to a string of early victories. Reagan lost the first four primaries to Ford. He also ceded virtually the entire Pennsylvania delegation to Ford without a challenge. A disastrous showing in Illinois all but eliminated Reagan from the race. But Reagan turned his campaign around with dramatic victories in North Carolina and Texas.

Numerous media critics have attributed Reagan's sudden rebirth to a switch in the campaign's advertising strategy beginning with North Carolina.[5] Until North Carolina, Reagan television ads featured short, man-in-the-arena film clips of Reagan speeches; the audience would applaud as Reagan confronted hostile questioners. The ads were created by Harry Treleavan and were reminiscent of the image-creation approach he took on Nixon's behalf in 1968. However, in 1976 the ads did not seem to be working. The campaign switched advertising formats.

In North Carolina, the Reagan campaign aired an edited version of an old Reagan speech. Reagan spoke simply and directly to viewers at home during a half-hour block of time purchased by the campaign. The speech contained the usual Reagan campaign lines; it would appeal to North Carolina's more conservative Republicans. Reagan won North Carolina with 52 percent of the vote.

The victory brought the campaign new money and momentum. A month later in Texas, Reagan soared to a dramatic two-to-one victory in winning the state's entire 100-person convention delegation. In the succeeding nominating contests he engaged Ford in a bitter battle for delegates. The fight for the nomination went down to the wire. The Republican convention was marked by enthusiastic floor demonstrations by the supporters of both candidates. Ford held on to win an extremely narrow 1187 to 1170 victory. The convention battle was so close that Reagan took the extraordinary step of attempting to win over marginal Ford delegates by announcing his vice-presidential choice in advance. If nominated, he would choose Pennsylvania Senator Richard Schweicker as his running mate.

But was it the new advertising approach that turned around the campaign for Reagan? The evidence points to an alternative explanation. In all likelihood, Reagan won North Carolina and Texas after losing the earlier rounds only because the Republican nominating contests had finally moved to the nation's more conservative states. Reagan's challenge to an incumbent President in his own party only drew sizable support in states with Republican constituencies responsive to his more ideological brand of conservatism. As political scientist Larry Bartels points out:

> Reagan's biggest primary victories came in Idaho, Nevada, Georgia, Texas, Alabama, and California—all strongly conservative Republican states in the West and South. By contrast, Ford's biggest victories came in New Jersey, Rhode Island, Michigan, and Massachusetts—all traditional strongholds of the moderate Republican establishment.[6]

It was ideology, not advertising, that dictated the state-by-state pattern of Reagan's successes and failures in 1976.

The General Election: "Are You Better Off. . . ?"

Throughout the general election Carter continued his personal image advertising. But his message was also one of retrospective rejection, urging voters to reject the mounting "stagflation" suffered under the Ford administration. The economic issue dominated the election. At the time of the first debate, unemployment was running at a national rate of 7.9 percent. Adding the unemployment and inflation rates together, according to Carter, amounted to a "misery index," which revealed the true extent of the nation's economic misfortunes under Ford. Democratic advertising attacked the nation's stagnating economic performance after eight years of Republican rule.

The Ford campaign was in fairly desperate trouble. Going into Labor Day, Ford trailed Carter by 18 points in the polls. The campaign had not even laid out an overall advertising strategy for the fall election; the President's political advisers had been too busy turning back the Reagan challenge and winning the nomination.

The initial Republican advertising approach was termed the Rose Garden strategy, as it attempted to wrap Ford in the symbols of the presidential office. These ads showed pictures of Ford hard at work in the Oval Office. Ford was the President; he was no mere candidate seeking to become President.

But as Carter's charges on the economic issue continued to hit home, the Ford campaign had to leave the Rose Garden strategy behind and rebut the Carter attacks. One Republican message was that Ford had brought down inflation. Eventually, the Republicans identified their theme—that people were feeling good about America and that Ford as President had restored respect and integrity to government. One campaign commercial featured a song written especially for the Ford effort. The visuals showed various images of proud and happy Americans at work and play while the voiceover sang out:

> *There's a change that's come over America*
> *A change that's great to see*
> *We're livin' here in peace again*
> *We're going back to work again*
> *It's better than it used to be.*
>
> *I'm feelin' good about America*
> *I feel it everywhere I go*
> *I'm feelin' good about America*
> *I thought you ought to know*
> *That I'm feelin' good about America*
> *It's something great to see*
> *I'm feelin' good about America*
> *I'm feelin' good about me!*[7]

The Republican ad campaign also sought to strengthen Ford's personal image, to offset the widespread impression that Ford was an unpresidential bumbler—a perception reinforced by Saturday Night Live comedian Chevy Chase, who repeatedly spoofed the President's clumsiness. The new Republican spots attempted to humanize Ford, even showing a picture of him in his football uniform at the University of Michigan. The new ads also sought to dispel any doubts about the President's intelligence: "He was graduated in the top third of Yale Law School, while holding a full-time job."

The Ford campaign rose from the depths. The final election was close; Carter won by only two points. To a great extent, Ford rebounded as the national economy began to recover. Ford's comeback was consistent with retrospective and "sociotropic" interpretations of voting: the public's support for the incumbent administration is greatly dependent on the broad perception of how well the economy is doing.[8] As political scientist Arthur Miller observes, the recovery in economic optimism in the few months prior to the election may have deflated the economic issue considerably.[9]

The story of Ford's comeback and its end is also the story of personal images built and lost in televised presidential debates. Post-debate polls showed that the public clearly saw Ford to be the winner of the first debate. Carter looked tentative and unsure of himself. Carter later admitted to having been somewhat intimidated in finding himself standing on the same platform confronting the President of the United States.

But Ford's momentum was brought to an abrupt halt by the second presidential debate. Press coverage of that debate, devoted to a discussion of foreign policy, was dominated by Ford's gaffe in responding to the question of whether or not the Soviets had gotten "the better of us" in certain signed agreements. As part of his question, *New York Times* associate editor Max Frankel asserted that "we've virtually signed in Helsinki an agreement that the Russians have dominance in Eastern Europe." Ford's response was to deny that there is Soviet domination of Eastern Europe and Poland. The reaction of the press was incredulous. In not being aware of the extent of Soviet domination of Poland and other Eastern European nations, Ford had again demonstrated his incapacities as President.

It is worth looking at Ford's comments in some detail to discover just what Ford said and how the press interpreted it. The most controversial of Ford's words are italicized:

> **Ford:** In the case of Helsinki, thirty-five nations signed an agreement, including the secretary of state for the Vatican. I can't under any circumstances believe that His Holiness the Pope would agree by signing that agreement that the thirty-five nations have turned over to the Warsaw Pact nations the domination of Eastern Europe. It just isn't true. And if Mr. Carter alleges that His Holiness by signing that has done it, he is totally inaccurate. Now, what has been accomplished by the Helsinki agreement? Number one, we have an agreement where they notify us and we notify them of any military maneuvers that are to be undertaken. They have done it in both cases where they've done so. *There is no Soviet domination of Eastern Europe* and there never will be under a Ford administration.
>
> **Frankel:** I'm sorry. Could I just follow? Did I understand you to say, sir, that the Russians are not using Eastern Europe as their own sphere of influence and occupying most of the countries there and making sure with their troops that it's a Communist zone, whereas on our side of the line, the Italians and the French are still flirting with the possibility of Communism?
>
> **Ford:** I don't believe, Mr. Frankel, that the Yugoslavians consider themselves dominated by the Soviet Union. I don't believe that the Romanians consider themselves dominated by the Soviet Union. *I don't believe that the Poles consider themselves dominated by the Soviet Union. Each of those countries is independent, autonomous.* It has its own territorial integrity. *And the United States does not concede that those countries are under the domination of the Soviet Union.* As a matter of fact, I visited Poland,

Yugoslavia, and Romania to make certain that the people of those countries understood that the President of the United States and the people of the United States are dedicated to their independence, the autonomy, and their freedom.

Moderator: Governor Carter, have you a response?

Carter: I would like to see Mr. Ford convince the Polish Americans and the Czech Americans and the Hungarian Americans in this country that those countries don't live under the domination and supervision of the Soviet Union behind the Iron Curtain.

Ford seemed unaware of the furor that his remarks would touch off. Frankel and Carter went in for the political kill.

What the postdebate commentary ignored was that Ford to a great extent was right! Ford had refrained from discussing the situation in Eastern Europe solely in terms of highly charged political stereotypes—stereotypes and emotions that Carter played to in his rebuttal to Ford. Ford was describing a pluralism in Eastern Europe that Americans as a whole, blinded by Cold War stereotypes, did not see. The Soviets did not control from the center all facets of life in Eastern European nations. Important variations and divisions continued to exist inside the Soviet bloc—as seen in the historic fissure between Yugoslavia and the Soviet Union, and in the continued strength of both the Solidarity movement and the Catholic church in Poland. The amazing events of 1989 and 1990—the success of the freedom movements in each of the East European nations, the reunification of Germany, and the elections of Vaclev Havel as President of Czechoslovakia and Solidarity leader Lech Walesa as President of Poland—would prove that Ford was right. The Soviets did not completely dominate Eastern Europe.

But the substantive accuracy of Ford's comments counted for little in the presidential politics of 1976. Carter had the politically astute sense to clearly identify himself with the cause of freedom-loving people in Eastern Europe. Yet, there was something absurd in seeing Carter attack Ford for failing to take a tougher stance on the Soviet presence in Eastern Europe "as if the conservative, hawkish President were soft on communism."[10] Throughout the campaign it was Ford, not Carter, who had insisted on a stronger commitment to defense spending. Carter's demagogic response to Ford's gaffe on Eastern Europe simply took advantage of "the bias of the news for the simple and symbolic."[11]

Voters saw Ford's remarks as significant only as the media told them they were. Viewers contacted within twelve hours of the second debate in fact saw Ford, not Carter, as the winner; 53 percent said Ford had won, and only 10 percent said the Poland remark was important. However, among voters contacted twelve to forty-eight hours after the debate, the results were much different. The percentage seeing Ford as the winner dropped to just 29 percent, and 60 percent saw the Poland remark as a major error.[12]

Studies show that the debates changed few voting decisions.[13] Still, in an election as close as 1976, Ford's stalled momentum in the wake of the second debate can be seen to have affected the final outcome.

A Partial Restoration of the New Deal Coalition

With the passing of the polarizations of the Vietnam era, the Democratic party enjoyed renewed unity. The Democratic New Deal coalition had been formed to a great extent in response to economic issues; and in 1976 economic issues once again dominated public concern.[14] As Warren E. Miller and Teresa E. Levitin observe in their summary of the polling data gathered by the Center for Political Studies, "[T]he 1976 election was as much a party election as those elections from the 1950s or early 1960s in which party was acknowledged to be a major determinant of voters' decisions."[15]

Social class had eroded as an influence on presidential voting behavior in 1968 and 1972. But in 1976, a class pattern to voting was once again apparent. Still, the class pattern observed in 1976 was less sharp than that observed during the New Deal, as typified by voting in the 1948 election (see Table 6.1). After the turmoil of the 1960s and early 1970s, the New Deal Democratic coalition could not be fully put back together again.[16]

Overall, in comparing the 1976 election with 1972, personal images were more important, ideology less important but still significant, and specific issues still less important than they had been four years previously.[17] In the wake of Watergate, both Ford and Carter attempted to persuade voters that they possessed the personal qualities of honesty, decency, integrity, and competence. Few prospective issue appeals were evident in 1976. One political scientist, J. David Gopoian, has observed the virtual absence of issue voting during the 1976 primaries.[18]

Yet, political observers who see the 1976 election as issueless do so only as they take a very strict and narrow definition of the issue voting.[19] Carter had asked voters if they were better off as a result of Republican rule. Few felt that they were. Ford's standing in the polls improved only when the economy showed signs of recovery. Voters divided along partisan lines in 1976, but this was no

Table 6.1 Democratic Percentage of the Presidential Ballots, White Voters by Socioeconomic Position, Selected Years, 1948–1976

	1948	1960	1968	1972	1976
All					
High SES	30	38	36	32	41
Middle SES	43	53	39	26	49
Low SES	57	61	38	32	53
Women					
High SES	29	35	42	34	41
Middle SES	42	52	40	25	46
Low SES	61	60	39	33	53
Under 30 years of age					
High SES	31	42	50	46	46
Middle SES	47	49	39	32	48
Low SES	64	52	32	36	52
College-educated	36	45	47	45	44
Noncollege	56	49	33	30	51

Source: Everett Carll Ladd, Jr., with Charles D. Hadley, *Transformations of the American Party System,* 2nd ed. (New York: W.W. Norton, 1978), p. 289.

mindless return to an earlier age of blind partisanship. Instead, economic issues were reflected in the partisan decision.[20]

The influence of both the economic issue and partisanship is evident if we take a look at Table 6.2. Economic performance evaluations are clearly related to the vote. Among self-identified Democrats, Republicans, and independents alike, support for Carter was greatest among voters who gave the Ford government a poor rating on dealing with inflation. But partisanship, too, remained a

Table 6.2 Vote by How Good a Job Government Was Doing Fighting Inflation, Controlling for Party Identification, 1976

	Democrats			Independents			Republicans		
	good job (6%)	fair (57%)	poor job (37%)	good job (16%)	fair (59%)	poor job (25%)	good job (22%)	fair (65%)	poor job (13%)
Vote									
Carter	62%	77%	93%	10%	41%	64%	7%	12%	31%
Ford	38	23	7	90	59	36	93	88	69
	100%	100%	100%	100%	100%	100%	100%	100%	100%

Source: Arthur H. Miller, "The Majority Party Reunited? A Comparison of the 1972 and 1976 Elections," in *Parties and Elections in an Anti-Party Age,* ed. Jeff Fishel (Bloomington, Ind.: Indiana University Press, 1978), p. 129.

strong influence on voting, so much so that Ford retained the loyalty of 69 percent of those Republicans who believed that the government did a bad job in handling inflation.[21]

Despite the candidates' purposeful attempts at ambiguity, surveys show that voters were able to distinguish between the candidates in terms of their economic policies.[22] Voter concern over inflation and unemployment—especially unemployment—was the dominant issue in the 1972 election.[23] In the general election, Carter ran as a traditional Democrat. As the campaign progressed, voters increasingly associated Carter with the Democratic party's traditional positions on issues.[24] Voters saw Carter as liberal and Ford as conservative.[25]

Watergate was a second major issue in retrospective voting in 1976.[26] Voters blamed Ford for pardoning Nixon. Ford's approval rating as president dropped eighteen points, from 71 to 53 percent, in the first poll taken after the pardon.[27] Ford never recovered his popularity among key groups. Carter won an extremely narrow 270-to-240 electoral vote victory. Kristen Monroe concludes that "While it is impossible to say exactly how great an impact the pardon had on voter calculus in the 1976 election, the evidence here strongly suggests that the pardon of Richard Nixon cost Ford that margin of popular support he needed to win the election."[28]

Arthur Miller presents further evidence that opinion on the pardon was strongly related to the vote irrespective of partisanship (see Table 6.3).[29] Thirty percent of those Republicans who disapproved of the pardon defected to Carter!

Despite the personalization of campaigns after Watergate, 1976 was not an issueless battle of professionally mediated image campaigns. In the primaries specific issues were important to pivotal electoral groups. In Iowa, Jimmy Carter won the votes of teachers and their families with his promise to create a cabinet-level Department of Education. Given the low level of participation in the caucuses, it can be argued that teachers and their families gave Carter his Iowa victory. Throughout the primaries Carter also won the votes of African-American citizens because of his record on civil rights. As Governor of Georgia he had even placed a portrait of Martin Luther King on his wall, an extraordinary gesture for a white, Southern, elected official at that time. Union members and Jewish voters, however, did not support Carter but, instead, "Scoop" Jackson, a Senator whose voting record favored their causes.[30] Similarly, in the Republican primaries differences in ideology explained the state-by-state pattern of the Ford-Reagan vote.

Table 6.3   Vote by Attitude toward Ford's Pardon of Nixon

	Total		Democrats	
	approved (43%)	disapproved (57%)	approved (25%)	disapproved (75%)
Vote				
Carter	24%	75%	56%	88%
Ford	76	25	44	12
	100%	100%	100%	100%

	Independents		Republicans	
	approved (52%)	disapproved (48%)	approved (72%)	disapproved (28%)
Vote				
Carter	30%	61%	8%	30%
Ford	70	39	92	70
	100%	100%	100%	100%

Source: Arthur H. Miller, "The Majority Party Reunited? A Comparison of the 1972 and 1976 Elections," in *Parties and Elections in an Anti-Party Age,* ed. Jeff Fishel (Bloomington, Ind.: Indiana University Press, 1978), p. 132.

Even in the general election, issues proved important as personal image factors alone were not decisive in the final vote. After the Watergate scandal, voters sought a candidate that they could trust. But it was Ford, not Carter, who won this image battle in 1976; voters saw Ford as more trustworthy.[31] Carter won the election as a result of retrospective performance evaluations, not personal imagery. According to Morris Fiorina, a retrospective voting model can account for 85 to 90 percent of the vote in 1976.[32]

1980: ANYONE BUT CARTER

By 1980 Jimmy Carter was an unpopular President. Some of the President's aides blamed his unpopularity and reelection defeat on the Iranian hostage situation. In November 1979 more than fifty members of the American diplomatic mission were seized in Teheran, Iran. Television emphasized the gravity of the crisis. CBS News anchor Walter Cronkite ended each evening's broadcast by counting the number of days of captivity for Americans in Iran. ABC instituted a new late evening news broadcast it originally titled "America Held Hostage." After the hostage crisis, the broadcast continued as "ABC News Nightline."

Table 6.4   Carter Approval Ratings on Three Issues*

	percentage approving						
	Nov. '79	Jan. '80	Feb. '80	Mar. '80	April '80	June '80	Aug. '80
Foreign Policy	28	45	48	34	31	20	18
Economy	21	27	26	23	21	18	19
Iran		55	63	49	39	29	31

*Questions: (1) Do you approve or disapprove of the way Jimmy Carter is handling foreign policy?
(2) Do you approve or disapprove of the way Jimmy Carter is handling the economy? (3) Do you
approve or disapprove of the way Jimmy Carter is handling the crisis in Iran? Each percentage is
the proportion approving Carter's actions on the stated issue.
Source: Kathleen A. Frankovic, "Public Opinion Trends," in The Election of 1980, ed. Gerald
Pomper (Chatham, N.J.: Chatham House, 1981), p. 100.

Had Carter been able to secure the release of the hostages before November, the outcome of the election might well have been
different. In 1991, eleven years after the election and well after the
revelations of the Iran-Contra affair, former Carter national security aide Gary Sick charged that the Reagan campaign secretly negotiated to give arms to Iran. In return, Iran agreed to delay until
after the election the release of Americans held captive. In office,
the Reagan administration did, in fact, help to arrange for the delivery of weapons to Iran. Yet, there was no firm evidence to support Sick's allegations of a preelection secret arrangement that
included a delay in the release of the hostages.

Whether there existed a secret deal or not, Carter's defeat cannot be blamed solely or even primarily on the hostage situation.
Polling data reveal that the President's approval ratings had plum-
meted due to the nation's mounting economic woes well before the
Iranian crisis emerged.[33] During Carter's term in office, inflation
hit 18 percent, the unemployment rate hovered around double-
digit levels, and homebuyers faced the daunting prospect of having
to pay 18 to 20 percent annual interest on loans. In the days immediately preceding the hostage-taking, only one in five Americans
expressed their approval of the President's economic performance
(see Table 6.4).

The Democratic Race: The Unmaking of "President" Kennedy and the Rediscovery of "President" Carter

Before the Iranian crisis altered the political landscape, Carter's unpopularity was so evident that the press, in a chorus of pack
journalism, portrayed him as a one-term President. According to

many commentators, the Democratic nomination was Edward "Ted" Kennedy's for the taking.

But Carter fought off Kennedy in a divisive intraparty struggle. The press had understated the resources available to an incumbent President. Carter's appointees in the bureaucracy helped steer federal aid projects to key primary states, including New Hampshire. Kennedy's weaknesses as a candidate were also soon to become apparent.

As Kennedy moved closer to announcing his candidacy, the press began to subject his candidacy to greater scrutiny. A special television program by CBS correspondent Roger Mudd was the key media event in Kennedy's undoing. Most damaging of all was the program's reenactment of the tragedy at Chappaquiddick, where Kennedy, a married man, on a summer evening in 1969 left a party on Martha's Vineyard in the company of a young political staffer, Mary Jo Kopechne. Kopechne drowned when the car driven by Kennedy plunged off a secondary bridge leading to the mainland. Kennedy did not immediately report the incident to authorities. Instead, in the hours immediately after the accident, he huddled with his close personal advisers. Kennedy claimed that his conduct was not improper, that in the dark he had inadvertently taken the wrong route to the main bridge. Kennedy also said that he did not immediately report the incident because he was suffering from a state of shock after having repeatedly plunged into the waters in an attempt to save Kopechne.

Mudd's television cameras seemingly contradicted Kennedy's account of the incident. Mudd showed that a definite turn had to be made for Kennedy's car to shift paths to the side road. As the car carrying CBS's camera left the main road, the television picture bounced up and down. No one could possibly have mistaken this secondary road for the main route to the bridge.

The Carter campaign exploited the opening offered by the morality issue. In one Carter man-in-the-street spot, both men and women voiced their doubts regarding Kennedy: "I don't think Kennedy's qualified to be President"; "I don't think he has any credibility"; "I don't trust him." Another Carter ad featured pictures of a happy and intact Carter family while an announcer informs viewers: "Husband, father, President. He's done these three jobs with distinction." Another ad was more biting still: "President Carter—He tells the truth."[34]

Put on the defensive, the Kennedy campaign attempted to reconstruct Kennedy's personal image, as seen in the following excerpts from one biographical ad:

 KENNEDY IMAGE ad (excerpt)

VIDEO: Shot of a family scene of Kennedy walking along the beach
with his wife and children.

AUDIO (Kennedy): "I suppose that the greatest source of happiness
in my life has been the relationships with my wife and my children, and my brothers, and my sisters, and my parents."

VIDEO: Switch to Kennedy sitting at home in a living room chair with
a newspaper on his lap. He speaks to a teenage boy, who appears to
be his son, carrying a lunch pail and a backpack.

AUDIO (Kennedy): "You're having a games day tomorrow?"

AUDIO (Boy): "Yeah. Yeah"

AUDIO (Kennedy): "Can I come, too?" (Laughter) "I want to play. Do
they have the dads? Do they play, too?"

These Kennedy image ads, however, were generally ineffective. Voters had heard too much—about Chappaquiddick, allegations as to Kennedy's continued philanderings and marital
problems, stories on his wife Joan's drinking problems—for the
new image-making to work.[35]

But it was not simply the question of Kennedy's character that
turned around the Democratic race. The intrusion of both the Iranian hostage situation and the Soviet invasion of Afghanistan created a crisis situation that allowed Carter to act and look
presidential, to regain his presidential stature. Americans tend to
unite behind the President in times of international crisis. This
rally-'round-the-flag pattern of public opinion was clearly apparent at the beginning of the hostage situation (see Table 6.4).

Yet, as Table 6.4 shows, Carter's rebound in the polls was not
as high as might have been expected. Even the intrusion of a foreign policy crisis could not totally resuscitate Carter's presidential
image. Further, any rebound in the public's perceptions of Carter
resulting from the hostage crisis did not spill over into the economic arena. In January and February, in the early months of the
crisis, still only one in four Americans approved Carter's handling
of the economy.

Carter responded to world events by adopting a Rose Garden strategy. In a time of crisis he would devote his full attention to the affairs of state. The news media covered his every pronouncement. In essence, he was campaigning by doing his job as President. His campaign ads only reinforced the image of a man hard at work handling the presidential job.

Carter's renewed presidential stature allowed him to easily beat Kennedy in the January Iowa caucuses and the February New Hampshire primary. Kennedy suffered a string of primary losses that virtually ensured Carter's renomination. Carter lost New York, in part due to the disaffection of Jewish voters outraged by the Carter administration's failure to veto a United Nations resolution condemning Israeli settlements on the West Bank.

As the hostage situation dragged on, the initial public rally behind the President began to fade (see Table 6.4). An ill-advised hostage rescue mission, aborted owing to the mechanical failure of three helicopters operating in desert conditions, only reinforced the public's perceptions of Carter's inabilities. Carter fared poorly in a number of the later primaries. But by then the race was already over; he had already amassed a large enough block of delegates to ensure his renomination.

The Republican Race: "I am paying for this microphone."

On the Republican side, Ronald Reagan, the front-runner, chose to bypass the Iowa caucuses where each of his lesser-known Republican rivals were attempting to gain the momentum of an early nominating season victory. It was a mistake. George Bush won Iowa and gained considerable publicity. In New Hampshire, Reagan would confront Bush directly.

Reagan effectively ambushed Bush in a pseudoevent that gained considerable media attention. After Iowa, Bush had sought to limit all Republican debates to the two top contenders, himself and Reagan. A local newspaper, the *Nashua Telegraph*, invited Bush and Reagan to participate in a two-person debate. But complications arose when the other Republican candidates complained and it was discovered that under federal finance rules, the local television station's sponsorship of such a debate would amount to an illegal contribution to the Bush and Reagan campaigns. The Reagan campaign resolved the problem by paying for the air time for the debate.

While Bush and Reagan were seated ready to begin the debate, four other Republican candidates suddenly paraded out from behind the stage. When the debate moderator refused to change the format to allow their participation, Reagan spoke in their defense. The moderator ordered that Reagan's microphone be turned off; Reagan countered by sharply replying, "I am paying for this microphone." The crowd roared its approval; the four candidates standing behind Reagan and Bush literally applauded Reagan's words. Reagan came across as the champion of openness and fairness. He even shook the hand of one Republican rival, John Anderson, as he escorted the four uninvited guests off the stage. Compared to Reagan, Bush seemed petty, unfair, and afraid. Reagan beat Bush handily, 53 to 22 percent, in New Hampshire.

But it was not personal imagery alone that won New Hampshire. After Bush's victory in Iowa, the Reagan campaign switched to a more issue-oriented advertising approach that emphasized the conservative values popular in Republican party circles. In the new ads, for instance, Reagan stressed his doctrinaire opposition to communism—a sharp contrast to Bush's campaign ads that emphasized his resumé and showed the former Ambassador to China greeting Chairman Mao.[36]

The new ads also stressed Reagan's opposition to taxes. They also hit hard at the record of the Carter years:

 JFK TAX CUT ad

VIDEO: Words scroll up from the bottom of the screen.

AUDIO (Announcer reads the words): "Ronald Reagan believes that when you tax something, you get less of it. We're taxing work, savings, and investment like never before. As a result we have less work, less savings, and less investment."

VIDEO: Reagan dressed in blue suit and red tie looks directly into the camera and speaks.

AUDIO (Reagan): "I didn't always agree with President Kennedy. But when his 30-percent federal tax cut became law, the economy did so well that every group in the country came out ahead. Even the government did so well that it gained $54 billion in unexpected revenues. If I become President, we're going to try that again."

News commentators criticized the distortions contained in the ad—whether the Kennedy tax cut was nearly as large as 30 percent and whether the government actually gained $54 billion in receipts because of the cut. Still, whatever its distortions, the ad proved effective in offering Americans a clear statement of policy direction; if elected, Ronald Reagan would cut taxes.

The General Election: Once Again, the Economy

Reagan's general election advertising contained a certain few specific policy promises intermixed with a clearly communicated sense of overall policy direction. In the October 17, 1980, "Reagan Speaks" commercial, Reagan sits on the edge of a desk in front of a twelfth-grade class at Luther High North in Chicago. He makes two specific prospective promises—to empower parents by enacting tuition tax credits and to replace the draft with a volunteer army:

> There is no reason for the nation to restore the draft at this time. And I am opposed to the advanced registration for the draft. I believe that we can make the volunteer military work if we adopt a pay scale commensurate with what we're asking the young men and women in uniform to do.

Reagan's ads promised a general conservative direction to government policy—to eliminate waste and inefficiency in government, to balance the budget, to look at the price tag before launching any federal programs, and to restore the nation's military defense capacity. Reagan also specifically promised to reduce taxes. Most importantly, though, the Reagan ads repeatedly hammered away at the Carter record, especially at the toll taken by the mounting rates of inflation during the Carter years.

REAGAN REPORTS FROM LIMA, OHIO ad (excerpts)

VIDEO: Reagan dressed in tie and white shirt stands in a supermarket and speaks directly into the camera.

AUDIO (Reagan): "Good evening. I've been campaigning today in western Ohio. And I'm speaking to you now from Lima, a community of about 60,000 persons. As I've traveled across the nation these past few months it's clear that there's one problem that cuts evenly across the board hurting everybody. And that's the common enemy of inflation. I'm here in a grocery store in Lima."

VIDEO: Camera pulls back to reveal a shopping cart full of gro-
    ceries. Reagan pulls a package of hamburger from the cart and
    holds it up.

AUDIO (Reagan): "A mother, a father, four years ago, before Jimmy
    Carter was elected, could come in and buy a pound of hamburger
    for 89 cents. Today that same pound of hamburger costs $1.39. And
    if we continue the Carter economic policies for another four
    years, it will cost no less than $2.17 in 1984. The same thing is
    true for other staples."...

VIDEO: Reagan holds up a loaf of bread.

AUDIO: (Reagan): "A loaf of bread. Four years ago bread cost 39
    cents a loaf. Today it's 85 cents. And with another four years of
    Carter inflation it will rise to $1.85. And so it goes. The in-
    flation we've endured under Jimmy Carter, the worst inflation
    since the Second World War, is literally robbing millions of
    Americans of their chance to keep good food on the table."...

AUDIO (Reagan): "Yesterday, Jimmy Carter said that the reason for
    inflation was that revenues, tax revenues, had not kept pace with
    the increased amount of government, of public spending. In other
    words, his approach to solving inflation would be more taxes
    taken from you. There is another way--reduce the costs of govern-
    ment. And that can be done. And that's what I'd like to do. And at
    the same time I promise to begin reducing those taxes which are
    also so punitive. I know it can be done."...

 BROKEN PROMISES ad

VIDEO: Still picture of a smiling face of Jimmy Carter.

AUDIO (Announcer): "Can we afford four more years of broken prom-
    ises? In 1976 Jimmy Carter promised to hold inflation to 4 per-
    cent."

VIDEO: Picture rotates to reveal a still picture of a scowling Jimmy
    Carter.

AUDIO (Announcer): "Today it is 14 percent."

VIDEO: The picture continues to flip-flop back and forth as Cart-
    er's bright promises are contrasted with the present-day reali-
    ties.

AUDIO (Announcer): "He promised to create more jobs. And now there
    are 8 million Americans out of work. He promised to balance the

budget. What he gave us was a $61 billion deficit. Can we afford four more years?"

VIDEO (Closing pictures of Reagan and Bush with the words): REAGAN & BUSH

AUDIO (Announcer): "The time is now for strong leadership. Reagan for President."

The ads urge voters to retrospectively reject the Carter record. Only in the area of budget deficits is the Reagan message troubling. As President, Reagan would incur budget deficits that would dwarf those of the Carter administration.

The 1980 campaign was marked by the activity of many so-called independent committees spurred on by the Supreme Court's 1976 *Buckley v. Valeo* decision. Although spending data for 1980 is somewhat suspect, the Republican advantage resulting from independent spending is considerable. In 1980 independent committees spent $13.3 million on behalf of Republican candidates; in contrast only $171,000 was spent by independent committees in ways that aided Democratic candidates.[37] Many of the ads aired by independent political committees on behalf of Reagan stressed retrospective evaluations of Carter's performance in office, especially in his handling of the economy:

ARE YOU SATISFIED? ad

VIDEO: Still picture of the Capitol in Washington. Switch to a still picture of a long unemployment line.

AUDIO (Announcer): "Jimmy Carter came to Washington promising to do something about unemployment, to give people who were out of work a chance to restore their hopes and dreams."

VIDEO: Film of Carter speaking directly into the camera. As he speaks, a sign appears at the bottom of the screen: '76 Carter Commercial.

AUDIO (Voice of Jimmy Carter): "7.8 percent unemployment is what you arrive at when incompetent leaders follow outdated, insensitive, unjust, wasteful economic policies."

VIDEO: Camera scans down the list of candidates on a voting
    machine.

AUDIO (Announcer): "Jimmy Carter did do something about
    unemployment--2 million more people became unemployed this year
    alone."

VIDEO: Sign at the bottom of the screen reads: 2 Million More
    Unemployed.

AUDIO (Voice of Jimmy Carter): "Are we satisfied with what we have
    or are we ready to try to change it for the better?"

VIDEO (White words project out against a blue background):
    ARE YOU SATISFIED?

Carter's only hope of victory was for the public's focus to be
shifted away from the record of the past four years to the dangers of
electing Reagan as President. The Democratic strategy was to
make the election a referendum on the personal qualities of the
two men. Reagan's own exaggerations, verbal missteps, and memory lapses only fueled the public's doubts as to his presidential capacity.

In the only Reagan-Carter debate of the fall campaign, Carter
steered discussion away from the economy. He attempted to focus
the debate on foreign affairs, especially on the dangers of nuclear
proliferation. According to Carter debate coach Samuel Popkin,
Carter's strategy in the debate was to attack; he needed to goad
Reagan out to make the Republican look like "a man with dangerous tendencies, dubious judgment."[38] But Reagan deflected every
Carter attack as a misrepresentation of his views. He began his response to one Carter attack with a simple and effective verbal
parry, "There you go again." Reagan's steady performance reas-
sured voters and put to rest the competency question.

Reagan concluded the debate with a virtual repeat of Carter's
strong retrospective message of 1976. Reagan urged voters to ask
themselves "are you better off now than you were four years ago?"

A Third Candidate: "The Anderson Difference"

John Anderson, a moderate Republican leader, ran as an independent candidate for President in 1980 after first losing his at-

tempt to gain the Republican nomination. His general election candidacy was novel. As a result, he provided the media with a good story and received news coverage disproportionate to the actual vote he finally received.[39]

He ran on the slogan of the "Anderson Difference," and appealed to "new collar" voters who identified with "new politics" issues. Anderson took strong stands on certain issues, which helped him to cultivate the image that he was different from most politicians—that he was an open, honest individual who was not afraid to take on special interests. Anderson publicly confronted the National Rifle Association on gun control. He also proposed a 50-cents-per-gallon tax on gasoline to promote energy conservation. His promise of a "bipartisan government of national unity," however, was vague, for he failed to delineate the principles on which a national consensus could be built or detail just how he would be able to govern in the absence of party support in Congress.

Anderson faced monumental difficulties in gaining access to the ballot in the various states. Excessive signature requirements and early filing deadlines acted to preserve the two-party monopoly in most states. Anderson's success in forcing the revision of state electoral laws was notable, but the energy his campaign spent in petition campaigns and court fights diverted resources that could have been used to help build his general election appeal. Anderson also faced difficulty in borrowing money to run his campaign. It was not clear that he would win enough votes to receive public funding and thereby be able to pay back his creditors.

Polls showed that Anderson's support represented a greater threat to Carter than to Reagan. Despite his roots in the Republican party, Anderson's appeal was mostly to new liberals, voters who did not find Reagan at all acceptable. As a consequence, Carter sought to keep Anderson from being a factor in the fall election. Rulings by the administration made it more difficult for potential creditors to advance Anderson's strapped campaign badly needed funds. Carter also sought to deny Anderson parity. The President would not participate in any debates that included Anderson. The Carter campaign's message to voters was simple: as Anderson was a minor candidate, a vote for Anderson was a vote for Reagan.

Reagan, of course, found it to his advantage to keep Anderson's candidacy as viable as possible. Thus, Reagan insisted on Anderson's inclusion in the debates. Carter steadfastly refused. As a result, the first presidential debate, sponsored by the League of

Women Voters, was a two-person affair between Reagan and Anderson.

Anderson suffered a serious blow when his standing in the polls fell below the 15 percent threshold arbitrarily set by the League of Women Voters for his inclusion in the debates. Consequently, the second debate, the one voters focused on, included only Reagan and Carter. Anderson was relegated to the heap of minor party candidates. He would finally finish with nearly 7 percent of the vote, enough to qualify for public funding.

A Retrospective Election, Not a Mandate: 1980

Studies show that there was no clear turn to the right by voters in 1980. Reagan beat Carter by 10 percentage points; yet the election was no prospective issue vote or ideological mandate for Reagan. According to polls, the public was more liberal than Reagan on a number of issues; on other issues the public had little idea where Reagan stood. As Kathleen Frankovic has shown, there was no strong shift to the right in public opinion from the time Jimmy Carter was elected in 1976 to Ronald Reagan's election in 1980 (see Table 6.5).[40]

Instead, the 1980 election was more simply a retrospective rejection of Carter's performance in office.[41] Poor economic conditions in particular helped to account for the voters' rejection of Carter.[42] Citizens were voting not so much for Reagan as they were against Carter. Issues were important only to the extent that they provided the reasons why voters rejected Carter.

Retrospective voting clearly dwarfed prospective issue voting in 1980. The work of Gregory Markus underscores the limited impact that prospective issues had on voter choice.[43] Markus reviews the surveys of the National Election Studies that polled voters throughout the course of the presidential campaign. As Table 6.6 shows, voters had no clear opinion whether the government should pursue inflation control even at the cost of increasing unemployment, or whether the government should reduce unemployment no matter what the effect on inflation. By October, 40 percent of the voters were unable to take any position on this issue, and an additional 22 percent located themselves at dead center. Voters were even less certain where Carter and Reagan stood on this issue. Apparently, the unemployment-inflation trade-off issue was too "hard" to guide most voters in 1976.

Voters showed less but still substantial confusion on the questions of whether federal expenditures for health, education, and

Table 6.5   Ideological and Issue Preferences, 1976 to 1980*

ideology	November 1976	November 1980
Liberal	20%	18%
Moderate	48	51
Conservative	32	31

domestic spending	November 1976	November 1980
Increase	23%	12%
Decrease	45	49
Keep the same	26	33

welfare payments	July 1977	November 1980
Not needed	54%	51%
Necessary	31	39

payments for abortions	January 1978	November 1980
Favor	42%	38%
Oppose	50	55

business regulation	January 1978	November 1980
Too much regulation	58%	65%
Right amount	31	27

regulate pornography sales to adults	January 1978	November 1980
Yes	42%	32%
No	53	63

effect of '60s programs	January 1978	November 1980
Made things better	31%	30%
Made things worse	14	20
Had no effect	46	42

*Questions: (1) Are you in favor of increasing government spending on domestic programs, reducing it, or keeping it about the same? (2) In your opinion, do you think that most people who receive money from welfare could get along without it if they tried, or do you think they really need this help? (3) The government should help a poor woman with her medical bills if she wants an abortion. Do you agree or disagree? (4) The government has gone too far in regulating business and interfering with the free enterprise system. Do you agree or disagree? (5) Should government, at some level, restrict the sale of pornography to adults, or should adults be permitted to buy and read whatever they wish? (6) There were many government programs created in the 1960s to try and improve the condition of poor people in this country. Do you think these programs generally made things better, made things worse, or do you think they didn't have much impact one way or the other?

Source: Kathleen A. Frankovic, "Public Opinion Trends," in The Election of 1980, ed. Gerald Pomper (Chatham, N.J.: Chatham House, 1981), p. 114.

Table 6.6   Respondent and Perceived Candidate Positions on the Inflation-Unemployment Trade-off (percent)

	reduce inflation (1-2)	3	4	5	reduce unemployment (6-7)	DK
Respondent						
February	15	10	24	10	11	31
April	17	12	23	8	11	30
June	16	11	22	9	12	29
September	9	10	22	11	10	38
October	8	9	22	11	9	40
Carter						
February	4	7	18	16	17	38
April	11	11	18	13	11	36
June	13	12	17	12	11	35
September	6	9	17	12	10	45
October	6	7	14	14	12	47
Reagan						
February	10	11	10	8	5	56
April	14	11	13	10	5	47
June	11	13	16	9	4	47
September	11	12	12	10	5	51
October	11	11	12	9	5	52

Source: Gregory B. Markus, "Political Attitudes During an Election Year: A Report on the 1980 NES Panel Study," *American Political Science Review* 76 (September 1982): p. 543.

related services should be cut (see Table 6.7). There is no consensus among voters for a sharp reduction in these services. In October, more than a third of the voters could not even identify Reagan's position on this important domestic issue. On the whole, voters were able to see some difference between the candidates, with Carter being in support of maintaining services and Reagan being in favor of cuts. It was Carter, not Reagan, who was somewhat closer to the average voter on this issue! Voters in 1980 do not appear to have used their ballots to provide government with a clear sense of policy direction on the issue of domestic spending. Of course, voter opinion would have been quite different had the question asked solely about cuts in welfare.

In the area of defense spending the results are a bit different (see Table 6.8). Again, many voters had a difficult time placing where the candidates stood on the issue. But overall the voters favored increased spending for defense, an opinion that accurately reflected Reagan's position on the issue. As Markus notes, Reagan's stance on this issue may have contributed to his advantage over Carter.

Table 6.7 Respondent and Perceived Candidate Positions on Domestic Services Expenditures (percent)

	cut in services (1-2)	3	4	5	no cut in services (6-7)	DK
Respondent						
February	13	11	15	16	29	17
April	15	12	15	12	28	18
June	14	12	15	12	27	20
September	16	13	15	13	26	17
October	16	11	17	11	26	18
Carter						
February	4	6	18	20	26	26
April	6	11	19	19	20	26
June	5	7	18	22	21	27
September	3	7	16	23	24	27
October	3	5	12	22	28	28
Reagan						
February	13	11	14	8	7	46
April	17	14	14	10	5	40
June	16	13	15	10	6	39
September	19	16	15	9	6	34
October	19	15	15	8	8	35

Source: Gregory B. Markus, "Political Attitudes During an Election Year: A Report on the 1980 NES Panel Study," *American Political Science Review* 76 (September 1982): p. 544.

That issues can dominate over personal imagery in a presidential election is easily demonstrated by the results of the 1980 campaign in the South. Democratic ads aired in that region attempted to exploit the fact that President Carter was a native southerner. Carter kicked off his fall campaign with a Labor Day speech at Tuscumbia, Alabama. Clips from this event were used to create commercials that emphasized Carter's solidarity with the region and the sense of pride that southerners felt in seeing one of their own in the White House. These ads showed pictures of a large, enthusiastic crowd lining the parade route as Carter arrived at the airport. Parade viewers commented: "He picked the best place— that's the South"; "I'm proud that he's a southerner"; and "He's coming back home." The announcer intones: "The arrival of the President is always a special event. But never more so than when he comes home to the South." Carter speaks from behind a podium with the presidential seal: "In the last few years, I've been to a lot of places, and I've seen a lot of people. But I just want to say

Table 6.8   Respondent and Perceived Candidate Positions on Defense Spending (percent)

	reduce spending (1-2)	3	4	5	increase spending (6-7)	DK
Respondent						
February	4	4	13	23	41	15
April	5	5	15	22	37	17
June	5	6	15	24	36	15
September	3	4	15	21	41	14
October	6	4	16	21	39	15
Carter						
February	5	10	18	22	22	22
April	10	13	23	20	12	23
June	11	13	23	20	11	21
September	12	16	23	18	9	22
October	16	19	18	12	10	25
Reagan						
February	4	4	9	13	23	47
April	3	7	11	17	25	37
June	3	4	11	19	27	36
September	3	3	7	18	41	29
October	2	4	6	15	43	30

Source: Gregory B. Markus, "Political Attitudes During an Election Year: A Report on the 1980 NES Panel Study," *American Political Science Review* 76 (September 1982): p. 544.

how great it is to be with folks who don't talk with an accent." The crowd laughs and cheers.

Yet, despite this personal-image merchandising, Carter lost the South to an outsider. Carter won the votes of southern blacks. But white southerners knew too much about Carter's liberalism for his "good ole boy" and southern-roots imagery to work. It was Reagan's conservative ideology that had a stronger appeal in this traditionalist region. As Kathleen Hall Jamieson observes, personal imagery cannot overcome deeply held beliefs and information:

> If, as [Carter media adviser Gerald] Rafshoon believes, Carter lost his Southern base in 1980 because he had proven more liberal than white Southerners had expected him to be, then no appeals to Southern values could have saved him. Advertising, whether brilliant or banal, is powerless to dislodge deeply held convictions anchored in an ample amount of credible information.[44]

The Republican nominating contest in 1980 further demonstrates that good advertising by itself cannot win a presidential election. Senate Majority Leader Howard Baker was a fresh candidate whose campaign for the Republican nomination was noted for its advertising excellence. Carefully chosen camera angles and skillful editing made the diminutive Baker appear to be a towering, powerful, dramatic leader. In one quite famous commercial, Baker is shown verbally putting down an Iranian student protester, much to the delight and amplified cheers and applause of his audience. Yet, Baker lost in Iowa and his campaign quickly dissolved. Good media was not enough for Baker.[45]

THE POLITICS OF RETROSPECTIVE APPROVAL: 1984

I n 1984 Ronald Reagan won reelection by a landslide. He won 59 percent of the popular vote and forty-nine states. Democrat Walter Mondale carried only his home state of Minnesota and the District of Columbia.

The 1984 election was an overwhelming retrospective vote of endorsement for the Reagan administration. The country was at peace, inflation had eased, and a sense of growth and prosperity had returned. As the Reagan ads proclaimed, "It's morning again in America." There was little reason for Americans to vote for a change.

Retrospective performance evaluations dominated the Fall election. Image politics, particularly the vaguely defined sense of candidate "momentum," had dominated the Democratic primaries. Yet, as we shall see, broad issue choices were at stake in both the spring and fall. Walter Mondale and Gary Hart drew support from quite different constituencies in the Democratic party. In the general election, Reagan and Mondale offered voters a clear choice between governmental directions. The electorate gave its endorsement to the changes Reagan had initiated during his first term in office. They voted to continue—not to reverse and not to expand—the general course of action as set by

Reagan. The issue of taxes also proved to be an important factor in the Fall election.

The 1980 and 1984 elections were no mandates for a particular Reagan brand of conservatism. In 1980 Americans voted to oust a President, Jimmy Carter, who could not handle the nation's mounting economic crisis. In 1984 Americans voted to return a President, Ronald Reagan, whose performance showed that he could do so.

THE 1982 MIDTERM ELECTIONS: REAGAN'S NADIR

The retrospective basis of voting in the 1980s becomes all the more apparent if we look at an election, the 1982 midterm congressional elections, at a time when Reagan and the Republicans were not so popular. In 1982 unemployment rates were at their highest since the Great Depression. The Republicans controlled both the presidency and the Senate. In 1982, unlike the presidential election two years previous, voters would blame the Republicans, the party of government, for the nation's poor economic performance.

In 1982 the Republicans lost twenty-six House seats—a major loss for the party of an incumbent President in a midterm congressional election. In a way, the Republicans were fortunate; they barely held on to a number of sharply contested Senate seats. Nineteen eighty had been no mandate for Republicanism or conservatism. The public had simply rejected Carter's and the Democrats' performance in office. Now, in 1982, they were rejecting the Republican performance as well.

Democratic ads seized on the poor state of the economy under the Republicans:

 STATE UNEMPLOYMENT ad

VIDEO: Scenes, shot in color, of people standing in what is meant to be a present-day unemployment line.

AUDIO (Announcer): "The Republicans in this state say that the record unemployment is only temporary. High taxes, only temporary. 'High unemployment is topping out,' the Republicans say. 'Why, prosperity is just around the corner.'"

VIDEO: The picture suddenly turns to black-and-white, as the contemporary unemployment line blends into one of Depression-era
clad people--a line of unemployed people during the Great Depression. Finish with a close-up of the face of one of the persons standing in line, that of a stereotypical, Depression-era
elderly gentleman.

AUDIO (Announcer): "Of course, the Republicans have said that before. The President was Hoover. The year was 1929."

VIDEO: White letters against a black background read: LET'S GET OUR
STATE WORKING AGAIN

AUDIO (Announcer): "Let's get our state working again."

AUDIO AND VIDEO: Closing message to vote for the local Democratic
candidate by name.

One particularly effective 1982 Democratic spot was a play off
a Republican commercial that had aired two years previous. In
their 1980 ad, the Republicans hired James "Buzz" Willders, a
stereotypical blue-collar worker, to stand inside a closed factory
and argue that if the Democrats are so good for working people,
then why are so many people not working? The spot had two ob-
jectives. It hit at the poor state of the economy under Carter. It targeted blue-collar voters who, dissatisfied with Democratic
welfarism and social liberalism, were no longer firmly anchored in
the New Deal Democratic coalition and might be persuaded to
cross party lines. Reagan won a majority of white working-class
voters in 1980.

But by 1982 it was a Republican administration that presided
over a deepening recession. Democratic National Committee advertising specialist Robert Hirschfeld heard rumors that Willders
was dissatisfied with the treatment and favors he had received from
the Republicans. Hirschfeld traveled to Baltimore to ask Willders
to do a new ad for the Democrats. But Hirschfeld added that he
was interested in producing the new spot only if Willders would
agree to appear in it without pay. The result was a classic retrospective appeal that urged a targeted group of voters to reject the
poor economic performance of the incumbent administration:

BALTIMORE WORKER ad

VIDEO: A worker clad in T-shirt and blue jeans walks through an idle
factory.

AUDIO (Worker addresses viewers): "Remember me? In 1980 the Republicans paid me to go on television because they promised us they
would make things better. And I believed them."

VIDEO: The worker's name appears at the bottom of the screen: James
A. Willders, Baltimore, MD.

AUDIO (Willders continues): "Well, since they've been in control,
unemployment is the highest since the Great Depression. And
businesses are closing down every day. Millions are without jobs,
and we've got to do something."

VIDEO: Willders turns and looks directly into the camera. For emphasis, he first points to himself, and then to the audience.

AUDIO (Willders): "I'm a Democrat, but I voted Republican once. It's
a mistake I'll never make again. And I didn't get paid to say
that!"

VIDEO: The words "Democrats will get this country working!" are
overlaid across Willders' picture on the screen.

AUDIO (Announcer): "Democrats will get this country working!"

The Democrats also attacked the lack of fairness in the tax and
spending cuts initiated by the Republicans. The fairness issue was
an important factor in 1982:

SOCIAL SECURITY ad

VIDEO: Super close-up of a Social Security card.

AUDIO (Announcer): "The Republicans all say they believe in Social
Security, a sacred contract with the American people. That's what
they say. Look what they do."

VIDEO: Pull back to show a pair of scissors repeatedly clipping off portions of the Social Security card until there's almost nothing left.

AUDIO (Announcer): "In 1981 they tried to cut Social Security by $60 billion. In 1982 they said either increase Social Security taxes or cut $40 billion just to balance the budget. When are they going to stop? Not until it hurts."

VIDEO: Still frame of scissors cutting the small portion of the Social Security card that still remains. Across the picture appear the words: "It isn't fair. It's Republican."

AUDIO (Announcer): "It isn't fair. It's Republican."

TRICKLE DOWN ad

AUDIO: Sounds of water dripping into a tin cup.

VIDEO: Water drips into a tin cup held by an arm clad in a plaid shirt, apparently that of a working man.

AUDIO (Announcer): "The big Republican tax cut. What does it mean to the average working person? About four bucks a pay check. Not much! But it means a lot to the wealthy!"

VIDEO: Suddenly a champagne glass, held by a hand clad in what appears to be a tuxedo, intercepts the trickle of water. The trickle suddenly turns into a gushing flow of champagne. The champagne overflows into the champagne glasses held apparently by other well-dressed party-goers.

AUDIO: Sounds of laughter at a high-class party.

AUDIO (Announcer): "It's the Republican theory called Trickle Down. Give to the rich, and it will eventually trickle down to every body else."

VIDEO: From the last champagne glass a few drops of water finally trickle down all the way to the bottom--into the tin cup.

AUDIO (Announcer): "But you have to ask yourself: just how much is trickling down to you lately?"

```
VIDEO: The tin cup is turned over to reveal that it is virtually
    empty. Freeze frame of the empty tin cup next to the words: "It
    isn't fair. It's Republican."

AUDIO (Announcer): "That's what we thought. It isn't fair. It's
    Republican."
```

The Republicans countered with ads of their own urging voters to "Stay the Course!" and complete the difficult job of cutting government spending and turning the economy around. The Republican ads also pointed out that Reagan had brought down inflation and interest rates from their exorbitant highs of the Carter years. The ads also pointed out that the Republicans had given the nation the greatest tax cut in its history.

The ads on both sides were incomplete and contained numerous distortions. For instance, the Democratic ad on Social Security did not mention that reforms were urgently needed to put the program on more solid fiscal footing. The ad also misled voters by seeming to imply that cuts had been made in the benefits provided the elderly. In fact, the initial cuts had been predominantly in the more peripheral Social Security programs. Likewise Republican ads on the Reagan tax cut did not address the question of who was receiving the lion's share of new tax reductions.

Still, despite distortions and incompleteness, the ads offered voters a choice of policy directions. A viewer who saw both parties' ads and heard the competing claims and arguments could choose accordingly. A citizen who wanted tax cuts and believed that bitter medicine was needed to control inflation and turn the economy around could vote Republican to stay the course. A citizen more concerned with fairness, protecting Social Security benefits, and the urgency of dealing with the recession could vote Democratic.

Given the poor state of the economy in 1982, it was the Democratic message that resonated with the public. Retrospective voting on the economy and the fairness issue both contributed to the Democratic victory. "Stay the course!" was the best argument that a Republican administration could muster in the midst of such difficult economic times; but it was not one that had great appeal to citizens suffering the hardships of the recession.

Only the lack of finances and the resulting inability of the Democrats to widely broadcast their message kept the Democrats from picking up even more extensive congressional gains in 1982. The Democratic National Committee prepared the spots but

lacked the money to air them nationwide. It was left up to each local Democratic campaign to decide whether to use the spots and to
find the money to pay for air time. As a result, the Democratic generic spots were not seen in many congressional districts.

Tactical decisions by national Republican party officials further helped to mute the impact of the advantages enjoyed by the
Democrats. The Republican party worked hard to recruit and
train a good class of congressional candidates. National party officials also made sure that funds, computer services, and other
forms of party campaign technical assistance were targeted to Republican candidates in competitive races. In contrast, much of the
Democratic funds were spent and effectively wasted by incumbents
in relatively safe districts.[1]

Overall, the 1982 House elections were a referendum on President Reagan.[2] 1982 was a retrospective vote against the Republican record.

1984: THE ECONOMY AND REAGAN CAME BACK

In February 1983, in the depths of the recession, Reagan's approval rating fell, in at least one national poll, to a low point of 35
percent.[3] But the President's ratings would soon rise with the improvement in national economic conditions. As Scott Keeter has
shown, Reagan's popularity virtually tracks the gains made in em-
ployment (see Figure 7.1).[4]

By 1984 unemployment was no longer the dominant issue that
it had been in 1982. The economy had rebounded. The 1984 election would be a referendum on peace and prosperity.

IMAGES AND ISSUES IN THE DEMOCRATIC PRIMARIES

The race for the Democratic nomination in 1984 turned on images
and the influence of momentum. Yet, as we shall see, issues—the
broad choice of policy direction—were not absent from the Democratic contest. Different constituencies in the Democratic party
voted for different candidates.

Walter Mondale, the front-runner, ran as an establishment
liberal committed to the party's New Deal and civil rights traditions. Mondale suffered serious image problems. His opponents
charged that he represented a tired, outdated political philosophy
that was incapable of meeting the challenges of the 1980s. Mondale also gained endorsements from numerous organizations, in-

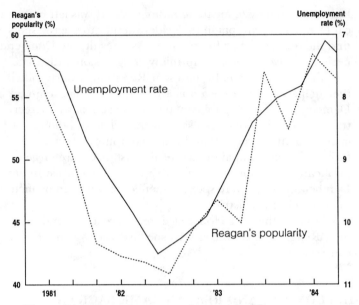

Figure 7.1   Unemployment and approval of Reagan

Source: Scott Keeter, "Public Opinion in 1984," in *The Election of 1984: Reports and Interpretations,* ed. Gerald Pomper (Chatham, N.J.: Chatham House Publishers, 1985), p.94.

cluding the National Organization of Women, the National Education Association, and the first-ever presidential endorsement of the AFL-CIO. These endorsements seemed to provide further evidence of Mondale's ties to the old political order. His opponents charged that he was the captive of special interests. As the former Vice-President, Mondale also bore the albatross of the failed policies of the Carter administration—an image problem that would hurt him in the general election more than in the Democratic primaries.

Ohio Senator John Glenn and Colorado Senator Gary Hart both offered themselves as candidates who represented the nation's future. Glenn's handlers hoped that their campaign would benefit from the Hollywood release of *The Right Stuff,* a film that glorified the early years of, and Glenn's role as an astronaut in, America's man-in-space program. Glenn's commercials were generally recognized to be of high quality. They projected his heroism, patriotism, and sensible centrism. But they could not overcome the handicaps stemming from the Senator's dull public-speaking style (he did not do well in candidate debates) and his campaign's general lack of organization.[5]

The Meteoric Rise. . .

Hart ran on a new generation image but sought to avoid Glenn's more conservative tag. Hart was deliberately ambiguous in the ideological image he projected. He sought to attract votes from all factions of the party dissatisfied with Mondale, from both conservatives and "new collar" antiestablishment liberals alike.[6]

Hart entered the first-in-the-nation Iowa caucuses as a relative unknown. He hoped that a good showing in Iowa would establish him as a major candidate and boost his chances for success the next week in New Hampshire. As Hart explained: "You can get awful famous in this country in seven days."

Mondale won the Iowa caucuses with 45 to 49 percent of the vote. (The exact percentage of vote that Mondale received is unclear as complex caucus voting procedures at times allow the supporters of a losing candidate to reallocate their votes to another candidate.) Yet it was Hart who emerged from Iowa as the big winner. Hart gained considerable momentum with 15 to 16 percent of the vote and a second-place finish that effectively separated him from the rest of the Democratic field. News coverage of the Hart campaign grew tenfold during the week following the Iowa caucuses, and equaled that given Mondale. Equally important, the new media coverage given Hart was virtually all upbeat.[7]

Hart's 37-to-32-percent upset win in the first-in-the-nation New Hampshire primary was a stunning surprise. One week later, Hart did even better, winning an amazing 70 percent of the vote in Vermont's nonbinding primary. Momentum was clearly with Hart. According to CBS/*New York Times* polls, Hart had been the choice of only 1 percent of Democrats before Iowa. One week after New Hampshire, Democrats said that they preferred Hart to Mondale by a 38-to-31-percent margin.[8]

. . .and Fall of Gary Hart

But as Hart moved clearly to the front, the press began to subject his candidacy to greater scrutiny. The press got tough on Hart; "compensatory journalism" began to slow Hart's momentum.[9] News stories criticized Hart for aping John Kennedy's mannerisms, for allegedly lying about his age, and for having changed his name from Hartpence to Hart.

Hart had run on a program of "new ideas." He called for a streamlined national defense that relied on smaller, more flexible, and cost-effective weapons systems. He proposed a national industrial policy geared to increased productivity and the development of high-technology industries. He rejected trade protectionism for insulating American industry from the demands of competition and adaptation. As a Senator he had angered organized labor by being one of the few Democrats to vote against the Chrysler bailout.

Since the beginning of the campaign, when Hart was still "Gary Who?," his organization had dutifully fed the press reams of position papers. The press, with few exceptions, ignored them. Issues were boring. A detailed examination of policy proposals did not make for interesting stories. Some members of the press derisively dismissed Hart as the thinking-man's candidate. But all this changed when Hart emerged as the new front-runner. The media now began to question whether there was any substance to Hart's new ideas.

In a March debate, Mondale borrowed a line from the Wendy's hamburger ads that had become part of the popular culture. Mondale said that when thinking about Hart's new ideas he was tempted to ask: "Where's the beef?" The sound bite was picked up and repeated nationwide. At various campaign rallies thereafter, Mondale would hold up an empty hamburger bun much to the delight of his supporters.

Mondale's "Where's the beef?" charge hit home as Hart had not been clear in identifying himself as either a liberal or conservative. According to political scientist Larry Bartels, ambiguity can be an effective strategy for a candidate early in the primary season, for voters can project their own preferred policy views onto a candidate who fails to take clear stands on issues. But later in the campaign, a candidate like Hart pays a price for this strategy as the press subjects his issue positions to more critical scrutiny.[10] Hart had tried to gain votes both from conservatives who saw Mondale as too liberal and from new liberals who saw Mondale as too conservative. But now many Americans began to wonder if Hart had any substance at all.

In addition, new rules changes in the Democratic party worked to Mondale's advantage, but to Gary Hart's and Jesse Jackson's disadvantage. As one of the changes, the Hunt Commission increased to 568 the number of seats awarded automatically to Senators, Congressional Representatives, key state and local elected officials, and party officeholders. Few of these superdelegates could be expected to support a political loner such as Hart or an outsider such as Jackson. Mondale, in contrast, had long-established contacts with many of these superdelegates. He had even campaigned and raised money for a number of them. As a result, Mondale had the support of an estimated 450 to 500 of the 568 superdelegates.

Mondale and Hart had finished the primary season virtually even in terms of the number of delegates actually won in the primaries and caucuses. As the primary trail progressed, however, it was Mondale's edge in superdelegates that helped influence public perception as to his lead.[11] Mondale's support among superdelegates also gave him effective control of the national convention.

A second change in the nominating rules shortened the primary season to make it more difficult for a dark horse candidate to use an early primary or caucus victory to build the resources necessary to win later races. However, compression of the primary schedule actually worked to Hart's advantage at first. The momentum from his Iowa showing carried Hart to victory the next week in New Hampshire. There was insufficient time for a new critical attitude in the press to emerge and burst the Hart bubble.

Soon thereafter, the compressed and frontloaded primary calendar worked as predicted. Hart was forced to take on Mondale in five states on a single day, Super Tuesday, only two weeks after New Hampshire. The Hart campaign by necessity had focused virtually every resource it had in Iowa and New Hampshire. As a result, the campaign had made virtually no advance effort in the three southern Super Tuesday states. His organization lacked time to effectively redeploy staff and take full advantage of the surge of financial contributions that flowed into the campaign following its success in New Hampshire.

When Super Tuesday came, Hart could not deliver the knockout blow the press expected. Hart won the Massachusetts, Rhode Island, and Florida primaries. But the big story of the day was Mondale's survival, as the former Vice-President won Alabama and Georgia.

Momentum was no longer with Hart. Mondale regained the lead as the primary trail shifted north to Illinois and other major industrial states.

Momentum and Ideology in 1984

Momentum was a key factor in the rise and fall of Gary Hart. Yet, ideology was also related to the vote in the Democratic primaries. Hart's greatest appeal was to the young, to yuppies, and to new collar voters. He made no special promises to blacks or labor and, therefore, found little support among those groups.[12] Hart did well in the early contests in more rural and ideologically moderate states and thereby established his momentum. But when the primaries moved to the more urban and industrial states, Hart found that he was campaigning among more traditional Democratic constituencies. His new ideas message was not well received by constituencies that preferred the civil rights and job protectionism promises of Mondale.[13]

Jesse Jackson had attempted to build a "rainbow coalition" of forgotten Americans of all colors. But this broad range of support for Jackson did not materialize in 1984. Jackson's support was centered in the nation's black communities. His best showings came in those southern and northern industrial states with large African-American populations.

As Hart had virtually no support among African-Americans, Jackson's showing came essentially at Mondale's expense. Had Jackson not been in the race, Mondale would have had an easier time putting down Hart's challenge. Jackson's candidacy probably cost Mondale victories in Wisconsin, Louisiana, Indiana, Ohio, and California.[14]

The media, as previously observed, generally did a poor job in covering the policy views of the candidates. Hart ran as the candidate of new ideas; but according to a CBS poll, only 9 percent of voters could identify any specific Hart new idea.[15]

Still, as Larry Bartels shows, despite the glaring inadequacies of news coverage, as the 1984 primary season progressed, voters learned much about the candidates and their ideologies, not only about their personal traits. General issue orientations did matter in 1984, even if voters did not clearly see the differences between Mondale and Hart on specific issues. New Deal adherents preferred Mondale to Hart, and social traditionalists viewed Mondale more favorably than they did the new-style liberal Hart. In contrast, younger, more upscale voters preferred Hart. Hart and Mondale were viewed by their respective constituencies as they should have been. If voters did not quite learn about candidates' stances on specific issues, they did as least learn about candidates' general styles and issue dispositions.[16]

Mondale won the nomination, but he did not win the loyalty of those more independent Democrats who supported Hart. According to a CBS/*New York Times* poll, one-third of those Democrats who supported Hart in the primaries defected to Reagan in the general election. Two-thirds of the self-described independents who supported Hart also voted for Reagan in November.[17]

THE GENERAL ELECTION

The Reagan campaign ads sought to make the 1984 election a referendum on the incumbent, on the President's handling of the economy and foreign policy. Reagan had brought inflation to heel. The nation was feeling a new sense of vibrancy. It was a nation at peace and a nation with renewed respect abroad.

During the spring, the Tuesday Team, as Reagan's advertising professionals were called, aired upbeat, warm-feeling ads that dwelled on the nation's improved economy and sought to associate the President with the images of a content and well-off America at work and on the move:

PROUDER, STRONGER, BETTER ad

VIDEO: Picture of a city harbor at daybreak. A fishing boat goes to work.

AUDIO (Narrator): "It's morning again in America."

VIDEO: Various shots of people at work--a businessman getting out of a taxi, a farmer on a tractor, a boy on his bicycle delivering newspapers, and a suburbanite on his way to work. Switch to a scene of a man and young boy carrying a new carpet into a home.

AUDIO: "Today more men and women will go to work than ever before in our country's history. With interest rates at about half the record highs of 1980, nearly 2,000 families today will buy new homes, more than at any time in the past four years."

VIDEO: Stereotypical scenes of a small-town wedding. An elderly lady dressed in white virtually explodes with happiness. A couple exchanges marital vows. The bride smiles. The happy couple kisses.

AUDIO: "This afternoon 6,500 young men and women will be married. And with inflation at less than half of what it was just four years ago, they can look forward with confidence to the future."

VIDEO: Picture of the U.S. Capitol at night. Switch to a picture of a young boy looking up as the American flag is raised. Various scenes of a small-town flag-raising. Close-up on Old Glory as it waves in the breeze.

AUDIO: "It's morning again in America. And under the leadership of President Reagan, our country is prouder, and stronger, and better. Why would we ever want to return to where we were less than four short years ago?"

VIDEO (Closing picture of Reagan next to the American flag, accompanied by the words): President Reagan: Leadership That's Working.

It was almost as if Reagan personally deserved credit for every young couple that married or every family that moved into a new home. The early Reagan ads emphasized imagery, but it was imagery based not on a candidate's personal attributes but on retrospective performance:

STATUE OF LIBERTY ad

VIDEO: Shots of people at work on a heavy industrial job. Male and female workers welding, hoisting, and so on.

AUDIO (Narrator): "It was a dream that built a nation. The freedom to work at the job of your choice, to reap the rewards of your labor, to leave a richer life for your children and their children beyond."

VIDEO: Camera pulls back to reveal that the workers have been on the scaffolding of the Statue of Liberty, working on the much-celebrated restoration of that national monument. Close with a shot of the Statue of Liberty, enveloped in its scaffolding, standing majestically in New York Harbor.

AUDIO: "Today the dream lives again. Today jobs are coming back. The economy is coming back. And America is coming back, standing tall in the world once again."

VISUAL (Closing picture of Reagan next to the American flag, accompanied by the words): President Reagan: Leadership That's Working.

AUDIO: "President Reagan. Rebuilding the American Dream."

A number of the themes of the Reagan campaign were encapsulated in a seventeen-minute biographic retrospective of the Reagan presidency, aired at the Republican convention and later televised as a paid broadcast. The program, as did all Reagan ads, mixed images and issues. The program detailed both Reagan's personal qualities for leadership and his achievements in office. The film even included pictures of a physically vigorous president riding horseback and chopping wood at his ranch outside Santa Barbara, California. These pictures were meant to dispel any qualms that the public may have had about Reagan's advanced age, that he was too old to serve another full term in office.

In the program, a cross-section of Americans talk about their new-felt sense of pride in America and how America is once again on the move owing to Reagan's presidency. Reagan himself recalls for viewers the vast gains in the economy made during his four years in office. The film associates Reagan with this renewed sense of patriotism and well-being. Numerous shots of a flag-waving and a strong America at work are shown while the words "I'm Proud To Be an American...God Bless the U.S.A." (from Lee Greenwood's song "God Bless the U.S.A.") are sung in the background. The song became the reelection campaign's unofficial anthem.

The film's image-building sought to underscore the faith that Americans can have in Reagan as a take-charge and effective world leader. The President, dressed in a military jacket, prays and dines with American troops stationed in Korea. He walks the Great Wall of China and shakes hands with Chinese officials at a banquet.

Yet, the most moving part of the film is not a simple personal-image appeal; rather, it mixes images with a message. Most poignant of all is the program's extended treatment of Reagan's emotional speech on the beaches of Normandy in commemoration of the fortieth anniversary of the D-Day invasion. Speaking on a windswept beach, the President tells the story of the heroism of the sixty-two rangers who, in the first wave of the assault, scaled the cliffs: "These are the boys of Pointe du Hoc. These are the men who took the cliffs." The camera pans the now aging veterans and their families in the audience, who later stand and applaud the President's remarks. Reagan continues:

> They were what General Marshall called our secret weapon, the best damn kids in the world. Where do we find them? Where do we find such men? And the answer came almost as quickly as I'd asked the question. Where we've always found them in this country. On the farms. In the shops, and the stores, and the offices. They just are the product of the freest society the world has ever known.

The D-Day memorial sequence concludes with Reagan reading the words of the daughter of one of the veterans, a man who died of cancer eight years previous to the memorial. Her father had "promised that he would return to Normandy," and she, in turn, promised her father:

> I'm going there, Dad. And I'll see the beaches and the barricades and the monuments. I'll see the graves, and I'll put flowers there just like you wanted to do. I'll feel all the things you made me feel through your stories and your eyes. I'll never forget what you went through, Dad. Nor will I let anyone else forget. And Dad (Reagan's voice breaks as he continues to read), I'll always be proud.

The camera switches to the audience where the woman in question, the daughter of the deceased veteran, is crying. Reagan concludes: "We will always remember. We will also be prepared so we may be always free."

The D-Day speech is not just a simple appeal to emotional imagery and patriotism. It is also meant to underscore Reagan's message of peace through strength, the need to be vigilantly armed in a dangerous world. Reagan's approach to national defense entailed military spending at levels far above those advocated by the Democrats.

Throughout the campaign, the Tuesday Team felt that the theme of leadership and America's regained international respect had great appeal to younger voters. Economics was a second area that the campaign saw as a key to getting the votes of young people. The Republican ads portrayed Reagan's policies of economic growth as providing today's younger citizens with continued opportunity. Throughout the fall campaign, the Tuesday Team contrasted Reagan's strength and the alleged indecisiveness of the Carter-Mondale White House. On election day, the oldest presidential nominee in the history of the nation carried a majority of the nation's youngest voters.[18]

The only ray of hope for Mondale came as a result of the first presidential debate. Reagan's unfocused and rambling answers, especially toward the end of the ninety-minute encounter, once again raised the age issue. Was the seventy-three-year-old President too old to serve another term in office? Reagan's poor debate performance only reinforced doubts raised by rumors of his daily afternoon naps. Reagan did not seem to be fully in control of the White House.

Media reports and commentary on the debate served to magnify the political significance of Reagan's showing. Immediately

after the debate, 43 percent of the public saw Mondale and 34 percent saw Reagan to be the winner. But two days after the debate,
after press discussions of Reagan's performance had time to sink
in, public opinion polls showed Mondale's victory margin to be
much greater—66 to 17 percent.[19]

In the wake of the President's faltering debate performance,
his campaign handlers decided on two strategy changes. First, the
Tuesday Team would reassure voters by airing commercials that
featured visuals of an effective, take-charge President in the Oval
Office. In a five-minute ad and in two thirty-second spots, Reagan
spoke directly to television viewers. Second, the campaign went on
the offensive by airing stronger anti-Mondale ads. These ads
would make Mondale's promise to raise taxes the key prospective
issue in the campaign.

Mondale had made his extraordinary tax promise in a desperate gamble to revive his flagging campaign. He had little hope of
victory unless he could focus the public's attention on the more
unsatisfactory aspects of Reagan's governance, particularly the
mounting budget deficits of the Reagan years. In his televised acceptance speech at the Democratic national convention, Mondale
argued that a tax increase would be necessary to ease the deficit,
no matter who was elected President in November: "Mr. Reagan
will raise taxes, and so will I. He won't tell you. I just did."

Mondale's tax vow was not popular with voters, and the
republicans took advantage of it. A generic ad run on behalf of
Republican congressional candidates showed a Democratic congressman stuck in an elevator frantically pressing buttons in an effort to escape as voters asked him whether or not he supported
Mondale's proposed tax increase. A second Republican ad compared Reaganomics and Mondalenomics, listing "Raise Taxes"
again and again on the Mondale side of the screen. The Tuesday
Team also hit home on the tax issue in what was arguably the most
effective single spot of the 1984 race:

TAX VIGNETTES ad

VIDEO: A grimy, sweaty construction worker is hard at work breaking
a street with a pickaxe. A truck unloads gravel in the background.

AUDIO: Sounds of city traffic.

AUDIO (Announcer): "Walter Mondale thinks that if you put in more overtime, you could pay for his promises with your taxes. What do you think?"

AUDIO AND VIDEO: Construction worker with the pickaxe looks up in frustration and says with great sarcasm: "Right!"

VIDEO: Scene of a housewife in a busy kitchen. In the background, her children fight, and the family dog barks. The housewife scrapes peanut butter from a jar and tries to spread it thinly among a number of sandwiches.

AUDIO: Sounds of kids playing and fighting and the dog barking.

AUDIO (Announcer): "Walter Mondale thinks you can squeeze more tax money out of your budget. What do you think?"

VIDEO: Housewife gives a look that could kill.

VIDEO: A farmer is busy lifting bales of hay.

AUDIO: Sounds of farm machinery.

AUDIO (Announcer): "Walter Mondale thinks that if you stay out in the field longer you could pay more taxes. What do you think?"

VIDEO: The farmer looks up in obvious disgust.

VIDEO (Closing picture of Reagan next to the American flag, accompanied by the words): "President Reagan: Leadership That's Working."

AUDIO (Announcer): "Vote for President Reagan. You have better things to do with your money than to pay for Walter Mondale's promises."

The second debate, which was to focus on foreign policy, would allow Reagan the opportunity to undo any of the damage done in the first debate. Alternatively, a second bad performance could compound his troubles and accelerate a voter move toward Mondale.

During the days preceding the debate, the Tuesday Team sought to run ads that would make the public more receptive to Reagan's foreign policy message. The ads generally underscored the peace that the United States enjoyed during the Reagan years. The most well-known political spot of the 1984 campaign, "The Bear," was run for six consecutive days.

 THE BEAR ad

AUDIO: Eerie music and sounds of heartbeat-like drumbeats.

VIDEO: Various scenes of a grizzly bear lumbering through the woods.

AUDIO (Announcer): "There's a bear in the woods. For some people, the bear is easy to see. Others don't see it at all. Some people say the bear is tame. Others say it is vicious and dangerous. Since no one can be sure who is right, isn't it smart to be as strong as the bear?"

VIDEO: The bear looks up and sees a man with what appears to be a rifle slung across his shoulder. The bear suddenly stops and appears to take a step backward.

AUDIO (Announcer): "If there is a bear." (Ominous background music trails off.)

AUDIO: Drumbeat continues. Then only the eerie music.

VIDEO (Closing picture of President Reagan accompanied by the words): PRESIDENT REAGAN. PREPARED FOR PEACE.

The bear in the ad, of course, was meant to symbolize the Soviet Union. The ad was designed to provoke public discussion of the United States' need to continue to deal with the Soviets from a position of strength.

The Bear ad was probably the most heavily tested political spot in history. It was shown to no fewer than 100 focus groups and got an amazingly high 75-percent recall among viewers.[20] The ad succeeded in provoking commentary. Yet, the spot was probably too obscure and abstruse to be truly effective. Many viewers did not know what the bear represented; many did not even recognize that it was a political ad. A number of television viewers even thought that the ad was a commercial for "The Life and Times of Grizzly Adams," a once-popular television show.

A Reagan quip in the early moments of the second debate quickly dashed any hopes that Mondale may have had for a come-back victory in November. Panelist Henry Trewitt of the Baltimore *Sun* asked Reagan about his continued ability to perform in office despite being "the oldest President in history." Reagan responded: "I want you to know also that I will not make age an issue in this campaign. I am not going to exploit for political purposes my op-ponent's youth and inexperience." The audience roared its laugh-ter and approval. Reagan looked sharp and reassuring. As the debate continued, he effectively parried Mondale's thrusts on the dangers of an accelerated arms race and continued nuclear prolif-eration. But the substance of the debate and the candidates' stands on policy matters counted for little. Reagan's performance had laid the age issue to rest.

Reagan's lead over Mondale had fallen to 12 percent in the wake of the first-debate disaster. His performance in the second debate, however, helped to restore a more comfortable ballot edge of 20 to 22 points.[21] Reagan's reelection was well in hand, enough that the President's advertising team chose not to use the tougher negative ads it had created attacking Mondale's two-faced voting record and his indecision on Grenada.

Instead, the campaign returned to its retrospective themes. In the campaign's final ads, Reagan once again spoke of the nation's economic accomplishments, his record of peace, and the hopes for a better future that his policies offered young people. One ad fea-tured pictures of a parade and flag-waving celebration as the peo-ple turn out to greet the President's train, according to the announcer, as if to tell the President thank you for all that he has done.

Mondale, in contrast, was unable to find a message that hit home. As a result, he switched from issue to issue in an effort to find one that would reach voters. A number of his ads attacked Reagan's deficits for the "mortgaging" of America that would be a burden on future generations. Another ad used the visuals of a roller coaster to challenge the up-and-down performance of the Reagan economic record. Perhaps the most effective Mondale ads were those that tapped the public's fear of nuclear catastrophe by pointing to the policy area that polls showed to be the one glaring weakness in Reagan's record—his failure to negotiate an arms control treaty.

THE FERRARO FACTOR?

Walter Mondale picked New York Congresswoman Geraldine Ferraro as his vice-presidential running mate. It was a landmark choice. Ferraro was the first female major party nominee for the vice-presidency.

Mondale's choice of Ferraro was designed to exploit the gender gap. Women in the United States differ from men somewhat in their policy attitudes and candidate preferences. In the 1980 presidential and 1982 midterm congressional elections, women voted less Republican than did men. Women as a whole are less supportive of militarism than are men. Women are also more prone to support caring social service programs. Reagan's advocacy of escalated military budgets and reduced social spending only served to raise the salience of those issues at the root of the gender gap. But any advantage that Mondale hoped to gain from this choice quickly dissipated as the press grilled Ferraro on the question of her tax returns and those of her businessman-developer husband.

In the November 1984 presidential vote, the gender gap was once again observed.[22] The exact size of the gender gap remained unclear, as it varied from poll to poll. Depending on the poll, women voted 4 to 9 points less Republican for president than did men. Still, Reagan's popularity was so great that he carried the majority of female and male voters alike.

Overall, the nomination of Ferraro for Vice-President had little impact on the final vote. Perhaps the choice of Ferraro appealed to those more feminist voters who, for the most part, were already disposed to vote Democratic. The first-ever major-party nomination of a woman neither greatly helped nor greatly hurt the Democratic ticket.

RETROSPECTIVE VOTING AND CANDIDATE IDEOLOGY IN 1984

The 1984 election can most simply be understood as a retrospective endorsement of the Reagan administration's performance in office. The Tuesday Team had presented the public attractive images based more on performance than on personality. The public's favorable evaluations of Reagan were colored by positive evaluations of his performance in office.[23] The public's assessments of Reagan's effectiveness as President overshadowed the more personal evaluations of Reagan.[24] His record in office, not his acting skills or Teflon coating, determined his reelection.

The 1984 election was essentially a referendum on the state of the economy.[25] Annual inflation was down from 12 percent to 4 percent. Interest rates similarly were down sharply, from 21.5 percent to 12 percent. Even unemployment, while still somewhat troublesome, stood at 7 percent, below the 10 percent level of 1982.[26] As the economy improved, Americans were answering that all-important economic question positively: Yes! They were better off now than they were four years ago.[27]

Mondale could not hope to win an election focused on retrospective performance evaluations. The Democrats had to shift voter concerns to other matters, more specifically to the impact of rising budgetary deficits on future generations and the dangers that could result from Reagan's reluctance to negotiate new controls on the nuclear arms race. Mondale was asking voters not to look simply at the past but also to the future.

But Mondale was not successful in these efforts. For most voters, present-day pocketbook concerns outweighed questions about possible future policy consequences. On one prospective issue the voters did have a clear opinion; they did not want Mondale's new taxes.

Mondale also faced the difficult task of getting a broad spectrum of Americans to address such hard issues as the arms race and the budget. Most of the public had little understanding of Strategic Defense Initiative technology—its capabilities, its costs, and its relative merits compared to alternative weapons systems. Similarly, few Americans could appreciate the exact size of the nation's annual budget deficits or the possible long-term economic harm posed by the accumulated national debt. Reagan's budget-cutting rhetoric and the traditional image of the Republicans as the party of fiscal conservatism only further confused the public about how bad the budget situation was and who was to blame.[28] The return of peace and prosperity, in contrast, were much easier for voters to feel and comprehend.

Whereas retrospective economic evaluations were paramount in 1984, the electorate's behavior in 1984 cannot fully be understood solely by retrospective voting. Mondale and Reagan also offered Americans fundamentally different visions.[29] As was the case in 1972 the presidential candidates in 1984 tended to take distinct stands on the policy issues. The public responded accordingly. The electorate clearly saw Mondale as the more liberal of the two major-party candidates. The voters were also able to see differences between the candidates when it came to specific issues. Paul Abramson and his colleagues studied public opinion in seven different issues areas in the 1984 election. They found that voters' issues positions were strongly related to candidate choice.[30]

Still, we should be cautious not to overstate the impact of specific issues, other than taxes, on the 1984 election. According to the work of Martin Wattenberg, the public saw itself as closer to Mondale than to Reagan on the issues. Wattenberg sees the 1984 election as a vote of endorsement for Reagan's performance in office, not for his specific policy positions.[31]

The 1984 election was neither a mandate for conservatism nor Republicanism. In their separate studies of national polling data gathered by the Center for Political Studies, both Paul Abramson and Warren Miller have concluded that the public in 1984 had a preference for moderate policies. They further report that in a number of policy areas the public preferred more liberal policy alternatives than those advocated with Reagan.[32] While the public approved of the general conservative direction of Reagan's first four years in office, they were skeptical of initiatives that would move the country in a still more conservative direction:

> The Reagan administration had achieved many of its domestic program cuts and had increased spending for defense. In both cases, the average respondent was saying that the shift in policy was just about right. There was no longer any overall sentiment for further domestic program reductions nor for increased spending for defense.[33]

As Miller concludes: "Ronald Reagan may have been reelected in part because he had moved the government to the ideological right; he was *not* reelected with a mandate to move further toward the goals of his conservative supporters.[34]

Overall retrospective voting was the key to Reagan's reelection. But economic performance alone does not explain Reagan's success. Foreign policy performance constitutes a second important element in voter positive evaluations of the Reagan years. Theodore Lowi has traced public opinion trends and observed that Reagan's upswing in popularity starting in his third year in office is associated with key international events with which the President shrewdly associated himself.[35] One big jump in the President's approval rating came after his strong rhetorical denunciation of the Soviets for shooting down a Korean Air Lines passenger plane. Another sharp upswing in the President's approval rating came after the Grenada invasion, a swift and successful invasion that proved immensely popular with Americans (see Figure 7.2). John Aldrich and his colleagues, too, have concluded that foreign policy was an

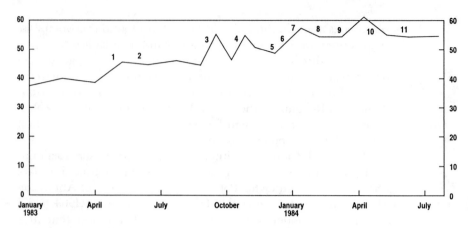

1. Terrorist bombing of U.S. embassy in Beirut and Reagan denunciation thereof; Secretary Shultz dispatched to Beirut.
2. Economic summit, Williamsburg, Va.
3. South Korean airliner downed; 2,000 more Marines to Lebanon.
4. Terrorist attack, killing 241 Marines in Beirut; Grenada invaded.
5. U.S. air attacks on Syrian positions near Beirut; 2 U.S. jets downed; Lt. Robert Goodman captured by Syria.
6. U.S. ships attack Syrian aircraft near Beirut.
7. Lt. Goodman released by Syria.
8. Redeployment of U.S. Marines, Beirut; Andropov dies.
9. Chernenko new Russian leader.
10. President's trip to China.
11. President's trip to Ireland and Normandy.

Figure 7.2   A profile of Ronald Reagan's popularity, 1983-1984

Source: Theodore J. Lowi, *The Personal President: Power Invested, Promise Unfulfilled* (Ithaca, N.Y.: Cornell University Press, 1985), p. 18. Reprinted in *The Elections of 1984,* ed. Michael Nelson (Washington, D.C.: CQ Press, 1985), p. 283.

important influence on the vote in both the 1980 and 1984 presidential elections.[36]

SUMMARY

Performance-based, not personal-based, images dominated the 1984 election. 1984 was an integral part of a retrospective voting era in American presidential elections:

> In sum, it would seem reasonable to conclude that the 1976 election, with its razor-thin edge going to Carter, was a very narrow rejection of Ford's incumbency, and 1980 was a clear and strong rejection of Carter's. In 1984 Reagan won in large part because he was seen as having performed well and because Mondale was unable to convince the public that he would do better.[37]

But it would be a mistake to view voting in 1984 purely in retrospective terms. Policy choices were at stake in 1972 when Richard Nixon and George McGovern offered Americans a clearcut choice of policy directions. In 1984 Mondale and Reagan offered voters a similarly clear choice. Once again voters were able to see distinct and important differences between the candidates.[38] The choice was pristinely clear on one particular issue. The voters knew what they did not want; they did not want Walter Mondale's proposed tax increase.

Both retrospective and prospective issue voting were at work in 1984. As Paul Abramson and his colleagues conclude: "[T]he 1984 election appears to be more like that of 1972, in that the retrospective evaluations were more important than the issue preferences, but the latter remained an important factor in the vote."[39] Substance—issues and performance evaluations, not simply personal-based imagery—determined the results.

THE TRIUMPH OF ISSUE-BASED IMAGES: 1988

Popular accounts that were circulated about the "flag and furlough campaign of 1988"[1] see the election to have turned on the creation of powerful televised images. Peter Goldman and Tom Mathews made these observations about the 1988 election:

> What was disturbing about the 1988 election, both for itself and as a harbinger of our future, was that ideals were never really in play. It was instead a contest between two men who could not say with any precision why they wanted to be president, or why they ought to be. In the circumstances, there was no agenda to fight for, only victory for its own sake. The result was a contest at manipulation, a war between high-tech button-pushers unburdened by contending vision or issues, and, whatever else one made of the outcome, the better button men surely won.[2]

Political scientist Marjorie Randon Hershey observes that media coverage of the three televised debates centered not on the substance of the candidates' issue positions but "on which candidate seemed the most relaxed, the most likable, with the best one-liners, as though the election were to result in the selection of a dinner guest, not a President."[3] It was "politics as spectator sport" where "[m]edia values had almost completely supplanted the values of governing."[4] Hershey's overall assessment is pejorative: "For when the 1988 presidential campaign came down to a choice between Willie Horton and the Pledge of Allegiance, the only people enriched were the campaign consultants."[5]

But was the 1988 campaign nothing more than a battle of personal images? As we shall see, the critics are in part right. In 1988 personal-based candidate images or, more accurately, the destruction of carefully cultivated candidate images, dominated the primary season. But the general election offered voters more—a fundamental choice between competing visions. Personal imagery alone did not win the day in 1988. Instead, the fusion of issues and images—the promulgation of issue-based images—turned the tide for George Bush. In both the paid and the free media, Bush evoked powerful symbols that underscored the fundamental alternative that he offered to the more liberal policy directions of Michael Dukakis.

Retrospective evaluations were also important in 1988. Bush's victory could not have been gained in the absence of the Reagan economic prosperity. Nineteen eighty-eight was essentially the second presidential election that turned on voter evaluations of the performance of the Reagan administration.[6]

CANDIDATE IMAGERY IN THE DEMOCRATIC RACE

The 1988 race for the Democratic nomination underscores the extent to which the presidential race is not in the total control of professional image-makers. Campaign managers and consultants cannot control the actions of the candidate. Nor can they dictate the course of events and the reactions of the mass media. As a result, 1988 saw the rapid deterioration of the presidential image of a number of Democratic contenders, contenders who were rapidly eliminated from the primary field.

Certain candidacies just never got off the ground despite the efforts of campaign handlers. Arizona Governor Bruce Babbitt and Illinois Senator Paul Simon both lacked the flair to come across well on television. Babbitt courageously called for raising taxes to reduce the national deficit. Well behind in the polls, he had little to lose by doing so. Simon, sporting an old-fashioned bow tie, sought to represent a return to the Democratic Party's ideals of the New Deal era. Simon finished a somewhat distant second in Iowa caucuses and lost momentum. He needed a better showing in a state neighboring his native Illinois.

Gary Hart and Joe Biden: Monkey Business and Plagiarism

The campaigns of two of the Democratic contenders, Gary Hart and Joe Biden, virtually self-destructed as the media focused on questions of personal character. Hart, the former Colorado Senator, was the clear early leader in the race owing to his nearly successful challenge for the Democratic nomination four years earlier. But he could not survive the scrutiny that the press gives a front-runner. Hart, dogged by repeated rumors as to his extramarital philanderings, sought to lay the suspicions to rest by challenging anyone interested in his sex life to "put a tail" on him. According to Hart, "They'd be very bored."

The Miami Herald responded to Hart's challenge. Following up a telephone tip, *Herald* reporters staked out and kept watch on the ex-Senator's Washington townhouse on a night when Hart's wife was out of town. The resulting exposé was anything but boring. Hart spent the night with a buxomy model, Donna Rice. Rice, herself, later revealed under questioning that she and Hart had previously spent a night on a yacht off Bimini. The yacht, quite appropriately, was named *Monkey Business.* *Washington Post* reporter Paul Taylor asked Hart the unprecedented question of whether he had ever committed adultery. Commentators in the press continued to speculate about the psychological and compulsive roots of Hart's behavior. Hart soon dropped from the race.

Delaware Senator Joe Biden was similarly forced to withdraw when media stories effectively demolished public perceptions of his presidential stature. Not counting Jesse Jackson, Biden was perhaps the most effective orator in the Democratic field, copying, it was said, John F. Kennedy's mannerisms. Unfortunately, that was not all that Biden copied. In an Iowa speech, he virtually repeated word-for-word, without attribution, a long section from a speech by British Labour Party Leader Neil Kinnock. With the media's attention now focused on Biden, it was soon uncovered that he had also lifted phrases from speeches by Robert Kennedy, that he inflated his college and law school grades, and that he had received an F in law school for plagiarizing a law review article.

Richard Gephardt: Self-Styled Populist

Missouri Congressman Richard Gephardt hoped to repeat Jimmy Carter's 1976 strategy of using an early win in Iowa to establish the momentum that would carry him to the nomination. Gephardt was, in fact, a Washington insider on the fast-track to a leadership position in Congress.[7] But as such a reputation would not sell in Iowa, Gephardt was recast for the campaign as a populist outsider running on behalf of the people against powerful established interests. He campaigned in Iowa as the champion of the family farm against corporate agriculture. By the end of the Iowa campaign, Gephardt's handlers even had him "shucking off his navy-blue business suits in favor of bright red parkas and farmer's caps."[8]

Gephardt also sought the votes of blue-collar workers by stressing the issue of trade protectionism and his record on tax reform. Gephardt hit hard against the allegedly unfair trade practices of Japan and South Korea. One powerful Gephardt ad claimed that Americans would have to pay $48,000 for a Korean-made Hyundai if the United States were to place the same taxes and tariffs on imported cars that Korea had placed on American-made cars. His "people's"-oriented message was encapsulated in the campaign slogan created by media adviser David Doak: "It's your fight, too."[9]

Gephardt won Iowa, but his focus on that state left him little time and money to adequately campaign in the New Hampshire primary, only one week away. Defeated by Michael Dukakis in New Hampshire, Gephardt was in a poor financial and organizational position to battle on Super Tuesday, when twenty-one states chose nearly one-third of the nominating convention delegates in a single day. Dukakis's ads effectively demolished Gephardt's populist image. These ads questioned how Gephardt could be fighting for the people when he had accepted large campaign contributions from corporate political action committees. On Super Tuesday, Gephardt won only one contest, his home state of Missouri.

Albert Gore: An Alternative Candidate

Conservative elements in the Democratic Party had crafted Super Tuesday with the hope that the early prominence of southern primaries would weed out liberal candidates and propel a southerner or conservative to the front of the pack. Senator Albert Gore of Tennessee hoped to vault into the race with a strong showing on Super Tuesday. Gore sought to portray himself as the only centrist or conservative candidate in a field of liberal contenders. Some commentators pointed to the liberal aspects of the Senator's voting record, which belied the candidate's campaign image.

Gore won six states on Super Tuesday but still was hopelessly behind Dukakis who had a better-financed and better-organized national campaign. On Super Tuesday Dukakis won Florida and Texas, two southern states that had received an influx of more liberal migrant voters from the northern states. He also won Maryland, Rhode Island, Washington, and his home state of Massachusetts.

Gore's lack of a national base quickly became evident. He made virtually no showing in the Illinois primary only a week after Super Tuesday. His candidacy came to an end in New York, where he gained only 10 percent of the vote, finishing far behind both Dukakis and Jackson.

Candidate Jesse Jackson

Jesse Jackson learned from the mistakes of his 1984 campaign and sought to broaden his base of support. In 1988 Jackson ran as a populist and did surprisingly well among white voters in economically depressed rural areas in Iowa, Minnesota, Maine, Vermont (where he received 25 percent of the vote among a virtually all-white electorate), Michigan, and Wisconsin. Still, Jackson's best showings came in contests where black voters composed a large percentage of the turnout. Jackson secured a stunning upset victory in the Michigan caucuses where, because of a low turnout statewide, the outpouring of the vote in black communities constituted a large percentage of the total vote. Jackson's campaign had taken on the appearance of a crusade among black citizens. On Super Tuesday, Jackson mobilized his base of black voters in the South to win Alabama, Georgia, Louisiana, Mississippi, and Virginia.

Despite these precedent-shattering victories, Jackson had no real chance at the nomination. He was still perceived by many whites as too extreme, inexperienced, and untrustworthy— especially in the critical area of foreign policy—to get their votes.

"Mike the Greek" Dukakis: Managerial Competence

The Dukakis campaign sought to win support from the diverse working-class and middle-class constituencies of the Democratic party by emphasizing the Governor's hard-working and ethnic roots. John Sasso, chief strategist for the Dukakis campaign, had transformed a technocratic governor, the son of a suburban doctor, into "Mike the Greek, a tough little ethnic scrapper fighting for the American Dream because his family had been blessed by it."[10] At the Democratic National Convention, Dukakis told how his parents, like millions of others, came to this country as immigrants and got ahead through hard work: "I believe in the American dream." The halls rang out with the strains of Neil Diamond's song, "Coming to America."

Mostly, Dukakis won the nomination on the basis of an image campaign that stressed his managerial record and presidential abilities. After eight years of Reagan, Dukakis, Sasso, and other members of the campaign staff figured that voters had had enough of divisive ideology. Instead of ideology, Dukakis would offer technocratic competence. His candidacy sought to offer the economic revival known as the Massachusetts miracle to the entire nation. In his acceptance speech, Dukakis proclaimed: "This election is not about ideology, it's about competence."

The Dukakis campaign suffered a damaging blow when John Sasso, implicated in leaking proof of Biden's plagiarism to the press, was forced to resign. In the absence of Sasso, the campaign lacked a capable, guiding strategist. Sasso would be brought back on board with just two months remaining before election day, way too late, when it was clear that the Dukakis campaign was in great trouble.

THE DE-WIMPING OF GEORGE BUSH

The Republican candidacies of Delaware Governor Pierre DuPont, Congressman Jack Kemp, and former Secretary of State Al Haig never caught on in 1988. These candidates tried, but failed, to grab the mantle of Reagan conservatism. They tried other ploys as well. DuPont, a member of the wealthy DuPont family, dropped the aristocratic-sounding monicker of Pierre and campaigned simply as the more everyday "Pete" DuPont. It did not work.

Pat Robertson, host of "The 700 Club," a religion-oriented television talk show, was able to mobilize his fundamentalist Christian following to good showings in the preliminary rounds of such low-turnout affairs as the Republican caucuses in Michigan and an advisory straw poll in Iowa. Robertson charged briefly into the national spotlight when he took nearly 25 percent of the vote in a second-place finish in the Iowa caucuses. But many Americans still distrusted Robertson; they were suspicious of a man they saw as a television preacher. It was an image that Robertson would unsuccessfully try to shake during the campaign. The press, not knowing how to treat a candidate whose religious claims were considered fantastic by many Americans, had been reluctant to criticize Robertson. But the press gained its opportunity to question Robertson's credibility when he alleged without evidence that Soviet missiles were based in Cuba—an allegation that was quickly denied by the Reagan administration.

The Republican race was essentially a two-man contest between Senate Minority Leader Robert Dole and Vice-President George Bush. Dole campaigned in Iowa as the champion of farmers. He tried to build on the record he had established in representing farmers in his home state of Kansas. Dole talked about his life growing up in a Kansas farm town during the Great Depression. Dole's handlers also convinced the Senator, who walked with a noticeable limp, to talk about the injuries he had sustained in the service during World War II, a matter that Dole had previously been reticent to discuss throughout his public life. Dole would be sold to the voters as a courageous, tough, and patriotic, yet caring, leader. His handlers portrayed Dole as a man of the people. In turn, they sought to paint Bush as the candidate of wealth and privilege.

Bush finished an embarrassing third place in Iowa, In part, the Vice-President had been victimized by the wrath of Iowa voters who blamed him and the Reagan administration's farm policy for the state's depressed farm economy.

Bush was also fighting what *Newsweek* magazine in a cover story labeled "The Wimp Factor," the public perception that he was a kind, decent, yet somewhat ineffective, man.[11] Bush was seen as Reagan's perpetual second-banana, the ever-loyal Vice-President who lacked the capacity to be President. Bush was also seen as a preppie. As the son of a United States Senator from Connecticut, he had attended elite schools at Andover and Yale.

Bush's image-makers would dispel the wimp notion. They recast Bush as a Texan, a man of the people who knew both bravery and the rigors of hard work. His campaign commercials showed vintage footage of Bush, then a young World War II aviator, stepping onto a naval ship after his plane had been shot down on a mission. Bush was shown to have spurned privilege, setting out on his own after the war to make his fortune in the rough and tumble days of the oil business in Texas. In interviews, Bush professed a love for fried pork rinds and country music. He also declared his voting residence to be in Texas, despite the time he spent at the

Bush family compound in Kennebunkport, Maine. Actually, the Vice-President's Texas residence amounted only to a hotel suite in Houston.

Roger Ailes worked with the Vice-President to make him a more effective public speaker. Bush was coached to be more assertive with his hand gestures and to avoid his penchant for using such unbecoming phrases as "deep doo-doo."

A "defining moment" for the Bush campaign, to use the lexicon of Ailes and campaign manager Lee Atwater, came in a January 25, 1988, live television interview with "CBS Evening News" anchor Dan Rather. Atwater feared that Rather would attempt to use the opportunity to undo Bush's candidacy, just the way that CBS reporter Roger Mudd had critically injured Ted Kennedy's 1980 presidential campaign with a disastrous taped program and interview. Ailes insisted that Rather conduct the interview live in order not to allow CBS an opportunity to edit Bush's responses to the Vice-President's disadvantage.

As Atwater feared, Rather did intend to focus the interview almost exclusively on the Vice-President's role in the Iran-Contra affair. American arms had been sold to Iran to raise funds for the Nicaraguan Contras, apparently in violation of federal law at the time. CBS planned to lead into the interview with a five-minute film that reviewed the Iran-Contra affair, pinpointing questions as to the Vice-President's involvement. Some staffers at CBS were bragging that the broadcast would be the end of the Bush campaign. Officials at the Bush campaign got wind of CBS's plans and alerted the Vice-President as to how he should respond to the trap.

Bush came out swinging. Instead of directly responding to Rather's first question following the film, Bush went on the offensive: "I find this to be a rehash and a little bit, if you'll excuse me, of a misrepresentation on the part of CBS, who said you're doing political profiles of all the candidates." Bush was challenging Rather, who, despite his own Texas roots, was now perceived by the public as a million-dollar, pampered, elite, New York network anchor. If Bush could do it right, it would be Rather, not Bush, who was put on public trial. When Rather declared that he did not mean to be argumentative, Bush's response was sharp and personal: "You do, Dan."

The strategy underlying Bush's response was similar to that of the man-in-the-arena format that Ailes had used in creating ads for the 1968 Nixon and 1976 Reagan campaigns. The sympathies of viewers back home rush to a besieged candidate who responds to an attack with self-assurance and courage. In his exchange with

Rather, Bush came across as a fighter, a street brawler, anything but a wimp. Atwater was enthusiastic: "I think it was the most important event of the entire primary campaign."[12]

In New Hampshire, Bush stepped up his increasingly aggressive style of campaigning. During the weekend before the primary, the Bush campaign flooded the state with a negative ad portraying Robert Dole as a two-faced senator who straddled votes on taxes and other key issues.[13] Badly organized, the Dole campaign was unable to muster new television ads to respond to this late broadside. Bush won the primary by nine points. The race had turned.

Dole was despondent over the turn of events. His televised comments after the returns came in only served to make matters worse. He sourly asked Bush to "stop lying" about his record. Dole looked unpresidential, very much like an embittered loser. If he could not stand up to Bush's attack in New Hampshire, how well could he stand up to the Soviets and all the other pressures of the presidential office?

THE MEDIA CAMPAIGN: PERSONAL AND ISSUE-BASED IMAGERY

At the time the Republican convention was to convene in New Orleans, the Bush campaign was in serious trouble. The size of Dukakis's lead had diminished a bit as the afterglow of the Democratic convention wore off. It was expected to diminish further still as the Republicans dominated the nation's airwaves with their week of speeches and festivities. Still, Dukakis's lead appeared strong. Furthermore, the Iran-Contra affair and revelations of the United States' dealings with the Panamanian dictator and drug trafficker Manuel Noriega had taken some of the gloss off the Reagan record. Unless something was done, the momentum seemed to be with Dukakis.

Bush campaign pollster Robert Teeter pointed to data that underscored a possible Republican opportunity. Voters had no strong impressions of Dukakis. For the most part, the governor of Massachusetts remained an undefined quantity in the eyes of the public. The Bush media campaign would seize the opportunity and define Dukakis for the public. The liberal elements in Dukakis's record would provide the Bush team with all the ammunition required. Dukakis's liberalism would become the dirty L-word of the 1988 campaign. Even Dukakis's past membership in the American Civil Liberties Union—an organization that opposed organized prayer in public schools—would be used to portray the Democrat as a left-winger out of step with the American public.

The pictures that had emanated over the airwaves from the Democratic convention in Atlanta made the Republican task easier. Jesse Jackson's supporters were bitterly disppointed when Dukakis asked Texas Senator Lloyd Bentsen, and not Jackson, to be his running mate. After all, their candidate was the second largest vote-getter in the Democratic primaries. They were outraged by what appeared to be a gratuitous snub when Dukakis did not even inform Jackson of his choice. Jackson learned of the decision from reporters at the airport; he was visibly stunned. The Dukakis team was confronted by the prospects of an embarrassing fight and large-scale revolt at the convention. This was not the image of managerial competence they had hoped to portray.

Dukakis's handlers quickly moved to patch up the spat. But it was not easy. The dispute, an interesting story in an otherwise storyless convention, dominated media coverage. Jackson was interviewed on one network after another. Some of his demands regarding reforms in the conduct of intraparty affairs were met. He was also given a prominent position on the convention schedule to address the concerns of the constituencies for which he spoke. While Jackson dominated the airwaves, Dukakis did not— at least until his acceptance speech at the convention's close. To the viewer at home it sometimes seemed that Jackson, not Dukakis, was the party's flag bearer. Furthermore, was Dukakis really presidential if he could be so easily forced to yield dominance to Jackson? The Democrats on television appeared to be the party of Dukakis *and* Jackson, an image that the Republicans would exploit in certain states, especially in the South, in the fall campaign.

Though the 1988 campaign is known for its negative ads, there were plenty of positive appeals as well. Dukakis stressed the upbeat message that "The best America is yet to come." Bush's handlers followed the maxim that a successful campaign could not simply go negative. You had to first establish positive images of your candidate to offer voters a credible alternative. Also, in the weeks before the November election, the Bush campaign closed with upbeat advertising, recounting the Vice-President's personal qualities and broad leadership experience. Such positive image creation was necessary for Bush to escape some of the stigma associated with negative campaigning.

Even at the Republican convention, the twenty-minute film used to introduce Bush reviewed his career experience and achievements and presented him as a warm and caring family man. The film contained images that would be used again and again in the various positive commercials run throughout the Fall campaign:

 FAMILY/CHILDREN ad

VIDEO: Young child running, probably one of Bush's grandchildren. Bush walks with his wife Barbara and the grandchildren. Child runs into Bush's arms. Scenes of Bush at a family picnic. Bush plays with the grandchildren; he makes a playful face at one. Switch to films of Bush's past, among them: Bush as a young World War II pilot boarding a submarine after his plane was downed; Bush as the U.S. ambassador to the United Nations; Bush being sworn in as Vice-President; Bush with British Prime Minister Margaret Thatcher. Close with Bush lifting and kissing his grandchild.

AUDIO AND VIDEO (Barbara Bush on camera): "I wish people could see him as I see him, thousands of people see him. You know, I always loved the time someone said to George, 'How can you run for President? You don't have any constituency.' And George said, 'Well, you know, I got a great big family and thousands of friends.' And that's what he has."

AUDIO (Announcer): "For more than forty years George Bush has met every challenge the country and the world has offered up to him. The truth is, the more you learn about George Bush, the more you realize that perhaps no one in this century is better prepared to be President of the United States."

CLOSING VIDEO: GEORGE BUSH

        EXPERIENCED LEADERSHIP
        FOR AMERICA'S FUTURE.

Bush's performance in delivering his acceptance speech was masterful. He appeared calm and in control. He paced his delivery well, pausing strategically, and using hand gestures where appropriate for emphasis. He spoke of the remarkable achievements of the Reagan legacy and portrayed himself as Reagan's loyal Vice-President. He then spent the rest of the speech setting himself out as his own man, attacking Dukakis, and establishing himself as presidential timber. He attacked the Massachusetts governor for opposing the death penalty and for failing to support the mandatory recitation of the Pledge of Allegiance in schools. He repeated his prior assault on Dukakis's record on prison furloughs and taxes. His own opposition to taxes was clear: "Read my lips. No new taxes!" He closed by leading the convention in reciting the Pledge of Allegiance.

The well-crafted speech was initially penned by Peggy Noonan, the noted Reagan speechwriter whom the campaign had recruited to help in what had been a previously troubled area.[14] The speech was far from negative in its tone. Bush reminded America of its strength and diversity, of the thousands of ethnic associations and voluntary and community organizations that were like the stars twinkling in the heavens, "a thousand points of light." Bush called for a "kinder, gentler nation." In a bit of personal imagery, he recounted how he had "learned a few things about life in a place called Texas," setting out after the war to run a business, living in a house with just one room for the three of them. It was a life of "high school football on Friday nights" and neighborhood barbecues. George Bush was one of us.

The convention conveyed the desired message to the public. By the time the convention was over, Bush was again leading in the polls, despite the flap that arose over the selection of Dan Quayle as the Republican vice-presidential nominee.

Still, it was the negativism of the attack ads that dominated the fall campaign and gave the 1988 general election its special flavor. At the end of May, when Bush was still trailing Dukakis by nearly 20 points, most of the Republican campaign braintrust— Robert Teeter, Lee Atwater, Roger Ailes, Nicholas Brady, and the Vice-President's chief of staff Craig Fuller—had assembled in Paramus, New Jersey, to help identify the themes they could use to turn around the election. From behind a one-way mirror, they viewed a focus group in which a Republican spokesperson informed thirty or so Democrats who had voted for Reagan in 1984 about numerous aspects of the Dukakis record. The Reagan Democrats were seen by the Republican campaign staff as the key to Bush's election chances. The Republicans were still narrowly the nation's minority party. A Republican candidate for the presidency needed the crossover vote of independents and disaffected Democrats. Reagan won this key constituency twice, but, as Teeter's polls showed, these voters were not yet there for Bush.

The focus group moderator informed the group that Dukakis had once vetoed a bill requiring teachers to lead the recitation of the Pledge of Allegiance in class. He also informed the group that Dukakis, a member of the ACLU, supported the nuclear freeze and gun control, but opposed the death penalty and prayer in schools. The Massachusetts governor also allowed Boston Harbor to become one of the filthiest city harbors in the nation. The spokesperson told the group the story about Willie Horton, a black man and a convicted murderer who was ineligible for parole but had been let out of Massachusetts prisons ten times on furlough. During his tenth furlough, Horton escaped to Maryland where he kidnapped a white couple, stabbing the man and raping the woman.

The results were dramatic. Prior to the session, the members of the focus group had been leaning toward Dukakis. After learning of the new information, half of the group said that they were switching to Bush. Lee Atwater assessed the situation: "I realized right there that we had the wherewithal to win."[15] Atwater told a Republican forum, "If I can make Willie Horton a household name, we'll win this election."[16] Ailes was reported as saying, with a touch of sarcasm, that the only question left in the campaign was in which of Horton's hands should they portray him holding the knife.[17]

The single most dominant ad in the campaign was the thirty-second Bush spot that used good visuals to portray Dukakis's furlough program as a revolving door.

REVOLVING DOOR ad

AUDIO: Opening "clang," a prison sound, followed by sounds of a guard's footsteps on metal prison steps.

VIDEO: Armed prison guard climbs a guard tower. Another guard patrols with a rifle. A long line of prisoners go in and then immediately back out of a revolving-door entrance to the prison.

AUDIO (Announcer): "As governor, Michael Dukakis vetoed mandatory sentences for drug dealers. He vetoed the death penalty. His revolving-door prison policy gave weekend furloughs to first-degree murderers not eligible for parole."

VIDEO: Sign across the bottom of the screen reads: 268 ESCAPED. It is followed by another sign that reads: MANY ARE STILL AT LARGE.

AUDIO (Announcer): "While out, many committed other crimes like
  kidnapping and rape. And many are still at large. Now Michael
  Dukakis says he wants to do for America what he's done for Massachusetts. America can't afford that risk."

CLOSING VIDEO: An armed guard on a prison wall.

Ailes had been careful to try to insulate the campaign against
charges of racism stemming from the ad; few black faces appeared
in the endless line of prisoners that filed through the turnstile.
Horton was not mentioned by name, nor was his picture shown.
Ailes asserted that the Republicans would have used the furlough
issue even if Horton had been white.

Still, critics charged that the ad played on white stereotypes of
blacks as criminals. At the time the ad was shown, the Horton
story was already well known. The Vice-President had mentioned
it in his speeches, and the media had discussed the Republican
charges at length. The commercial could evoke these preconcep-
tions and fears without having to directly mention Horton or show
his face.

Horton's face did appear in a televised ad, although not in one
produced by the official Bush campaign. In California, an independent group showed an ad that lingered on a picture of Horton.
The Bush campaign disavowed the spot, pointing out that independent committees do not clear their actions with the official
campaign.[18] But critics questioned just how independent such
groups really are. They charged that the Bush campaign effectively had its cake and ate it too. The Republicans could deny direct involvement; yet the fact that Horton was black was raised and
extensively repeated by the media. Most viewers saw the ad and
Willie Horton's face only due to its exposure on the free media of
television news.

An amateurish attempt at image-building by the Dukakis
camp provided Bush's advertising consultants with the opportunity to create another effective thirty-second spot. The Dukakis
campaign had staged a pseudoevent to counter perceptions that
the Massachusetts Democrat was soft on defense. Dukakis rode a
new tank that had just come off the assembly line. He wore a tank
driver's helmet and headset. He looked out of place and ridiculous, and media commentators had a field day deriding the event.
Footage of the ride provided the grist for a Republican ad that

quite effectively exploited perceptions of Dukakis's weakness on defense:

 TANK RIDE ad

VIDEO: Filmed footage of Dukakis, with helmet, riding in the gun turret of a tank. Words scroll up from the bottom of the screen. The announcer reads them to underscore their seriousness.

AUDIO (Announcer): "Michael Dukakis has opposed virtually every new defense system we developed. He opposed new aircraft carriers. He opposed antisatellite weapons. He opposed four missile systems, including Pershing II missile deployment. Dukakis opposed the Stealth bomber and a ground emergency warning system against nuclear attack. He even criticized our rescue mission to Grenada and our strike on Libya."

VIDEO: "Words no longer appear on the screen. Camera moves in for a close-up on Dukakis, who appears to be smirking.

AUDIO (Announcer): "And now he wants to be our commander-in-chief. America can't afford that risk."

CLOSING VIDEO: AMERICA CAN'T AFFORD THAT RISK

The prison turnstyle and Dukakis-tank-ride spots were among the most famous of the campaign ads produced in 1988. Other ads produced by Ailes hit hard at Dukakis's claims to competence. They sought to debunk any notion that the governor had an economic miracle in Massachusetts. The ads portrayed Massachusetts as suffering from continued economic woes due to a series of Dukakis tax hikes. A controversial ad sought both to destroy Dukakis's image of managerial competence and seize the advantage on the environmental issue:

 BOSTON HARBOR ad

VIDEO: Opening sign reads: THE HARBOR. Switch to shots of floating garbage, oil slicks, and other disgusting pictures of pollution

of the harbor. Close-up of a sign on the edge of the water that
reads: DANGER. RADIATION. NO SWIMMING.

AUDIO (Announcer): "As a candidate, Michael Dukakis called Boston
Harbor an 'open sewer.' As governor he had the opportunity to do
something about it but chose not to. The Environmental Protection
Agency called his lack of action the most expensive public policy
mistake in the history of New England. Now, Boston Harbor, the
dirtiest harbor in America, will cost residents $6 million to
clean. And Michael Dukakis promises to do for America what he's
done for Massachusetts."

The adeptness of the Republican campaign was not confined
only to the paid media. Skillful orchestration even allowed the Republican campaign to escape what could have been its single great
political disaster, the selection of Dan Quayle as the vice-
presidential nominee. After Quayle's selection, it was revealed that
Quayle had gotten into an Indiana National Guard unit during
the height of the Vietnam War, apparently with the help of his
family's political connections. In the midst of an otherwise quiet
convention and with little to do, reporters focused on the Quayle
story. Reporters soon discovered that in college Quayle had been a
better golfer and socializer than a student. Overall, Quayle looked
to be a lightweight, a man incapable of handling the responsibili-
ties of the Oval Office if called on to do so.

The top Republican campaign echelon met to discuss a damage limitation strategy. Bush had to maintain his image of looking
strong and presidential; Quayle would not be dumped from the
ticket. The Republicans would not repeat the mistake made by
Democrat George McGovern who looked weak in giving in to the
pressure to remove Thomas Eagleton from the ticket in 1972 after
the press revealed that Eagleton had undergone electroshock therapy to treat depression.

The campaign group made the decision to play to the press's
norm of neutrality to get the press to back off the Quayle story. Republican spokespersons again and again publicly accused the press
of engaging in a "feeding frenzy" in covering the story out of proportion to its merits. Immediately after the Republican convention. Quayle was flown to his hometown, Huntington, Indiana, to
meet the press before a public forum. In a variant of the man-in-
the-arena format, a partisan hometown crowd booed reporters as
they pressed their questions. The cheers and jeers from the audi-

ence cued television viewers at home. The sympathies of television viewers rushed to Quayle as he fended off the attack by the press.

The press had inadvertently become part of the story. With its own objectivity now under attack, the press gave less emphasis to the Quayle affair. For the rest of the campaign, the Republican handlers did their best to hide Quayle, having him speak only in safe states and in secondary media markets where he would not draw a large press following.

Dukakis did not quickly respond to Bush's negative campaigning. He did not believe that the voters would be greatly influenced by charges he saw as so tangential to the presidency. By the time Dukakis finally responded, the Bush ads and themes had already defined the playing field for the campaign.

In an act of desperation, a series of Dukakis ads attempted to warn voters against being manipulated by the Bush ad team. These spots portrayed a group of well-dressed, professional Republican campaign consultants discussing how they purposely twisted and distorted Dukakis's record. In one of the ads a younger consultant asks, "How long do you expect to get away with this?" The obviously senior consultant replies by calling out, "How long to the election, Bernie?" They cynically laugh. While the ads were good theater, they were too complex and confusing to have any real impact on voters. Viewers only casually glancing at their television sets would not even know if they were watching a Bush or a Dukakis campaign ad.[19] Furthermore, the ads offered no convincing reasons for people to vote for Dukakis.

Dukakis finally appeared in other ads saying "I'm sick of it"—regarding distortions contained in the Republican spots. Bush ads retorted that it was Dukakis who was distorting the truth.

THE DEBATES: ONE LAST CHANCE

The spirits of the Dukakis campaign were briefly revived during the vice-presidential debate in which Democrat Lloyd Bentsen appeared eminently more distinguished and presidential than Quayle. When, in responding to a question, Quayle observed that he had as much experience as John Kennedy when Kennedy was elected President, Bentsen went for the jugular with a sound bite that was picked up by virtually every news program across the nation: "Senator, I served with Jack Kennedy. Jack Kennedy was a friend of mine. Senator, you're no Jack Kennedy." Democratic ads played on the public's fears of having Quayle only a heartbeat away from the presidency.

For all intents and purposes, the last chance for Dukakis came down to the final televised debate. He had to carry the attack to Bush. He would have to give Americans a clear reason to vote for him. And he would have to dispel voter perceptions of him as overly dispassionate and distant; a cool and detached robot.

Unfortunately for Dukakis, his chance came to an end in his answer to the first question, put to him by CNN reporter Bernard Shaw: "If Kitty Dukakis were raped and murdered, would you favor an irrevocable death penalty for the killer?" Dukakis answered the question in legalistic fashion by repeating his opposition to capital punishment and pointing to alternative crime control measures. He did not mention his wife, Kitty, in his answer. Nor did he respond with any visible emotion to the hypothetical situation of seeing his wife raped and murdered. Many voters need to see their President as a warm and caring human being. Dukakis's answer came across as cold, almost inhuman. He had compounded his image problem. Nor did he appear "tough" on crime.

On election day, Bush won handily, carrying forty states to a 426 to 112 electoral-vote victory. The only rays of hope for presidential Democrats were that, despite having run an inept campaign, their candidate did better than expected in holding Bush to 54 percent of the popular vote. The Democrats also did fairly well in the upper Midwest and the West, regions that had not been very kind to the Democrats in recent presidential elections. In these regions Dukakis won Iowa, Wisconsin, Minnesota, Washington, and Oregon; he also made good showings in Michigan, Ohio, Illinois, Missouri, and California.

In Congress, the Democrats did even better. The strength of incumbency and the rise of split-ticket voting acted to insulate incumbents against any presidential trend. Bush had virtually no coattails. He not only failed to bring new Republican legislators into office with him; Republicans actually lost one Senate and three House seats.[20]

THE ISSUES IN 1988

Dramatic televised images dominated the fall election. Yet, the choice presented voters was not simply one of competing personal images. Americans were able to distinguish meaningful differences between the candidates in 1988. As Paul Abramson, John

Aldrich, and David Rohde note in introducing their extensive data analysis of the 1988 campaign:

> Clearly, the election offered policy alternatives, and as we shall see, voters saw clear policy differences between Bush and Dukakis. Although voters could not reelect Reagan, they could vote to continue his policies. Electing Dukakis would not overturn Reagan's reforms, but it would clearly lead to major revisions. Americans could also vote to support the traditional values espoused by Bush or the more liberal views advanced by Dukakis.[21]

Abramson and his colleagues report that voters were able to distinguish differences between the candidates on issues in 1988, more so than in several other contemporary presidential elections. Voters could even see differences when it came to prospective issues, what the candidates promised to do in the future. And 62 percent voted for the candidate they saw to be closer to them on the issues,[22] leading to the conclusion "that prospective issues were quite important in the 1988 election, but they cannot account for Bush's victory."[23] Citizens also cast ballots retrospectively to continue the general policy directions of the Reagan administration.

Issues were important in 1988. Martin Wattenberg has shown performance evaluations to be more important than policy issues in determining the 1988 vote. Yet, in examining voter responses to the open-ended questions of the National Election Study, Wattenberg also found that voters gave five issues prominent mention—crime, abortion, taxes, a weak military position, and liberal ideology—in explaining why they voted against Dukakis.[24]

Voters were aware of the competing action orientations of the two major candidates. The importance of issues can be denied only by critics who consider crime and the Pledge of Allegiance to be only matters of secondary importance that diverted voter attention away from the more pressing concerns of the day. These critics charge that the voters ignored the real issues—important issues like the deficit and the savings and loan bailout—while focusing on phony issues concocted by campaign strategists.

Yet, it is elitist for self-proclaimed experts to assume that they know just what issues voters should have focused on in an election. For many voters, crime was a more pressing matter than was the subject of the mounting budget deficit. Other Americans were concerned with maintaining a strong and vigilant position of national defense. Other voters, still, were concerned with the patriotism inherent in the Pledge debate. Candidates can only successfully push those concerns that citizens are willing to see as issues. It is worth repeating Jean Bethke Elshtain's observation that "[v]oters and candidates are co-constructors of issues." As Elshtain goes on to explain: "To claim, then, that candidates are trafficking in nonissues because they immerse themselves in weighty symbolism is to presume that which does not exist—a clear-cut division between the symbolic and the real, between issues and emotional appeals."[25]

The policy area of criminal justice cannot be dismissed as irrelevant or of only secondary importance when choosing a President. The President appoints an attorney general and sets the nation's law enforcement posture. He helps to determine the priorities and budgets of law enforcement agencies. He also nominates Supreme Court justices. Over time, the President thereby indirectly helps to determine the permissibility of certain law enforcement procedures and even the constitutionality of the death penalty.

Of course, the candidates did not offer the voters clear policy choices in all areas. Bush's promise to be the environmental President and the education President blurred any voter perceptions of stark policy differences in these areas. When it came to child care, Dukakis promised expanded grants-in-aid for child care while Bush offered a program of tax credits. The difference was lost on most voters. Both candidates also failed to detail plans for reducing the budget deficit. Bush's call for a "flexible freeze" on federal spending was especially vague. Still, there was one policy area in which there was a basic difference. Bush was adamant in opposing new taxes; Dukakis was more equivocal.

The candidates were clearly distinguishable in other areas besides taxes. Dukakis was pro-abortion; Bush was pro-life. Voters could also discern a choice on national defense, as Barbara Farah and Ethel Klein underscore in reviewing public opinion trends:

> Bush's lead was based on values implicit in keeping America strong, rather than on a policy of increased militarism.... Voters withdrew their support from Dukakis because they feared he would weaken the nation's defenses. Nothing in the Dukakis campaign made voters think that he would keep America strong. Instead, what voters heard about were all the weapon systems that the Democrat would get rid of and the inexperience of Dukakis in dealing with other nations.... Two weeks before the general election, 41 percent agreed that Dukakis would weaken national security.[26]

Bush had used his Republican convention speech to clarify the choice offered voters when it came to international action in world affairs: "He [Dukakis] sees America as another pleasant country in the U.N. roll call, somewhere between Albania and Zimbabwe. And I see America as leader, the unique nation with a special role in the world." Bush continued, "Strength and clarity lead to peace; weakness and ambivalence lead to war." Bush was describing a clarity of vision that would lead him as President to use force in Panama and the Persian Gulf. When it came to international affairs, Bush and Dukakis had offered Americans an extremely important choice of action orientations.

The Tank Ride ad further served to distinguish Bush from Dukakis on the issue of national defense. The ad cited the governor's opposition to numerous weapons systems. Dukakis's camp cried that the ad was deceptive in that the Democratic candidate did indeed support a number of weapons systems. Nonetheless, the ad communicated a difference between the candidates on an issue of importance to Reagan Democrats; Dukakis was less disposed than Bush to continued high levels of defense spending.

Crime was another area where differences between the candidates could be perceived. Bush supported the death penalty; Dukakis did not. Marjorie Randon Hershey, who as we earlier observed is underwhelmed by the level of issue discussion in 1988, has admitted that broad, general differences in orientations could be observed in the field of crime: "Ads featuring Willie Horton and the ACLU did suggest that George Bush associated himself with a different vision of crime and punishment than did Michael Dukakis."[27]

Overall, important differences between the candidates did emerge in 1988. Even *Washington Post* journalist Paul Taylor, who is otherwise so critical of the "mediaocracy" evident in the 1988 election, concludes that voter preferences had a lot to do with the election's outcome: "[T]he voters in fact wanted a great many contradictory things (more services *and* lower taxes, for example) and by the time they weighed them all, the rational choice was George Bush."[28]

Taylor continues, "in a video-literate society" citizens "know how to cut through what Key called the 'buncombe' of campaigns."[29] In 1988 the media campaign gave voters reasons why they should vote for or reject a candidate. Even in the 1988 primaries, George Bush's comeback in New Hampshire was due to his clear stance on the tax issue: his stern opposition to new taxes contrasted with Robert Dole's more vacillating position on the matter.

In the fall election, the candidates continued to offer the voters a choice of direction in several policy areas. Bush, for instance, staked out his opposition to the ill effects of government overregulation of business. Dukakis, in contrast, pointed to the necessity of workplace regulation. Dukakis specifically contrasted his support of legislation requiring a business to give workers a sixty-day notice in case of a plant closing with Bush's vote against such a measure. One Dukakis ad showed pictures of Bush and Quayle with the word "NO" stamped across the words "60 Days' Notice of Plant Closings?" The spot ended with the narrator declaring that, "The choice is clear." The ad underscored the clear and contrasting specific stands that the candidates had taken on the issue.

Another Dukakis spot used the visual of a young man of college age tossing dough in a pizza parlor. This young man could have attended college, but, as the narrator in the ad informs viewers, the Republican administration had cut student loans for working-class families. Dukakis, on the other hand, promised a new college loan program to ensure that any student could afford to go to college. Even without spelling out the specifics of the proposed loan program, this ad was an issue ad. It informed voters of the contrasting policy directions offered by the candidates.

In the closing days of the campaign, Dukakis clearly and unabashedly laid out the choice before voters. In the "On Your Side" ads, Dukakis spoke directly into the camera and asked:

> On the things that matter most to you, who do you trust to be on your side? We know where Mr. Bush stands. He wants to cut taxes by $30,000 a year for the wealthiest one percent of this nation. He's on their side. I want to see us teach our children, and house our homeless, and care for our elderly, and ask once again what we can do for our country and not just ourselves.

A clear choice of policy orientations was at stake in 1988 but was missed by critics who expected more: that election campaigns would present voters with a dialogue on the relative merits of detailed policy proposals. No contemporary major national American campaign can meet such a rigid test. Only broader choices are at stake in an election. If voters in 1988 were not quite offered specific formulations on each issue, they were presented with a basic choice of policy directions or values.[30]

RETROSPECTIVE VOTING IN 1988

Even where prospective issues were avoided, the Republicans raised questions of retrospective judgment and evaluation. In ad after ad they asked voters if they wanted to continue the policies of the past administration that had brought peace and prosperity, the nation's longest period of economic expansion. Apparently the voters did.

Democratic claims that the Republicans had purchased this prosperity only at the cost of an outrageous national debt that had mortgaged the future of America's children fell on deaf ears. Martin Wattenberg's study of presidential approval ratings in 1988 found that the public's performance assessment of the economy and national security were the most important factors in explaining Reagan's popularity. Attitudes toward the national debt did not seem to greatly affect the public's attitude toward Reagan: "People apparently cared little about a balanced budget as long as the state of the nation remained healthy."[31]

Bush won not just because he had the better advertising team but also because he had the better message; he had the broad issue themes that best fit the times. Had the nature of the times been different, a quite different set of issues and images would likely have dominated the election.

As we saw in Chapter 7, the Democrats made impressive gains in the midst of the 1982 recession, picking up twenty-six House seats in the midterm congressional election so soon on the heels of Reagan's 1980 landslide victory. To a great extent, the candidates in the 1988 presidential election reiterated the same basic themes that the parties staked out in 1982. Dukakis scored the Republicans for cutting Social Security. He promised to continue to provide necessary government programs of assistance to the elderly, the middle class, and the poor. Bush, in turn, reiterated the Republican stance of opposing new government taxes, regulation, and spending.

But 1988 was not 1982. The times had changed. The economic recession of 1982 had been displaced by boom times, with the result that job insecurity and the provision of economic and social assistance were no longer salient concerns for most Americans. The campaign themes and issues Democrats had used so effectively in 1982 could not win the election for Dukakis in the greatly altered economic landscape of 1988. In 1988 Bush was heir to the political benefits provided by the Reagan economic prosperity.

Wattenberg sees performance evaluations, not issues, to be the key to explaining Bush's victory. According to Wattenberg, voters in the candidate-centered age have an increased tendency to base their evaluations on short-term results, especially on results that are economic in nature. Bush won despite voter disagreement with him in a number of policy areas. As Wattenberg writes, in the

1980s "many voters were torn between the candidate they thought would adopt the best policies and the candidate they thought would perform better."[32] In 1988 the public's attitudes toward Bush were determined more by performance evaluations than by policy concerns.[33]

ASSESSING NEGATIVE ADVERTISING IN 1988

There is a disturbing note in the 1988 campaign. It goes beyond charges of racism implicit in the Willie Horton issue. It even goes beyond the alienation of citizens from the electoral process that has been exacerbated by the seemingly endless exchange of unsubstantiated allegations and personal attacks. The most troubling note of the 1988 campaign stems not from the negative nature of much of the campaigning but from the distortions in the ads that undermined the ability of citizens to use elections as instruments of policy control and government accountability.

Communications expert Kathleen Hall Jamieson and other critics have scored the serious deceptions inherent in political advertising. Jamieson is particularly scornful of the erroneous impressions purposely left by such ads as the Revolving Door spot. The Revolving Door spot gives viewers the impression that during Dukakis's term in office many murderers and dangerous prisoners escaped and that many are still at large. In fact, only four of the 268 escapees were first-degree murderers; and fewer than one percent of the convicts on furlough escaped. She further observes that the audience at home views such ads from the conventions of entertainment television, with the tendency to "suspend disbelief and all critical acuity."[34] Viewers tend to uncritically accept staged showings as representations of reality.

The Revolving Door ad clearly contains intentionally misleading inferences. The setting is also unreal. Paid actors go in and out of a door in a prison that, as Jamieson notes, is actually in Utah, not Massachusetts. The revolving door itself is a stage prop. But all this really is of little import. The ad effectively portrays candidate differences in policy orientations in an area that many Americans deemed to be of great importance.

Nor could Dukakis's supporters successfully decry that the ad was misleading in that it blamed Dukakis for a furlough program that had in fact been enacted by his Republican predecessor. The furlough program, they point out, was also later repealed. They also charge that a large number of convicts on furlough had escaped from federal prisons during the Reagan-Bush administration. The Dukakis campaign made these arguments, belatedly, in ads of its own. The voters simply were not convinced. Dukakis was a progressive on penal matters, and the voters did not want a progressive in this issue area.

As governor Dukakis had commuted the life sentences of twenty-eight murderers.[35] He had shown little inclination to curtail Massachusetts' furlough program, even in the immediate wake of the Willie Horton episode. The furlough program was repealed not as a result of the governor's actions but by the state legislature in response to a public referendum. There was a basic difference between Bush's and Dukakis's orientations toward criminal justice. The Revolving Door ad underscored this difference. So did Dukakis's intellectual but weak response in refusing to endorse the death penalty even when asked what he would do if his wife had been raped and murdered.

Negative ads can provide information that helps citizens to distinguish candidates' issue positions and dispositions. Attack campaigning is not intrinsically bad. Of course, like positive ads, negative ads tell only part of the story, the part that the candidate wants voters to know. An opponent in turn has the opportunity to present ads that present competing facts and interpretations and tell the other side of the story. The voters can then choose.

Electioneering by its nature entails the partial or one-sided representation of arguable claims. Virtually all political advertising—pamphlets, broadsides, partisan speeches, public addresses, print ads, radio ads, and television spots—contain distortions. No candidate admits weaknesses or discloses countervailing facts that can be used against his arguments or policy positions.

But positive ads can deceive just as well as negative ads. For instance, in 1988 one Republican ad clearly overclaimed the Vice-President's role in arms control. The narrator informs television viewers that "It was George Bush who led the way" in signing the 1988 arms reduction treaty. An informed follower of public affairs would have to wonder at this rewriting of history. Just what role did President Reagan play in opposing arms reductions agreements for so long before finally, later during his term in office, negotiating this treaty? It was President Reagan, not Vice-President Bush, whose actions determined the nation's policy in this critical area.

More serious distortions occur when a candidate or his handlers misrepresent events to mislead voters in attempting to escape the political consequences of unpopular actions. The most blatant distortion in the 1988 campaign involved not the Willie Horton and Revolving Door ads but Bush's Boston Harbor ad. The Boston Harbor spot implied that Dukakis bore responsibility for the toxicity of the city's filthy harbor. Dukakis's administrative incapacities in failing to clean up the harbor were certainly fair target for a Republican attack. But it was the Reagan administration, not the Dukakis administration, that had the poorer environmental record, especially in the area of pollution control. It was the Republican administration in Washington that had sought to relax the enforcement of environmental protection statutes and free business from some of the harmful effects of regulation.[36]

The power of the Boston Harbor ad results from its deceptive use of visuals. The ad was shot on a drizzly, dreary day that made the water in the harbor look worse. An open pipe that dribbled waste into the harbor looked more offensive in slowed-down, stop-frame treatment. The sign that read "Danger / Radiation Hazard / No Swimming" had been left over from a long-closed submarine base.[37]

The ad succeeded on two levels. It inoculated Bush in an issue area that, because of the Reagan administration's record, had been a political soft spot for Republicans. By pinning the blame for the lack of pollution enforcement on Dukakis's, the ad also questioned Dukakis's record on the environment and his managerial capacities as governor.

Later in the campaign, Dukakis would counter that it was the Republican administration that had undercut effective pollution control. But his response was too little, too late. By then the image of a sickly Boston Harbor had been fixed in the public's mind.

Taxation is another issue area where it can be argued that deceptive rhetoric undercut the ability of voters to use elections as instruments of policy control. In 1990, only two years into his presidency, Bush retreated from his vow against new taxes. He had opposed new taxes throughout his first year in office, but now he approved an agreement negotiated with congressional leaders that called for tax increases to help balance the budget.

If Bush knew during his 1988 campaign that the mounting national debt would eventually force a tax increase, then his no-new-tax vow was deceptive. On the other hand, Bush as President had opposed a number of proposals for new taxation. His midterm change on the issue can be seen as a necessary adjustment to the demands of governance in the face of changing fiscal and political realities. Presidents need to be flexible; to be able to learn in office.

In the New Hampshire primary Bush had used the Straddle ad to skewer Bob Dole on the tax issue. Dole was fresh from his victory in Iowa. Bush's victory in New Hampshire ended the momentum of the Dole campaign and changed the contours of the 1988 Republican nominating race. In 1990, just two years after the New Hampshire contest, Dole as Senate Minority Leader was asked by President Bush to help round up votes for a budget package that contained tax increases. One can only wonder what Dole felt.

SUMMARY

The 1988 election shows the ability of modern political handlers to manufacture carefully constructed and powerful symbolic images. The ability of the Bush paid-media effort to define the campaign dialogue was especially effective because the Dukakis campaign did not initially choose to challenge the claims advanced by the Bush campaign.

Yet, it is too easy to see the 1988 election solely as a battle of professional image merchants. Retrospective performance evaluations were prominently related to the vote in 1988. Voters could also discern important policy differences between the candidates. Indeed, the paid media effort, including the negative ads, helped voters to discern the competing action orientations of Bush and Dukakis in such issue areas as crime and defense spending. Negative ads provided the voters with information. The informational value of certain negative ads, however, was diminished by the distortions contained in those ads.

THE FUTURE OF AMERICAN POLITICS

A s we have seen in this book, issues exert a much greater influence on presidential elections than many commentators admit. Whereas Americans seldom meet the standards for prospective issue voting, presidential voting has, nonetheless, a substantive basis. Voters are capable of retrospectively evaluating a candidate's past performance. Economic evaluations have become a dominant factor in national elections. Voters are also able to distinguish the basic choices of direction offered by the two major-party candidates. They are capable of responding to the most salient issues of the day—especially "easy" issues.

Partisanship exerts a declining, but still significant, pull on voting behavior. Personal imagery continues to be part of the presidential race. The electorate will not vote for a candidate who appears unpresidential. But partisanship and personal imagery do not alone determine the outcome of presidential elections. Substantive evaluations of the candidates are important, too.

THE DIALOGUE OF TELEVISED DEMOCRACY: THE ISSUES ARE IN THE ADS

Many commentators continue to bemoan the lack of issue voting and the poor quality of public debate in presidential campaigns.

These commentators portray presidential elections as little more than the product of the behind-the-scenes manipulation of advertising consultants and other media strategists. According to this critique, the campaign dialogue is geared to sound bites and puffery. Candidates seldom present voters with a detailed discussion of policy alternatives. The voter is thereby deprived of a meaningful choice at the ballot box.

Yet, despite the much-alleged poor quality of issue discussion in presidential elections, the public has, in fact, been able to differentiate between presidential candidates. In certain elections— 1964 (Johnson-Goldwater), 1972 (Nixon-McGovern), and 1984 (Reagan-Mondale)—the differences between the candidates were sharply drawn by the elite dialogue; the public could easily discern competing issue dispositions. But even in an election such as in 1988, where one candidate failed to effectively participate in the campaign debate and where (as critics charge) phony issues dominated the campaign dialogue, the public was still able to see important differences between the candidates. Dukakis was perceived as the more liberal candidate. Bush was seen as the candidate more clearly opposed to new taxes, but more willing to spend on national defense.

Why is it that the pejorative view of presidential campaigns has missed the role played by issues? With its focus on the rise of the professionally mediated televised campaign, the critics of the American presidential election process have failed to recognize one important point: the issues are often in the advertisements! Of course, campaign strategists and advertising consultants continue to portray presidential candidates as embodying desirable personal leadership attributes. Personal image commercials are a prominent feature of the televised campaign. Yet, despite their prominence, it would be a mistake to conclude that presidential campaign dialogue offers voters little other than personal imagery. Presidential campaigns utilize both personal image ads and more substantively based ads. Different appeals are used to reach different markets of voters.

One notable study has pointed to the issue-based nature of contemporary presidential advertising. Thomas E. Patterson and Robert D. McClure found that 42 percent of the televised ads in the 1972 race were "primarily issue communications" while another 28 percent "contained substantial issue material."[1] According to Patterson and McClure, the ads presented voters with "solid reasons" based on "issue appeals."[2] Although the information provided in the ads was far from complete and lacking in richness and nuance, the information was no more one-sided or incomplete than that contained in candidate speeches, party campaign pamphlets, and other more traditional campaign media. Patterson and McClure find that their evidence leads them to dismiss the pejorative view of contemporary presidential campaigns:

> Political spots, then, are not entirely the mindless creatures developed in advertising darkrooms that some observers have claimed them to be. Presidential advertising is instead a blend of soft imagery and hard issue material. The image content is intended to draw an emotional reaction. The issue content is intended to make voters think. In the past, commentary about televised political advertising has fixed on the image content, condemned it, and ignored the issue content.[3]

The degree of issue-orientation of the 1972 ads may be a bit atypical. The issue-based character of the 1972 ads may be simply a result of the McGovern insurgency or the extraordinary politicization of the late-Vietnam War era. The issue-based dialogue of the paid media in 1972 may also reflect the relatively long length of the ads featured in the campaign. Only two percent of the ads shown in 1972 were thirty-second spots—the vehicle that has proved so popular in more recent presidential campaigns.

Richard Joslyn directly contradicts Patterson and McClure's assertion that presidential advertising communicates substantive issue material. Joslyn observes that the learning from the 1972 ads was quite limited and was greatest among low-interest voters. More concerned citizens learned little from paid television. The information presented in the ads was likely to be redundant:

> It appears, then, that campaign spot ads contribute to learning about candidate issue positions *in certain circumstances*. That is, ads are most effective for those who know the least to begin with and for those who care so little about the campaign that they are exposed to hardly any other campaign communication. . . . For those who are moderately informed or interested, and in those cases in which the advertising campaigns are making conflicting claims, the effect is minimal. *If* the perceptions gleaned from the spot ads are accurate, and *if* the citizens affected by these portrayals would have remained uninformed otherwise, it could be said that these presentations actually contribute more to the ideal of an informed electorate than does either television news (as a result of its content) or newspaper coverage (as a result of the lack of exposure to it). Those, however, are two big ifs.[4]

Joslyn's point of view is fortified by his review of an admittedly unscientific sample of 506 televised political commercials used in presidential and nonpresidential races. His findings are consistent with those of the pejorative view of political campaigns. Political ads tend to market candidates on the basis of their personal attributes, often doing little more than attempting to portray a candidate as a benevolent leader. Whereas political ads may emphasize retrospective satisfaction or dissatisfaction with performance, future actions or policy intentions are seldom revealed. According to Joslyn, only 15 percent of the ads contain appeals based on prospective policy choices. He concludes that televised spot ads do little to enable effective citizen participation or to educate the public regarding the policy alternatives represented by the candidates.[5]

Joslyn's assessment, however, can be challenged on several grounds. First of all, retrospective voting is based on relevant, not inconsequential, substantive evaluations. Retrospective performance may even provide a more dependable basis than prospective promises for assessing the action orientations of presidential candidates. Second, even when voters do cast their ballots on a candidate's personal qualities, those personal qualities are often relevant to the demands of the presidential job. Voters need to select a candidate of experience whose judgment they can trust. In office, a President faces numerous issues and newly emergent crises that could not have been anticipated at the time of the election.

Third, Joslyn's findings are influenced by the inclusion of nonpresidential ads in his sample. In relatively invisible elections for lesser offices where voters know little about the candidates, personal-image appeals may well prove to be the core of a winning advertising strategy. However, in a presidential race where virtually all voters are likely to know *something* about the candidates or have opinions on salient issues, personal-image appeals by themselves do not suffice.

Most importantly, Joslyn understates the issue content of the ads he analyzes. This understatement is readily apparent if we review his treatment of the televised advertising of the 1964 election—especially two ads that we reviewed in Chapter 5. Joslyn classifies the Daisy Girl and Khrushchev (Pledge of Allegiance) spots not as issue ads but only as "elections-as-ritual appeals" that evoke symbolic appeals to prevailing norms of cultural values. Joslyn considers Daisy Girl merely a "minimelodrama," a "truncated and simplistic" commercial that uses the "elements of intensified peril, conflict, suspense, and villainry to communicate a message."[6] He likewise excoriates Barry Goldwater's Khrushchev ad for appealing to prevailing cultural stereotypes and for its simplistic message "that if one is opposed to communism then one should vote a particular way."[7]

What Joslyn fails to see, however, is that the two ads in question did, in fact, succeed in informing viewers of clear differences between the candidates on matters of national significance. Daisy Girl and similar ads aired on behalf of Lyndon Johnson reminded voters of Goldwater's less-than-prudent statements on the use of nuclear weapons—an issue certainly of great importance to the future of both the nation and the world. As we already discussed in Chapter 5, this difference in action orientations may well have been of monumental importance in the post-1964 period. Faced with a failing war effort in Vietnam and his loosening hold on the presidency, Johnson did not resort to the use of nuclear weapons in Southeast Asia. It is uncertain whether Goldwater, given his statements on the nuclear weapons issue, would have shown equal restraint as President.

Goldwater's Khrushchev (Pledge of Allegiance) ad likewise presented voters with a choice on another issue of importance. The ad showed Goldwater to be the more intent of the two candidates on stopping the spread of communism. Critics of the campaign dialogue in 1964 point out that Johnson was no dove. As President he acted to greatly escalate the United States' involvement in the war in Vietnam. But Johnson also called periodic bombing halts and placed numerous restrictions on American military action in an effort to pursue a negotiated peace. Goldwater sharply criticized each of these restrictions and the pauses in the bombing. Goldwater was, as his ads had shown, the more strident in his opposition to communism. He would not fight a limited war; nor would he risk bombing halts in the pursuit of peace.

Both the Khrushchev and Daisy Girl ads contained substantive messages that went beyond mere melodrama or ritual. Both used symbolism—but it was symbolism that effectively communicated the competing action dispositions of the two presidential candidates.

It is Joslyn's and other critics' standards, not the ads themselves, that are lacking. Joslyn considers an ad as issue-oriented only if it provides voters with a clear-cut statement of policy intentions. These are the standards of prospective issue voting, not retrospective and directional voting. Joslyn's standards represent the idealized standards of issue voting that ignore the way many citizens incorporate issues into their voting decisions. Voters do not need a public policy expert's understanding of program details. Instead, voters need only to discern and understand the basic choice of policy directions offered to them by the two major-party candidates. Do they want more of what the Democratic or the Republican candidate has to offer? Do they want to continue the present course of policy or do they want a change?

In 1964 the Daisy Girl and Khrushchev ads and other spots on Social Security, Medicare, and foreign policy helped voters to perceive the basic choice offered by Johnson and Goldwater. Did these ads contribute information and thereby help to shape voter perceptions? Or did the spots simply reinforce what voters had learned from other sources of information? We do not have studies that would allow us to answer this question for 1964. But evidence from 1988 would seem to show that presidential ads do increase citizen learning. In answering open-ended questions about reasons for voting against Dukakis, respondents identified Dukakis's lenient attitude toward crime, his weakness on military and defense issues, and his support of taxes—themes that dominated the Republican media effort.[8]

Voters learn from television—from paid advertising. Presidential spot ads provide voters with information. Personal-based image ads are supplemented by numerous more substantive ads that give voters a reason to vote a preferred way.

Once the informational content of political advertising is recognized, television is no longer the extreme danger to democracy that its detractors would purport. Televised political dialogue is in many ways shallow and far from perfect—just as its critics have charged. Yet, the televised debate is far from issueless. In the race for the presidency, the issues are in the ads. We only have to be willing to look to see them.

COPING WITH NEGATIVE ADVERTISING

Contemporary accounts of presidential elections have focused on the supposed ills of negative or attack campaigning. Yet, any serious discussion of this phenomenon must come to grips with the different forms of attack advertising. Some negative ads focus on legitimate questions of policy and performance. This form of advertising actually adds to voter knowledge of the records and positions of the candidates. These ads provide a more issue-oriented basis for the voting decision than do vacuous positive ads that do little more than celebrate a candidate's leadership traits or present him as being a family man in tune with everything that is good about America.

Negative ads are one-sided. They never do full justice to the discussion of an issue. But positive ads are equally blameworthy in this regard. They, too, exaggerate claims, resort to the manipulation of symbols, and present equally shallow and distorted discussions of complex issues. No political ad—positive or negative—readily admits what is suspect in a campaign's position or what is defensible in an opponent's position. Yet democracy does not require that each candidate make his opponent's arguments for him. Instead, it is up to the voters to choose among the competing claims and arguments of the candidates.

Yet, not all forms of negative advertising are as salutary as the more issue-oriented negative ads discussed above. Spot ads that circulate unsubstantiated allegations, launch personal attacks irrelevant to job performance, or purposely distort a candidate's policy positions and past records provide no useful information in a democracy. They only increase the public's cynicism regarding politics.

Within elections is a safeguard against the excesses of negative advertising. Each candidate has the ability to respond with news conferences and ads of his own that point to the unfairnesses, distortions, and exaggerations in the opponent's attack. Perhaps negative campaigning was so influential in 1988 because Michael Dukakis failed to respond quickly and effectively to the initial Republican attacks. Dukakis's failure, though, will help ensure against a repeat situation in the future. Candidates have learned the lesson of 1988; they must respond immediately and effectively to each attack ad. Charges raised in attack ads will not go uncontested. The technology of the modern electoral politics has evolved to the point that a well-organized campaign can even put together and air a response to an attack levied during the weekend before election day.

During the primaries, accessibility of the airwaves is very much dependent on the candidate's finances. Any candidate strapped for funds has only a limited ability to respond to an opponent's attack. In the general election, public funding has helped to ensure that the two major party candidates have relatively equal media access. Each will have the ability to answer the other's charges. However, independent spending by political action committees (PACs) has helped to undo some the equality of media access. In the presidential race, independent PAC spending has favored Republican candidates by a large margin; the public is more likely to see Republican-oriented than Democratic-oriented ads.

PAC sponsorship of negative ads raises additional problems by undoing some of the natural policing built into American campaigns. No presidential candidate can afford to push an attack that is seen to be too personal or too unfair. Such an attack risks a backlash against the candidate who launched or sponsored the attack. But hard-hitting, even scurrilous, attacks can be launched with impunity by independent organizations. The candidate who benefits from the attack can deny responsibility for the ad in question. He may even point to the law that prohibits coordination between the independent committee and his official campaign organization. A politically astute candidate will gain the benefits of an attack, while at the same time taking the political high road of condemning the ad in question. This was the strategy George Bush adopted when questioned about the more controversial Willie Horton attack ad.

One piece of proposed legislation has sought to deal with the problem of attacks from independent committees by requiring that broadcast stations give candidates free air time to respond to certain ads sponsored by independent committees. But the merits of this legislative proposal are open to debate. Legislation that limits what can be said in a political ad may violate First Amendment free speech rights and may not survive court challenge. Also, as few organizations will pay for an ad giving an opponent free response time, the proposed piece of legislation in question, if enacted, may lead to the virtual elimination of such ads. This would have the detrimental effect of diminishing the volume of information available to the voting public.[9] Political ads inform voters.[10] Citizens need to hear competing claims and charges. They need to hear free debate regarding possible deficiencies in a candidate's past record or proposed program.

Another proposed measure for dealing with the problem of negative advertising seeks to bar ads that refer to an opponent unless a candidate appears personally in the ad to make the charge. Here again, the proposed measure might be a violation of free speech protections. But even if constitutional, such a measure would make for boring, ineffective ads with messages that are not likely to be remembered. Any reform measure must come to terms with the fact that different citizens have different learning processes. Lower-status voters tend to get their information from spot ads. As Alexander Heard reminds us: "Advertising is a way of retailing information that narrows the 'information gap' between better-informed citizens and those traditionally less knowledgeable about public affairs—the young and the old, the poor, the less educated, women."[11] Any proposed reform measure to restrict political advertising must be cautious not to limit the volume of information provided the general public.

An alternative route for dealing with the problem posed by negative advertising calls for greater press vigilance. More aggressive reporting by the news media can help hold political organizations accountable for the distortions and half-truths contained in ads. Indeed, as the problem of negative advertising has become more salient, journalists have begun to move away from outdated definitions of journalistic neutrality, and have taken a more aggressive stance in monitoring the claims presented in political ads. In recent state and local elections, numerous local television stations and newspapers devoted stories and columns to dissecting political ads.

Yet, there is a limit to what such vigilant reporting can hope to achieve. Throughout the course of a campaign, viewers are likely to see the exaggerated and distorted claims of an ad many times. They may see the news media's critical analysis of that ad once, if at all.[12] News coverage of and commentary on a controversial ad may even inadvertently give wider circulation to the claims contained in the spot—as was the case when the free media in 1988 repeatedly broadcast the message of the Willie Horton and the Revolving Door ads. Furthermore, journalists are ill-equipped to deal with the more subtle distortions contained in political spots. Reporters will point out claims that are fabricated. But they are less likely to question ads that are truthful in their statement of facts but unfair in their unspoken inferences. For example, reporters are not likely to point to the subtle deceptions that occur when the video or soundtrack in an ad is creatively altered, or when a negative ad juxtaposes audio and video so as to exaggerate the sense of foreboding or the seeming ill that has been alleged.[13]

Some political observers have called for the resurrection of the Fair Campaign Practices Committee (FCPC) from the 1950s.[14] The FCPC was a blue-ribbon, nonprofit citizens' organization that tried to instill a sense of morality into the conduct of political campaigns. The Committee possessed no statutory or coercive power. It could only investigate and publicize violations of a code of fair campaign practices.

The findings of such a committee today could provide the basis for news stories pointing to the excesses of a political campaign.[15] But, as we pointed out above, such news stories devoted to negative campaigning are unlikely to have nearly as much impact as the ads in question. Furthermore, as the decisions of the FCPC do not make for a good news story, they are unlikely to receive extensive media coverage.

More creative measures for offsetting the role of negative advertising have been proposed. Journalist Paul Taylor has advanced one such proposal.[16] Instead of attempting to eliminate or restrict attack ads, which might be contrary to democracy in action, Taylor has proposed that a new forum of communications be created to compete with the political spot. During the last five weeks of the campaign, each major candidate for President would be given five minutes of free air time a night—on alternating nights—to appear personally on every television and radio station in the country. Continuous appearances before a national forum would virtually force candidates to enunciate substantive policy positions. Candidates would also have a forum to respond almost immediately to attacks made by an opponent or independent committee.

The feasibility of Taylor's proposal remains to be seen. As Taylor admits, there is no constituency for the free-time proposal. Broadcasters can be expected to strongly line up against the proposal unless they are reimbursed for lost air time. Also, just what constitutes fair access accorded to third-party candidates is still the subject of much debate.

It appears that the problem of negative advertising is here to stay. Candidates will resort to negative attacks so long as voters respond to them. Negative ads will disappear only when they no longer prove to be an effective strategy for winning votes.

REALIGNMENT: A NEW ELECTORAL ERA

It seems undeniable that some sort of realignment or permanent shift in voter loyalties has taken place. The Democratic New Deal majority no longer dominates presidential elections. As Republicans have won five of the six presidential elections from 1968 to 1988, it might even be more accurate to talk about a Republican as opposed to a Democratic presidential majority.

Yet, whatever realignment has taken place is incomplete. No clear-cut majority of Republican identifiers-in-the-electorate has emerged to replace the Democratic majority of the New Deal era. Also, despite their disastrous record in recent presidential elections, the Democrats continue to win the majority of congressional and statehouse races. Instead of ushering in a new Republican majority at all levels, the realignment of the 1970s and 1980s resulted in a new era of voter independence and volatility—a "rootless" politics characterized by high levels of party switching, split tickets, split results, and divided government.

While there has been no single critical election or flashpoint to signal the realignment, the American party system has clearly evolved. Among the changes that Everett Carll Ladd notes is the inversion of the New Deal class order, where high-status whites are now more supportive than low-status whites of liberal or equalizing change. Also notable is the emergence of a two-tier party system where the dynamics of candidate selection and voting at the presidential level are quite different from the dynamics of congressional elections.[17] The Republicans have successfully emphasized broad ideological themes to capture the presidency. The Democrats, in turn, have parlayed their edge in partisanship and the advantages of incumbency and redistricting to retain control of congressional, especially House, elections. More recent polling data, however, has shown that the Democratic edge in partisanship has slipped substantially over time.

The change in voter alignments has come gradually. Its roots can be found in 1948 when the white South, in reaction to the civil rights planks of the Democratic platform, began to split off from the national Democratic party. The changes continued over three decades. Ladd notes that the group alignments evident by 1984 were vastly different from those of the New Deal era. In 1936, 85 percent of white Southerners voted for Roosevelt; twenty-eight years later, just over a quarter voted for Mondale. But white southerners were not the only group to alter their voting allegiances. During the New Deal alignment, blue-collar voters and Catholics were mainstays of the Democratic coalition. In 1984, in sharp contrast to the New Deal patterns, the majority of voters in each of these groups cast their ballots for Reagan, not Mondale. African-Americans today are more solidly aligned with the Democratic party than they were during the New Deal era.[18]

The issue of race alone does not fully explain the change in voting alignments. Economics, too, has played a large role. Changing times have redefined the economic issue. While economic hard times, especially during a Republican administration, will work to the political advantage of the Democrats, it is now the Republicans—not the Democrats—who have the advantage on such economic issues as inflation, taxes, and management of the economy. As a result, the Democrats can no longer rely on economic issues to rally a presidential majority as they did during the New Deal era. There is no longer a Depression-era, submerged middle class in need of the economic and social assistance programs promised by the Democrats. Voters now take for granted major Democratic legislative victories, such as the enactment of Social Security, Medicare, and other basic social welfare protections. At the same time, many of these voters resent rising taxes and the extension of programs to provide benefits to the undeserving poor. Secure in their jobs, the increasingly white-collar, middle-class, and professional electorate is more apt to worry about the toll taken by taxes and inflation than by unemployment.

During the New Deal era the Democrats were seen as the party of recovery and prosperity; the Republicans, in contrast, were the party of Depression and Hoovervilles. But memories of Hoover, Roosevelt, the Depression, and the New Deal have all faded deep into the past. They have been supplanted by general partisan images of a more recent vintage—of Jimmy Carter's and the Democrats' inability to handle the economy compared to the general economic prosperity brought by the Reagan years. Younger voters, in particular, are likely to be influenced by perceptions based on more recent political events. Generational change, too, helps to explain the changing partisan balance in presidential elections. The Democrats can no longer hope to win by running on what is essentially a New Deal, or even a Great Society, platform.

DEMOCRATIC STRATEGY

The Democrats have essentially two options. Under the first, they unflinchingly adhere to the party's activist New Deal and Great Society orientations. Under the second, the party adapts to the changed political contours of a post-New Deal electorate.

The first option is usually advanced by the party's more liberal factions. They argue that the party must remain true to its progressive traditions. They argue further that the electorate has voted Republican for President for reasons other than political outlook or philosophy. They argue that Humphrey lost in 1968 because the Democratic party was divided by the Vietnam War. Nixon also enjoyed the benefit of having a more professional advertising team— a team that sold a "new" Nixon to the people. In 1972 McGovern's presidential image was destroyed by the Eagleton fiasco. In 1980 Reagan was elected only as a repudiation of Jimmy Carter's inadequacies as President. Four years later, Reagan won reelection without having to declare his stance on specific issues. In 1988 the Democrats lost an election they could have won. Republican strategists rescued a failing Bush presidential effort, and Dukakis ineptly failed to inoculate himself against the attacks.[19]

According to this argument, the Democratic party does not need to reexamine its programs and philosophy. It needs only to offer better candidates and run better campaigns. This argument, however, fails to recognize that the times and the electorate have changed. By persisting with the past, Democrats have helped produce a Republican presidential majority.

Martin Wattenberg has noted the tendency of political parties during times of transition to resist change and to continue to nominate candidates with diminishing voter appeal. In the *cementing* elections immediately following the critical elections of 1896 and 1932, the losing party opted for continuity instead of "trying to shift away from what had been a disastrous course four years earlier."[20] During the 1970s and 1980s, the Democrats similarly opted for continuity rather than change, and cemented in place new partisan images that worked to the Democrats' disadvantage. As Wattenberg underscores:

> The point is that voters may forgive a party that has gone astray once, but twice in a row may transform short-term change into long-term change. The Democrats' nomination of Carter's vice-president in 1984 can thus be seen as an invitation for realignment history to repeat itself.[21]

If the Democratic party continues to nominate avowedly liberal candidates—or even candidates whom the Republicans can easily portray to be liberals—the party cannot hope to win the presidency except by accident. It would take a major economic recession, failed foreign policy engagement, a scandal of the magnitude of Watergate, or a glaring campaign error by the Republican nominee for the electorate to turn to the Democrats.

The second or alternative Democratic strategy, however, does not passively wait for the intervention of fortuitous outside events. Instead, it seeks to address the root cause of contemporary Democratic defeats; that in postindustrial America, the Democrats have not offered candidates and platforms acceptable to pivotal voting groups. Unless Democrats adjust and do a better job of meeting voter expectations, they will continue to be the presidential minority.

More liberal Democrats object that strategy based on adaptation represents a sell-out of the party's traditions and principles. Yet, a Democratic presidential nominee can be politically viable and still offer voters a program substantially to the left of that offered by the Republicans. Studies have shown that presidential elections in the 1980s did not constitute a mandate for specific conservative or Republican programs. In many policy areas, the Republicans were perceived to be more conservative than the public at large. To win, the Democrats do not need to mimic the Republican platform. But they do need to offer candidates and a general policy orientation that voters are willing to accept.

Concern for winning does not denote a sacrifice of the party's principles. Winning is important. Only by winning can the Democratic party advance its programs in the areas of antipoverty policy, civil rights, women's rights, workplace regulation, environmental protection, nuclear nonproliferation, and foreign affairs. Only by winning the presidency can the Democrats gain control of nominations to the Supreme Court and begin to redirect the Court away from its more recent conservative drift on civil rights, civil liberties, and abortion rights.

To win, Democrats must learn which issues they should emphasize and which they should not in presidential elections. First of all, Democrats must recognize the *ideological / operational split* in American public opinion.[22] More Americans identify themselves as conservative than as liberal. When asked about government in a broad ideological sense, Americans tend to give conservative answers. They oppose activist big government, taxation, regulation, welfarism, and redistribution. They prefer state and local power to national power. Yet, when asked about specific programs—that is, when broad principles are given operational definition—the public proves much more supportive of government action. The public supports continued expenditures for Social Security, Medicare, unemployment assistance, antipoverty programs (as long as they are not labeled "welfare"), the relief of homelessness, the rebuilding of cities, job training, improving the economic conditions of minorities, student aid, and the provision of assistance to needy children. Voters claim to be against government regulation, but they support strengthened measures to ensure airline and workplace safety, environmental protection, and the regulation of daycare centers.

The lesson for Democrats is clear. Democrats should avoid broad, philosophical statements regarding the role of the government in the social and political economies. Instead, they need to argue for the virtues of specific programs where the public can clearly see the benefits of government action.

As Kevin Phillips has pointed out, the Democrats can also remain true to their party's populist heritage by attacking the intensifying inequalities of the Reagan years. The Democrats can once again paint the Republicans as the party of the rich: the party of billionaires and yacht owners insensitive to the needs of everyday working people. The rich have prospered. Newspapers are filled with the accounts of leveraged buyouts, junk bonds, and the savings and loan crisis. Yet, the homeless populate America's streets, newlyweds face the lost dream of owning a home of their own, and even two-income families find it difficult to pay for their children's education at the college of their choice.[23]

Democrats can also carry the populist attack to the Republicans on the issue of taxes. Democrats must repeatedly point out that Republicans during the Reagan-Bush era cut the top income tax bracket from 70 percent to 28 percent, created the "bubble" under which many middle-class Americans pay a higher tax rate than do millionaires, and reduced taxes on corporations and unearned income.[24] Democrats can also attack George Bush's proposed reduction of capital gains rates as one more tax break for the rich.

Democrats must be careful to avoid Walter Mondale's grave political mistake of advocating new taxes as the path to deficit reduction. The advocacy of new taxes is an abandonment of populism. Middle-class voters are suspicious that they will be the ones to bear the brunt of any new levy, even when they are promised that the burden of a new tax will fall on the rich. Even if new taxes are needed to cope with the deficit, the Democrats must let the Republicans as the party of government take the lead. Democrats in Congress should not vote for any tax measure that fails to get anything less than unambiguous Republican presidential support and a party-line Republican congressional backing. If Republicans remain divided over the issues of taxes, they will simply charge that it was once again the Democrats who forced new taxes on the American people.

The new inequalities of the Reagan era also afford the Democrats new political opportunities in the nation's heartland. Traditional Democratic job-based appeals and promises to save the family farm should win votes in much-troubled farm states and the economically depressed rustbelt cities in the Midwest.[25]

Democrats can also argue for equalizing programs that provide benefits across class lines. By pursuing the passage of programs that provide benefits to the middle class and the poor, the Democrats can remain true to their party's progressive traditions and still avoid the electorally damaging stigma of welfaristic liberalism. The Democrats can count on continued public support (especially among the elderly) for Social Security and Medicare. They can also count on middle-class support for new programs in the areas of college tuition assistance, day-care provision, and health-care financing. The provision of assistance to first-time homebuyers represents still another program area where positive government action can attract middle-class votes.

Democrats can even target assistance to the poor so long as they are careful to emphasize benefit programs tied to education and the workplace. Democrats can propose expanded funding for schools, job training, day care, and even cash relief tied to a recipient's work effort. The benefits provided by these job training and social assistance programs can be generous, but they must be conditioned on a recipient's efforts at self-improvement, such as attendance in high school, GED classes, or enrollment in a job training program. Such a Democratic policy would reflect the party's traditions of providing assistance to people in need and provide a level of benefits much higher than that of conservative workfare proposals. Yet, such a policy of conditioned assistance also recognizes the value that the American public places on work.

The environment represents a potentially potent issue for Democrats. Americans overwhelmingly support more aggressive governmental action in the area of environmental protection.[26] Democratic presidential candidates can push for an activist program of environmental protection, including measures for recycling, pollution reduction, toxic waste clean-up, and energy conservation. Democrats cannot be content with reminding voters of the horror stories of the underenforcement of environmental statutes during the Reagan administration, for the Reagan administration has already become part of a seemingly distant past. Instead, Democrats must concentrate their fire on the inadequacy of the environmental record of the Bush administration. Democrats can attack the Bush administration for failing to adequately protect public land from development and exploitation. They can also charge Bush with having formulated an energy plan that pays virtually no attention to the need for energy conservation. Announced in the wake of the Gulf War, the Bush energy plan emphasizes expedited energy development, not conservation, as the means of reducing America's dependence on imported oil.

The environmental issue provides fertile political ground for the Democrats. Yet, Democrats must still be cautious in approaching this issue. Public opinion behind environmental protection certainly seems strong. Seventy percent of the public views current environmental regulations as "not strong enough," and 65 percent express their willingness to protect the environment even if it means that some people will lose jobs and the government will have to spend a great deal of money. Seventy-eight percent agree that environmental standards cannot be too high and that environmental improvements must be continued regardless of cost. Yet, when an October 1989 Gallup poll asked "Would you be willing to pay $200 more taxes each year to increase federal spending for. . . reducing air pollution?" 71 percent said no. More than half the public also expressed their opposition to a 25-cent-per-gallon gasoline tax increase that would be used to control pollution.[27] Democrats must be careful not to advance proposals that lead the public (and the Republicans!) to focus on the costs rather than the benefits of environmental clean-up.

The Democrats can also take advantage of the public's support for women's rights. Younger and more professional women may be attracted to the Republican party's conservative economic philosophy, but they are less comfortable with the Republicans' record on women's and life-style issues. The Republicans have been too tied to the profamily orientations of New Right traditionalists to respond to the more liberal life-style concerns of younger, career-oriented women. The Democrats can exploit this dissonance by pointing to their support of measures to ensure women's equality. They can contrast their record with that of the Republicans, including the Republican party's opposition to the passage of the Equal Rights Amendment.

Democrats can also advocate the protection of abortion rights, an issue that might increase in salience if states impose new restrictions on abortions in the wake of the Supreme Court's *Webster* decision. But a pro-choice Democrat must do more than observe that abortion is a woman's private choice. He must also point to the futility of attempting to roll back rights in this area. To minimize the loss of votes on the abortion question, a Democrat must also make clear that abortion is a last resort and is not a desired course of policy. He must emphasize that government needs to do more in the area of pregnancy prevention, including giving teenagers a sense of a stake in the future, to reduce the number of abortions.

Social and life-style issues alone, however, will not win back younger voters for the Democrats. Reagan and Bush won the votes of younger Americans who saw the Republicans as the party of a better economic future. To win the votes of younger Americans, Democrats, too, must be seen as the party of economic opportunity. Democrats must favor partnerships with business to promote economic adaptation and a growing economic pie. While Democrats can propose more equitable measures than those of the rapacious profiteering of the Reagan boom period, they must seek to become known as the party that promotes growth and prepares America for a high-tech economic future.

In foreign and defense policy, the Democrats can take advantage of the public's fears of nuclear war. Democrats can campaign for arms reduction and nuclear nonproliferation. Democrats can stress the need for continued arms control talks and point to Republican footdragging in this area.

But Democrats must also recognize that a policy of nuclear arms reduction will not be enough to win voter confidence in the foreign policy area. Assessments of a candidate's ability to handle foreign policy are crucial when Americans go to the polls to elect a President. Americans want a President who can lead, one who is capable of taking decisive action especially in times of crisis. A President must be willing to use force when needed.

In the area of national defense, voters have not seen Democratic candidates as potential world leaders. Instead, many voters view the Democrats as though they are still the party of George McGovern; a party so plagued by the post-Vietnam War syndrome that it is incapable of using force when needed in foreign policy. These foreign policy images hurt Dukakis badly in 1988 and were exploited by the Republicans in their ads. Unfortunately for the Democrats, this dovish image of the party was only reinforced by the virtual party-line vote in Congress on the use of force in the Persian Gulf. George Bush came out of the Gulf War looking like a world leader; the Democrats did not.

To win the presidency, a Democratic candidate must convince voters that he is prepared to lead in the world arena. While a Democrat can express great reluctance to commit American troops overseas, he must also convince voters that he is capable of using America's military force should the mantle of leadership require him to do so.

Democrats can begin to rebuild their image in foreign policy by being more supportive of defense spending. Changes in the Soviet Union and the Eastern bloc have reduced America's defense requirements. Yet, the public recognizes that the world continues to be a dangerous place. For most Americans, the quick victory of allied forces against Iraq was the payoff of years of weapons modernization. Televised press briefings during the war included dramatic footage of American bombs dropped down the airshafts of key Iraqi installations. These pictures seemingly underscored the virtues of high-tech weaponry. Democrats must support those weapons systems that are worth the cost, just as they must continue to oppose those weapons systems that are not. No Democratic presidential nominee can oppose weapons system after weapons system and still hope to maintain foreign policy leadership credibility in the eyes of the public.

In both foreign and domestic policy Democrats must also learn the importance of political symbols. Patriotism, the Pledge of Allegiance, and respect for the flag are not minor or inconsequential issues in a presidential race. Nor are they simply the specious creations of advertising specialists. Instead, they are important issues to the millions of Americans who express outrage when they see these cherished symbols violated.

Democrats can win presidential elections, but only if their program and candidates escape the taint of big-government, welfaristic, dovish-on-defense liberalism. The L-word hurt Dukakis in 1988; it needs to be avoided in the future. To win, the Democrats need to find a candidate who can escape the liberal tag, yet remain true to the party's progressive traditions. The candidate must be capable of unifying the diverse constituencies that make up the party but still be able to reach out to more independent voters. It will be no easy task for the Democrats to find such a candidate. Even if they do, there is no guarantee that he or she will survive the primary and caucus selection system.

Geography provides one additional clue to the path of a possible Democratic presidential victory. The 1990 census recorded the further shift of population and electoral votes to the Sunbelt. National Democrats have not done well in the South in recent years, and they are unlikely to do so in the future. Even Jimmy Carter did not carry the South in his race against Ronald Reagan. However, the Pacific states—California, Oregon, and Washington— each contain strong pockets of social and political liberalism. These states may well provide the pivotal battleground for future presidential races. If so, the Democrats may do well to recruit candidates who can appeal to voters in these Pacific states and not just to traditional Democratic constituencies in the Northeast and the Midwest. In choosing a presidential candidate, Democrats can profitably heed the advice: "Go West, Young Democrat!"[28]

REPUBLICAN STRATEGY

The strategic advice for Republicans is more straightforward than that given Democrats: keep on doing what has produced the Republican winning record in recent presidential elections. Republicans should keep the campaign dialogue at the ideological level where the public is attuned to the party's more conservative appeal. Republican candidates should declare their staunch opposition to big government, taxes, bureaucracy, and regulation. They should seize upon symbols—patriotic symbols included—in tune with America's ideological conservatism. They should also continue to portray the Democrats as the party of an effete, trendy, liberal intellectual elite out of step with the majority of Americans.

Economics provides a key area for Republicans. The Republicans can continue to present themselves as the party of a prosperous economic future. Republican economic policies are designed to preserve jobs at home by making American industry more competitive globally. When Democrats charge that Republican tax and economic policies are inequitable, the Republican response is simple: The Republicans give tax cuts and a brighter economic future to all Americans! Democrats, in contrast, offer only the antiquated prescriptions of another era. The GOP needs to portray the Democrats as a party too constrained by its obligations to big labor and other special interests to undertake those actions that will make the American economy more competitive and bring benefits to all Americans.

The Republicans can offer youth the ideal of the American Dream—vertical mobility in an opportunity society. Democrats, in contrast, offer only downward mobility. The Republican opportunity society will create new professional jobs for college graduates. It will also create new entry-level jobs for unskilled workers. These jobs will be an alternative to welfare.

In the domestic arena, four specific issues afford the Republicans great electoral advantage. First is the issue of crime. As the 1988 election showed, many Americans continue to see the Democrats as soft on crime. The crime issue remains ripe for Republican exploitation.

The second area is affirmative action. A majority of Americans do not accept the arguments made on behalf of affirmative action. Instead they see affirmative action simply as reverse discrimination, a policy that violates merit principles by awarding unfair advantages to certain individuals on the basis of skin color, gender, or ethnicity. Given the constituent make-up of the Democratic party, Democratic presidential candidates in all likelihood will continue to support affirmative action programs, if not quite numerical quotas. The Republicans should attack that there is no real difference between affirmative action programs and quotas. The public fails to see how the granting of positive preferences or the setting of numerical hiring goals differs from the establishment of quotas. By pressing their attack on affirmative action and quotas, the Republicans also increase their chances of gaining new support among Asians, Jews, and other racial and ethnic groups who see their opportunities limited by the hiring and promotional preferences given to others.

The third issue, school prayer, has not been a salient factor in recent presidential elections. Yet, it has indirectly affected presidential elections by helping to shape the general public's perceptions of the two parties. Public opinion surveys reveal overwhelming support for prayer in public schools. While civil libertarians and Democrats may object that organized school prayer violates the separation of church and state, such arguments carry little weight with voters. Republicans can use the school prayer issue to paint the Democrats as a party more in touch with the ACLU than with the values of everyday Americans. In dealing with school prayer and other religion-related issues, though, Republicans must be cautious not to be seen as the agents of New Right, Christian fundamentalist groups—groups that do not enjoy great public confidence.

The fourth issue, public choice, crosses several substantive policy areas. Republicans have made increased public choice part of their governing philosophy. Americans are dissatisfied with the state of public services and with their dependence on public bureaucracies. Americans are particularly dissatisfied with the state of public schooling. Republicans can offer the public tax credits, vouchers, and other public choice programs that will give parents the ability to reclaim control over their children's education. These programs will allow parents to withdraw their children from schools that perform poorly and send them to schools that perform better. Republicans can offer competition, restructuring, and reform as the answers in education. They can attack Democratic solutions as rewarding unionized teacher bureaucracies and doing little more than throwing good money after bad to schools that do not teach.

Of course, choice programs need not be restricted to the area of education. A program of tax credits can expand the public's choice of day-care and adult-care arrangements. Tax incentives can also increase the variety of health insurance plans offered by employers to workers.

There are dangers and electoral pitfalls that face Republicans. Republicans must remain aware of America's operational liberalism. Their options must not be so conservative as to lose the votes of middle-class Americans. A conservative revolution that leads to major service cuts in programs favored by the middle class can only endanger Republican political standing. Republicans must be very cautious in how they approach retrenchment in areas that have become political entitlements. Republicans can effect cuts in Social Security, Medicare, tuition assistance, and other big-spending, middle-class programs only at great political risk.

The potential alienation of the middle class is the Republican Achilles' heel. As Kevin Phillips warns, unabated pursuit of the policies of the Reagan era can only raise populist resentment against the Republicans. The public resents the unfairness of a government that gives major tax breaks and other incentives to the wealthy while at the same time it imposes service cutbacks and a savings and loan bailout plan that increases the burden shouldered by average Americans.

The Republicans run a similar risk of alienating voter affections if they pursue deregulation and economic growth policies that are harmful to the environment. The environment has become a new and important political symbol. Republicans recognized this in using the Boston Harbor ad to turn the environmental issue on Dukakis. George Bush further recognized the electoral significance of this issue in his promise to become the nation's environmental President. As President, he forged an acid rain policy and took several other actions in the environmental field stronger than those taken during the Reagan administration. Future Republican presidential candidates will find themselves on safer political ground if they follow the more balanced environmentalist stance of George Bush as opposed to the more ideological, antienvironment policies of Ronald Reagan. A major environmental crisis or enforcement scandal has the potential of doing grave harm to a Republican administration that is not perceived to be a friend of the environment.

The area of social regulation represents still one more potential danger for Republicans. The endorsement by young Americans of the Republican economic performance does not necessarily translate into an equivalent endorsement of Republican social policies. Many of the same young voters who support Republican growth economics will be turned off by a Republican party that seeks to force traditional or conservative life-styles on them. These voters are quite independent. Should the Republican party be captured by a fundamentalist Christian or ideological New Right philosophy, voters might suddenly rediscover a fondness for the

Democrats' tolerance of diversity. Strident Republican opposition to abortion—especially to *all* abortions, including abortions in cases of rape and incest—may lose the party some support among more moderate voters.

The area of foreign and defense policy has proven to be an electoral asset for Republicans. The Republicans can continue to run as the party of proven strength and leadership in foreign policy. Yet, one major setback overseas can quickly alter the public's partisan perceptions in this area. Republicans must also be aware of voter ambivalence in the areas of foreign and defense policy. Americans want the nation to be adequately prepared in the area of defense. They also want a President who is capable of exerting skilled leadership in the foreign arena. They do not want a crusading foreign policy that will unnecessarily cost the lives of many Americans and drain the country's economy. Americans will continue to support quick and winnable, but not long-term and costly, commitments overseas. The invasions of Grenada and Panama, the bombing of Libya, and the war in the Persian Gulf provide the model for a politically acceptable course of foreign policy interventionism.

Overall, Republicans should present themselves as the party of the sensible middle as opposed to Democratic elite liberalism. To do so they must avoid being captured by the party's more ideological and evangelical wing. Republicans must be careful not to mistake their present popularity as a permanent fixture on the American political scene. The realignment of the 1970s and 1980s has been incomplete. Voters remain quite independent. The Republicans will continue to be popular so long as they continue to run the sort of candidates and advocate those policies that Americans approve.

The lesson provided by the fate of British Prime Minister Margaret Thatcher is instructive. Thatcher resigned under pressure after eleven years in office during which she transformed the British social and economic systems. Her more recent actions had made her unpopular; she became an electoral liability for the Conservative party. Thatcher vocally opposed Britain's participation in a fully economically integrated Europe despite clear public sentiment in favor of European integration. She also adamantly pushed the much-despised community charge or poll tax, which the British public saw as unfairly favoring the rich while imposing new tax burdens on the poor and the middle class. Thatcher would not withdraw the poll tax even in the face of riots and demonstrations, the defeat of various Conservative candidates for local and national office, and opinion surveys that showed the overwhelming unpopularity of the new tax measure.

The Thatcher example shows that voters do react to the policy positions of a party and its candidates. The Thatcher example particularly points to the political dangers inherent in an ideological approach to governance that voters might consider extreme. Republicans, too, must be aware of the political dangers inherent in extremism and an ideological approach to governance. Moderate-conservative Republican presidential candidates who avoid major political gaffes can, in all likelihood, expect to win voter support. But an extreme Republican party that ignores the policy concerns of middle-class voters faces the risk of political rejection.

CONCLUSION

This book is written in the tradition of V. O. Key, Jr. The voters are not fools. Image manipulation and television alone do not win presidential elections. Today's more independent electorate responds to broad-based issue concerns as well as to images. The most effective political campaigns are those that mix personal-based images with issue-based themes.

The lesson of this book is simple. When they go to the polls to choose a President, Americans know why they vote as they do. The political party that ignores their values and issue preferences will, in all likelihood, lose.

NOTES

Chapter 1. The Economy, the Gulf War, and the Prologue to the 1992 Election

1. David S. Broder, "Democrats Must Rethink Defense Policy," *Washington Post* Writers Group, March 9, 1991.
2. Janet Hook, "Bush Back on World Stage," *Congressional Quarterly Weekly Reports* (August 24, 1991): 2323.
3. Sam Roberts, "War of Words: Gulf War May Figure in Cuomo's Future," *New York Times,* February 7, 1991.
4. Howard L. Reiter, *Selecting the President: The Nominating Process in Transition* (Philadelphia: U. of Pennsylvania Press, 1985).

Chapter 2. The Changed Setting of Presidential Elections

1. Frank J. Sorauf, *Money in American Elections* (Glenview, Ill.: Scott, Foresman; Boston: Little, Brown, 1990), pp. 208–9.
2. Theodore White, *The Making of the President 1960* (New York: Atheneum, 1961).
3. David Mayhew, *Congress: The Electoral Connection* (New Haven, Conn.: Yale U. Press, 1974), pp. 52–77, identifies various ways by which incumbent members of Congress claim credit and secure their reelection.
4. See, for example, Richard E. Cohen, "Strains Appear as 'New Breed' Democrats Move to Control Party in the House," *National Journal* (June 25, 1983): 1328; and Charles S. Bullock III and Burdett A. Loomis, "The Changing Congressional Career," in *Congress Reconsidered,* 3d ed.,

eds. Lawrence C. Dodd and Bruce I. Oppenheimer (Washington, D.C.: CQ Press, 1985), pp. 65–84.

5. Peter Goldman, Tom Mathews, et al., *The Quest for the Presidency 1988* (New York: Simon and Schuster, Touchstone, 1989), pp. 129–32.

6. Ibid., pp. 75–76, 117.

7. Paul Taylor, *See How They Run: Electing the President in an Age of Mediaocracy* (New York: Alfred A. Knopf, 1990), pp. 207–8.

8. See Chapter 3 for a review of the literature pointing to the increased influence of issues in American elections and the continuing debate on the subject of issue voting.

9. John Kenneth White, *The New Politics of Old Values,* 2d ed. (Hanover, N.H.: University Press of New England, 1988), pp. 145–84.

10. Jean Bethke Elshtain, "Issues and Themes in the 1988 Campaign," in *The Elections of 1988,* ed. Michael Nelson (Washington, D.C.: CQ Press, 1989), p. 117.

11. Raymond E. Wolfinger and Steven J. Rosenstone, *Who Votes?* (New Haven, Conn.: Yale U. Press, 1982), pp. 13–36, 89–93.

12. Martin P. Wattenberg, *The Decline of American Political Parties, 1952–1988* (Cambridge, Mass.: Harvard U. Press, 1990), p. 139.

13. Walter DeVries and V. Lance Tarrance, *The Ticket-Splitter: A New Force in American Politics* (Grand Rapids, Mich.: Eerdmans, 1972), pp. 48–55.

14. Ibid., pp. 57–90.

15. Angus Campbell, Philip E. Converse, Warren E. Miller, and Donald E. Stokes, *The American Voter,* abridged ed. (New York: John Wiley & Sons, 1964), pp. 83–85.

16. Walter Dean Burnham, *Critical Elections and the Mainsprings of American Party Politics* (New York: W. W. Norton, 1970), pp. 90–134.

17. Wattenberg, *The Decline of American Political Parties, 1952–1988,* pp. 92–98.

18. Ibid., pp. 92–98.

19. Everett Carll Ladd, Jr., with Charles D. Hadley, *Transformations of the American Party System* (New York: W. W. Norton, 1978), pp. 19–27 and 275–76; James L. Sundquist, *Dynamics of the Party System: Alignment and Realignment of Political Parties in the United States* (Washington, D.C.: Brookings Institution, 1973), pp. 376–411.

20. Public opinion data reporting public support for strengthened environmental regulation despite the general public attitude toward deregulation are reported by Robert Cameron Mitchell, "Public Opinion and Environmental Politics in the 1970s and 1980s," in *Environmental Policy in the 1980s,* eds. Norman J. Vig and Michael E. Kraft (Washington, D.C.: CQ Press, 1984), pp. 51–74.

21. Paul Allen Beck, "A Socialization Theory of Partisan Realignment," in *Controversies in American Voting Behavior,* eds. Richard G. Niemi and Herbert F. Weisberg (San Francisco: W. H. Freeman, 1973), pp. 396–411.

22. Wattenberg, *The Decline of American Political Parties, 1952–1988,* pp. 120–24.

23. Ladd and Hadley, *Transformations of the American Party System,* pp. 162–69.

24. See, for example, Donald Kinder and D. Roderick Kiewiet, "Sociotropic Politics: The American Case," *British Journal of Political Science,* 11 (1981): 129–61.

25. Walter Dean Burnham, "Insulation and Responsiveness in Congressional Elections," *Political Science Quarterly,* 90 (1975): 411–35; and Gary C. Jacobson, *The Electoral Origins of Divided Government* (Boulder, Colo.: Westview Press, 1990).

26. William Crotty and John S. Jackson III, *Presidential Primaries and Nominations* (Washington, D.C.: CQ Press, 1985), p. 28. Crotty and Jackson provide a good overview of the reforms of the nominating process and their effects.

27. Ibid., pp. 34–35.

28. See ibid., pp. 44–49, for an overview of the more limited delegate selection reforms instituted by the Republicans.

29. Jeane Kirkpatrick, *The New Presidential Elite: Men and Women in National Politics* (New York: Russell Sage Foundation, Twentieth Century Fund, 1976), pp. 281–347; Denis G. Sullivan, Jeffrey L. Pressman, Benjamin I. Page, and John J. Lyons, *The Politics of Representation: The Democratic Convention, 1972* (New York: St. Martin's Press, 1974), pp. 17–40.

30. Kirkpatrick, *The New Presidential Elite,* pp. 3–34, 281–331. Also see Austin Ranney, *Curing the Mischiefs of Faction: Party Reform in America* (Berkeley, Calif.: U. of California Press, 1975), pp. 150–54; and Sullivan et al., *The Politics of Representation,* pp. 30–34.

31. Kirkpatrick, *The New Presidential Elite,* pp. 53–54.

32. Thomas R. Marshall, "Turnout and Representation: Caucuses versus Primaries," *American Journal of Political Science,* 22 (February 1978): 169–82.

33. Herbert Kritzer, "Representativeness of the 1972 Presidential Primaries," in *The Party Symbol,* ed. William Crotty (San Francisco: W. H. Freeman, 1980), pp. 148–54.

34. Crotty and Jackson, *Presidential Primaries and Nominations,* pp. 89–95.

35. Herbert McClosky, Paul J. Hoffman, and Rosemary O'Hara, "Issue Conflict and Consensus Among Party Leaders and Followers," *American Political Science Review,* 56 (June 1960): 406–29.

36. Warren E. Miller and M. Kent Jennings, with Barbara G. Furah, *Parties in Transition: A Longitudinal Study of Party Leaders and Party Supporters* (New York: Russell Sage Foundation, 1986). Also see Nelson W. Polsby and Aaron Wildavsky, *Presidential Elections,* 7th ed. (New York: Free Press, 1988), pp. 127–30.

37. ABC News/*Washington Post* poll results, cited in Polsby and Wildavsky, *Presidential Elections,* p. 135.

38. Polsby and Wildavsky, *Presidential Elections,* pp. 127–43.

39. Crotty and Jackson, *Presidential Primaries and Nominations,* p. 137.

40. *Buckley v. Valeo,* 424 U.S. 1 (1976). In *FEC v. NCPAC,* 105 S.Ct. 1459 (1985), the Supreme Court essentially reaffirmed its view as to the legality of independent expenditures in a publicly financed campaign.

41. Herbert E. Alexander and Brian A. Haggerty, *Financing the 1984 Election* (Lexington, Mass.: D. C. Heath, 1987), pp. 173–74.

42. Ibid., p. 403.

43. Ibid., pp. 177–80.

44. Ibid., pp. 335–40.

45. Herbert E. Alexander, "Making Sense about Dollars in the 1980 Presidential Campaigns," in *Money and Politics in the United States,* ed. Michael J. Malbin (Chatham, N.J.: Chatham House, 1984), pp. 19–24; Alexander and Haggerty, *Financing the 1984 Election,* pp. 329–31.

46. Herbert E. Alexander, "Financing the Presidential Elections, 1988," in *The Quest for National Office,* eds. Stephen J. Wayne and Clyde Wilcox (New York: St. Martin's Press, 1992), pp. 45–49.

47. Herbert E. Alexander, *Financing Politics* (Washington, D.C.: CQ Press, 1976), p. 250.

48. Campbell et al., *The American Voter.* We review the findings of early stud-
    ies of American voting behavior, including *The American Voter,* in Chapter
    3 of this book. More recent studies pointing to the possible changing nat-
    ure and increased issue-orientation of American voters are reviewed in
    Chapters 3 and 5.

Chapter 3.   The Debate over Issue Voting

1. Richard G. Niemi and Herbert E. Weisberg, eds., *Controversies in Voting
   Behavior* (Washington, D.C.: CQ Press, 1984), p. 102.
2. Angus Campbell, Philip E. Converse, Warren E. Miller, and Donald E.
   Stokes, *The American Voter* (New York: John Wiley & Sons, 1960). Page
   references to *The American Voter* cited in this chapter will be to the
   abridged edition published in 1964.
3. Paul F. Lazarsfeld, Bernard Berelson, and Hazel Gaudet, *The People's
   Choice* (New York: Columbia U. Press, 1944).
4. Bernard R. Berelson, Paul F. Lazarsfeld, and William N. McPhee, *Voting*
   (Chicago: U. of Chicago Press, 1954).
5. Ibid., pp. 19–21.
6. Ibid., p. 27.
7. Ibid., p. 322.
8. Angus Campbell, Philip E. Converse, Warren E. Miller, and Donald E.
   Stokes, *Elections and the Political Order* (New York: John Wiley & Sons,
   1966).
9. Campbell et al., *The American Voter,* p. 33.
10. Ibid., p. 72.
11. Ibid., p. 76.
12. Ibid., p. 29.
13. Ibid., p. 44. Also see Herbert McCloskey, Paul J. Hoffman, and Rose-
    mary O'Hara, "Issue Conflict and Consensus Among Party Leaders and
    Followers," *American Political Science Review* 54 (June 1960): 406–27.
14. Campbell et al., *The American Voter,* p. 98.
15. Ibid., p. 105.
16. Philip E. Converse, "The Nature of Belief Systems in Mass Publics," in
    Ideology and Discontent, ed. David E. Apter (New York: Free Press, 1964),
    Chap. 6. Christopher A. Achen, "Mass Political Attitudes and Survey
    Response," *American Political Science Review* 69 (December 1975): 1218–31,
    criticizes that some of the low correlations over time that Converse re-
    ports are the artifact of inadequate survey methods, more precisely the
    low reliability of survey questions. As the choices in questions do not
    closely match voter beliefs, respondents' answers vary a bit over time,
    even when their opinions do not change. When Achen corrects for the
    lack of reliability of the survey instrument, he finds that voters have more
    stable opinions. Other political scientists, however, charge that Achen has
    inadvertently inflated the apparent level of ideological thinking by over-
    compensating for the lack of reliability of survey questions.
17. Campbell et al., *The American Voter,* pp. 116–17, 135.
18. Ibid., p. 142.
19. V. O. Key, Jr., *The Responsible Electorate* (New York: Vintage Books, 1966),
    pp. 7–8.
20. Ibid., p. 37.

21. Ibid., p. 55.
22. Ibid., p. 92.
23. Ibid., p. 56.
24. Also see Everett Carll Ladd, Jr., with Charles D. Hadley, *Transformations of the American Party System*, 2d ed. (New York: W. W. Norton, 1978), pp. 129–30.
25. Key, *The Responsible Electorate*, p. 57. Also see Arthur H. Miller and Martin P. Wattenberg, "Throwing the Rascals Out: Policy Evaluations of Presidential Candidates, 1952–1980," *American Political Science Review* 79 (1985): 359–72.
26. Also see Miller and Wattenberg, "Throwing the Rascals Out," p. 365.
27. Richard G. Niemi and Herbert F. Weisberg, eds., *Controversies in American Voting Behavior* (San Francisco: W. H. Freeman, 1973), pp. 165–66.
28. Michael Margolis, "From Confusion to Confusion: Issues and Voters, 1952–1972," in *Parties and Elections in an Anti-Party Age*, ed. Jeff Fishel (Bloomington, Ind.: U. of Indiana Press, 1978), pp. 116–17.
29. David E. RePass, "Issue Salience and Party Choice," *American Political Science Review* 65 (June 1971): 389–400. The quotation appears on p. 390.
30. Margolis, "From Confusion to Confusion," pp. 120–21.
31. Ibid., p. 119.
32. Gerald Pomper, "The Impact of *The American Voter* on Political Science," *Political Science Quarterly* 93 (Winter 1978): 625.
33. Norman H. Nie, Sidney Verba, John R. Petrocik, *The Changing American Voter* (Cambridge, Mass.: Harvard U. Press, 1976), pp. 70–73.
34. Ladd and Hadley, *Transformations of the American Party System*, p. 320.
35. Gerald Pomper, *Voters' Choice* (New York: Dodd, Mead, 1975), p. xiii. Also see Pomper, "From Confusion to Clarity: Issues and American Voters, 1952–1968," *American Political Science Review* 66 (June 1972): 415–28.
36. Ibid., pp. 11–12.
37. Ibid., p. 180.
38. Ibid., p. 114.
39. Ibid., pp. 170–73.
40. Ibid., p. 178.
41. Margolis, "From Confusion to Confusion," p. 117.
42. Ibid., pp. 117–19.
43. Nie et al., *The Changing American Voter*, especially Chapter 8. Also see Norman H. Nie and Kristi Anderson, "Mass Belief Systems Revisited: Political Change and Attitude Structure," *Journal of Politics* 36 (August 1974): 540–90.
44. Converse, "The Nature of Belief Systems in Mass Publics."
45. George F. Bishop, Alfred J. Tuchfarber, and Robert W. Oldendick, "Change in the Structure of American Political Attitudes: The Nagging Question of Question Wording," *American Journal of Political Science* 22 (May 1978): 250–69; and Eric R. A. N. Smith, *The Unchanging American Voter* (Berkeley, Calif.: U. of California Press, 1989), pp. 117–35.
46. John L. Sullivan, James E. Piereson, and George E. Marcus, "Ideological Constraint in the Mass Public: A Methodological Critique and Some New Findings," *American Journal of Political Science* 22 (May 1978): 233–49.
47. Norman H. Nie and James N. Rabjohn, "Revisiting Mass Belief Systems Revisited: Or, Doing Research Is Like Watching a Tennis Match," *American Journal of Political Science* 23 (February 1979): 139–75.
48. John L. Sullivan, James E. Piereson, George E. Marcus, and Stanley

Feldman, "The More Things Change, the More They Stay the Same: The Stability of Mass Belief Systems," *American Journal of Political Science* 23 (February 1979): 176–86; and George F. Bishop, Alfred J. Tuchfarber, Robert W. Oldendick, and Stephen E. Bennett, "Questions About Question Wording: A Rejoinder to Revisiting Mass Belief Systems Revisited," *American Journal of Political Science* 23 (February 1979): 187–92.

49. Philip E. Converse and Gregory B. Markus, "Plus ça change . . .: The New CPS Election Study Panel," *American Political Science Review* 73 (March 1979): 32–49.

50. Philip E. Converse, Warren E. Miller, Jerrold G. Rusk, and Arthur G. Wolfe, "Continuity and Change in American Politics: Parties and Issues in the 1968 Election," *American Political Science Review* 63 (December 1969): 1083–1105.

51. Arthur H. Miller, Warren E. Miller, Alden S. Raine, and Thad A. Brown, "A Majority Party in Disarray: Policy Polarization in the 1972 Election," *American Political Science Review* 30 (September 1976): 753–78; Warren E. Miller and Teresa E. Levitin, *Leadership and Change: The New Politics of the American Electorate* (Cambridge, Mass.: Winthrop, 1976), pp. 45–62, 119–66.

52. Edward G. Carmines and James A. Stimson, "The Two Faces of Issue Voting," *American Political Science Review* 74 (March 1980): 78–91.

53. Morris P. Fiorina, *Retrospective Voting in American National Elections* (New Haven, Conn.: Yale U. Press, 1981), p. 83 and chap. 6; John E. Jackson, "Issues, Party Choices, and Presidential Votes," *American Journal of Political Science* 19 (May 1975): 161–85; and Charles H. Franklin, "Issue Preferences, Socialization, and the Evolution of Party Identification," *American Journal of Political Science* 28 (August 1984): 459–78. For a brief review of the revisionist literature that sees party identification as a response to adult political experiences and policy attitudes, see Michael M. Gant and Norman R. Luttbeg, *American Electoral Behavior* (Itasca, Ill.: F. E. Peacock, 1991), pp. 30–33.

54. Fiorina, *Retrospective Voting in American National Elections*, p. 200. Emphasis in the original.

55. Carmines and Stimson, "The Two Faces of Issue Voting," p. 79.

56. Fiorina, *Retrospective Voting in American National Elections*, pp. 10–11.

57. Ibid., p. 10.

58. Ibid., p. 5.

59. This point is also made by Anthony Downs, *An Economic Theory of Democracy* (New York: Harper and Row, 1957), pp. 38–40.

60. See, for instance, D. Roderick Kiewiet, "Policy-Oriented Voting in Response to Economic Issues," *American Political Science Review* 75 (1981): 448–59; Donald R. Kinder and D. Roderick Kiewiet, "Sociotropic Politics: The American Case," *British Journal of Political Science* 11 (1981): 129–61; Donald R. Kinder, Gordon S. Adams, and Paul W. Gronke, "Economics and Politics in the 1984 Presidential Election," *American Journal of Political Science* 33 (May 1989): 491–515; and Robert S. Erikson, "Economic Conditions and the Presidential Vote," *American Political Science Review* 83 (June 1989): 567–73.

61. Fiorina, *Retrospective Voting in American National Elections*, pp. 100, 127–28; and Arthur H. Miller, "Partisanship Reinstated? A Comparison of the 1972 and 1976 United States Presidential Elections," *British Journal of Political Science* 8 (1978): 129–52.

62. Kathleen A. Frankovic, "Public Opinion Trends," in *The Election of 1980,* ed. Gerald M. Pomper (Chatham, N.J.: Chatham House, 1981), pp. 97–118; Gregory B. Markus, "Political Attitudes During a Presidential Year: A Report on the 1980 NES Panel Study," *American Political Science Review* 76 (1982): 538–60.
63. George Rabinowitz and Stuart Elaine MacDonald, "A Directional Theory of Issue Voting," *American Political Science Review* 83 (1989): 93–121.
64. Ibid., p. 94.
65. Ibid., p. 115.
66. Carmines and Stimson, "The Two Faces of Issue Voting," pp. 78–91.
67. It should be noted that the Carmines and Stimson article analyzes the impact of the Vietnam War and race on voting in the 1972 presidential election. It is likely that their conclusions also apply to the 1968 election. In their book *Issue Evolution: Race and the Transformation of American Politics* (Princeton, N.J.: Princeton U. Press, 1989), pp. 123, 137, Carmines and Stimson state that race was at the center of voters' ideology or "issue bundles" in 1968.
68. See Carmines and Stimson, *Issue Evolution: Race and the Transformation of American Politics,* pp. 11–12.

Chapter 4. The New Deal Era

1. Gerald Pomper, "The Impact of *The American Voter* on Political Science," *Political Science Quarterly* 93 (Winter 1978): 625.
2. V. O. Key, Jr., *The Responsible Electorate* (New York: Vintage Books, 1966).
3. V. O. Key, Jr., "A Theory of Critical Elections," *Journal of Politics* 17 (February 1955): 3–18; Walter Dean Burnham, *Critical Elections and the Mainsprings of American Politics* (New York: W. W. Norton, 1970), pp. 1–10.
4. Walter Dean Burnham, "The Changing Shape of the Political Universe," *American Political Science Review* 59 (March 1965): 7–28, reprinted in Walter Dean Burnham, *The Current Crisis in American Politics* (New York: Oxford U. Press, 1982), p. 49.
5. Samuel Lubell, *The Future of American Politics,* 2d ed. (Garden City, N.Y.: Doubleday, 1951, 1956), p. 40.
6. Ibid. The nature of Bryan's appeal is also discussed by Everett Carll Ladd, Jr., *American Political Parties: Social Change and Political Response* (New York: W. W. Norton, 1970), pp. 120–24.
7. E. E. Schattschneider, *The Semi-Sovereign People* (New York: Holt, Rinehart & Winston, 1960), p. 79. The phrase "the system of 1896" is also from Schattschneider.
8. Burnham, "The Changing Shape of the Political Universe," p. 50.
9. Lubell, *The Future of American Politics,* pp. 35–43. Also see Key, "A Theory of Critical Elections," pp. 4–11.
10. Gerald H. Gamm, *The Making of New Deal Democrats* (Chicago: U. of Chicago Press, 1989), pp. 188–90; Duncan MacRae, Jr., and James A. Meldrum, "Critical Elections in Illinois: 1888–1958," *American Political Science Review* 54 (1960): 669–83; and Jerome M. Clubb and Howard W. Allen, "The Cities and the Election of 1928: Partisan Realignment?" *American Historical Review* 74 (April 1969): 1205–20.
11. Kristi Anderson, "Generation, Partisan Shift, and Realignment: A Glance Back to the New Deal," in Norman H. Nie, Sidney Verba, and John R. Petrocik, *The Changing American Voter* (Cambridge, Mass.: Har-

vard U. Press, 1976), pp. 74–95. Everett Carll Ladd, Jr., with Charles D. Hadley, *Transformations of the American Party System*, 2d ed. (New York: W. W. Norton, 1978), pp. 31–87, presents the opposite point of view, that the "conversion" of former Republicans, not "generational replacement," accounts for realignment. The argument that both conversion and generational replacement occurred during a continuing process of realignment is made by Robert S. Erikson and Kent L. Tedin, "The 1928–1936 Partisan Realignment: The Case for the Conversion Hypothesis," *American Political Science Review* 75 (December 1981): 951–62; and Courtney Brown, "Mass Dynamics of U.S. Presidential Competitions, 1928–1936," *American Political Science Review* 82 (December 1988): 1153–81.

12. Gamm, *The Making of New Deal Democrats*, pp. 3–104, 183–202.

13. Paul Allen Beck, "A Socialization Theory of Partisan Realignment," in *Controversies in American Voting Behavior*, eds. Richard G. Niemi and Herbert F. Weisberg (San Francisco: W. H. Freeman, 1973), pp. 396–411.

14. Edwin Diamond and Stephen Bates, *The Spot: The Rise of Political Advertising on Television* (Cambridge, Mass.: MIT Press, 1984), p. 41.

15. Ibid., pp. 46–47.

16. J. Leonard Reinsch, *Getting Elected: From Radio and Roosevelt to Television and Reagan* (New York: Hippocrene Books, 1988), pp. 79–80.

17. Ibid., p. 82.

18. Diamond and Bates, *The Spot*, p. 52.

19. Ibid., p. 54; and Stanley Kelley, Jr., *Professional Public Relations and Political Power* (Baltimore: Johns Hopkins Press, 1956), p. 188.

20. Kelley, *Professional Public Relations and Political Power*, pp. 193–95.

21. Nixon's strategy in preparing for the Checkers speech is discussed by Diamond and Bates, *The Spot*, pp. 66–75; Kelley, *Professional Public Relations and Political Power*, pp. 177–84; and Kurt Lang and Gladys Engel Lang, *Politics and Television* (Chicago: Quadrangle Books, 1968), pp. 24–29.

22. Angus Campbell, "A Classification of the Presidential Elections," in *Elections and the Political Order*, eds. Angus Campbell, Philip E. Converse, Warren E. Miller, and Donald E. Stokes (New York: John Wiley & Sons, 1966), pp. 69–79.

23. Diamond and Bates, *The Spot*, pp. 95–96.

24. Philip Converse, "Religion and Politics: The 1960 Election," in *Elections and the Political Order*, eds. Campbell et al., p. 124.

25. Ithiel de Sola Pool, Robert P. Abelson, and Samuel L. Popkin, *Candidates, Issues, and Strategies: A Computer Simulation of the 1960 Presidential Election* (Cambridge, Mass.: MIT Press, 1964), p. 117. See their more extensive discussion, pp. 115–18.

26. According to Kathleen Hall Jamieson, *Packaging the Presidency: A History and Criticism of Presidential Campaign Advertising* (New York: Oxford U. Press, 1984), pp. 136–39, the Kennedy campaign also used the saga of the PT-109 rescue mission to portray a physically vigorous and quite capable Kennedy, thereby keeping under wraps knowledge of Kennedy's affliction with Addison's disease.

27. Marshall McLuhan, *Understanding Media* (New York: McGraw-Hill, 1964), pp. 287–88. Reinsch, *Getting Elected*, pp. 133–53, provides a good account of the strategy involved in the debates from the perspective of the Kennedy camp.

28. Lang and Lang, *Politics and Television*, pp. 212–49, and Sidney Kraus, ed., *The Great Debates* (Bloomington, Ind.: U. of Indiana Press, 1962), analyze the impact of the 1960 debates.

29. Key, *The Responsible Electorate,* p. 56.
30. Ibid., p. 57. Also see Arthur H. Miller and Martin P. Wattenberg, "Throwing the Rascals Out: Policy Evaluations of Presidential Candidates, 1952–1980," *American Political Science Review* 79 (1985): 359–72.
31. Arthur H. Miller, Martin P. Wattenberg, and Oksana Malanchuk, "Schematic Assessments of Presidential Candidates," *American Political Science Review* 80 (1986): 521–40.
32. Miller and Wattenberg, "Throwing the Rascals Out," p. 365.

Chapter 5. The Rise of Issues in Presidential Elections: 1964–1972

1. Edwin Diamond and Stephen Bates, *The Spot: The Rise of Political Advertising on Television* (Cambridge, Mass.: MIT Press, 1984), pp. 122–24.
2. Ibid., pp. 124–26.
3. Aaron Wildavsky, "The Goldwater Phenomenon: Purists, Politicians, and the Two-Party System," *Review of Politics* 27 (1965): 386–413.
4. For details about the Johnson campaign's continued use of the nuclear weapons issue even after the withdrawal of the Daisy Girl ad, see Diamond and Bates, *The Spot,* pp. 129–36.
5. Kathleen Hall Jamieson, *Packaging the Presidency: A History and Criticism of Presidential Campaign Advertising* (New York: Oxford U. Press, 1964), pp. 177–78.
6. Ibid., p. 176.
7. David E. RePass, "Issue Salience and Party Choice," *American Political Science Review* 65 (June 1971): 389–400.
8. Norman H. Nie, Sidney Verba, John R. Petrocik, *The Changing American Voter* (Cambridge, Mass.: Harvard U. Press, 1976), pp. 123–30. Also see Norman H. Nie and Kristi Anderson, "Mass Belief Systems Revisited: Political Change and Attitudinal Structure," *Journal of Politics* 36 (August 1974): 540–87.
9. Nie, Verba, and Petrocik, *The Changing American Voter,* p. 336.
10. Gerald Pomper, *Voters' Choice: Varieties of American Electoral Behavior* (New York: Dodd, Mead, 1975), p. 178.
11. Donald E. Stokes, "Some Dynamic Elements of Contests for the Presidency," *American Political Science Review* 60 (March 1966): 19–28.
12. Aage R. Clausen, Philip E. Converse, and Warren E. Miller, "Electoral Myth and Reality: The 1964 Election," *American Political Science Review* 59 (June 1965): 321–32.
13. Ibid., p. 331.
14. Ibid.
15. Arthur H. Miller, Martin P. Wattenberg, and Oksana Malanchuk, "Schematic Assessments of Presidential Candidates," *American Political Science Review* 80 (1986): 528–29.
16. R. Kenneth Godwin, *One Billion Dollars of Influence* (Chatham, N.J.: Chatham House, 1988), pp. 101–2; Herbert E. Alexander, *Financing the 1964 Election* (Princeton, N.J.: Citizens' Research Foundation, 1966); and Frank J. Sorauf, *Money in American Elections* (Glenview, Ill.: Scott, Foresman; Boston: Little, Brown, 1988), p. 26.
17. Theodore H. White, *The Making of the President 1968* (New York: Atheneum, 1969), p. 61.
18. Ibid., pp. 3–5.

19. Ibid., pp. 71–72.
20. Ibid., p. 70.
21. Timothy Crouse, *The Boys on the Bus* (New York: Ballantine, 1972), p. 196.
22. Richard M. Scammon and Ben J. Wattenberg, *The Real Majority* (New York: Coward-McCann, 1970), pp. 85–87.
23. Philip E. Converse, Warren E. Miller, Jerrold G. Rusk, and Arthur G. Wolfe, "Continuity and Change in American Politics: Parties and Issues in the 1968 Election," *American Political Science Review* 63 (December 1969): 1095. Also see Scammon and Wattenberg, *The Real Majority,* p. 91.
24. Nelson W. Polsby, *Consequences of Party Reform* (New York: Oxford U. Press, 1983), pp. 24–26; White, *The Making of the President 1968,* p. 218.
25. Scammon and Wattenberg, *The Real Majority,* p. 142.
26. Joe McGinniss, *The Selling of the President 1968* (New York: Trident Press, 1969), p. 20.
27. Ibid., p. 22.
28. Ibid., p. 83 (emphasis in the original).
29. Scammon and Wattenberg, *The Real Majority,* p. 174.
30. Converse et al., "Continuity and Change in American Politics...the 1968 Election," p. 1097.
31. Scammon and Wattenberg, *The Real Majority,* pp. 200–211.
32. Ibid., pp. 35–71.
33. Benjamin I. Page and Richard A. Brody, "Policy Voting and the Electoral Process: The Vietnam War Issue," *American Political Science Review* 66 (1972): 979–95.
34. Converse et al., "Continuity and Change in American Politics...the 1968 Election," p. 1098.
35. Ibid., p. 1099.
36. Diamond and Bates, *The Spot,* p. 187.
37. Crouse, *The Boys on the Bus,* pp. 46–47.
38. Ibid., pp. 46–65.
39. Jeane Kirkpatrick, *The New Presidential Elite* (New York: Russell Sage Foundation, 1976), pp. 305–15; Denis G. Sullivan, Jeffrey L. Pressman, Benjamin I. Page, and John J. Lyons, *The Politics of Representation: The Democratic Convention 1972* (New York: St. Martin's Press, 1974), pp. 330–34; and William Crotty, *Party Reform* (New York: Longman, 1983), pp. 143–51.
40. Crotty, *Party Reform,* pp. 155–202, details the expulsion of the "Daley 59" from the 1972 Democratic convention.
41. Crouse, *The Boys on the Bus,* pp. 339–53.
42. Jamieson, *Packaging the Presidency,* pp. 320–21.
43. Ibid., pp. 322–23.
44. Ibid., p. 304.
45. Everett Carll Ladd, Jr., with Charles D. Hadley, *Transformations of the American Party System* (New York: W. W. Norton, 1975), p. 234. See pp. 181–246 for Ladd and Hadley's larger description of the changed pattern of class alignments in the postindustrial era.
46. Pomper, *The Voter's Choice,* pp. 190–91.
47. Edward G. Carmines and James A. Stimson, "The Two Faces of Issue Voting," *American Political Science Review* 74 (March 1980): 78–91.
48. Warren E. Miller and Teresa E. Levitin, *Leadership and Change: The New Politics and the American Electorate* (Cambridge, Mass.: Winthrop, 1976), p. 1.
49. Ibid., p. 127.

50. Ibid., pp. 133–39.
51. Arthur H. Miller and Warren E. Miller, "Issues, Candidates, and Partisan Divisions in the 1972 American Presidential Election," *British Journal of Political Science* 5 (1975): 393–431.
52. Arthur H. Miller, Warren E. Miller, Alden S. Raine, and Thad A. Brown, "A Majority Party in Disarray: Policy Polarization in the 1972 Election," *American Political Science Review* 30 (September 1976): 753–78.
53. Samuel Popkin, John W. Gorman, Charles Phillips, and Jeffrey A. Smith, "Comment: What Have You Done for Me Lately? Toward an Investment Theory of Voting," *American Political Science Review* 70 (September 1976): 779–813.
54. Ibid., p. 801.
55. Ibid., p. 794.

Chapter 6.   The Politics of Retrospective Rejection: 1976–1980

1. Gerald R. Ford, *A Time to Heal* (New York: Harper & Row, 1979).
2. Edwin Diamond and Stephen Bates, *The Spot: The Rise of Political Advertising on Television* (Cambridge, Mass.: MIT Press, 1984), p. 235.
3. Larry M. Bartels, *Presidential Primaries and the Dynamics of Public Choice* (Princeton, N.J.: Princeton U. Press, 1988), pp. 172–75, 201–3.
4. Jonathon Moore and Janet Fraser, eds., *Campaign for the President: The Managers Look at '76* (Cambridge, Mass.: Ballinger, 1977), pp. 92–93. Quoted in Bartels, *Presidential Primaries and the Dynamics of Public Choice,* p. 44.
5. For instance, see Diamond and Bates, *The Spot,* pp. 241–44; and Kathleen Hall Jamieson, *Packaging the Presidency* (New York: Oxford U. Press, 1984), pp. 355–56.
6. Bartels, *Presidential Primaries and the Dynamics of Public Choice,* p. 211.
7. Diamond and Bates, *The Spot,* pp. 241–44.
8. Donald R. Kinder and D. Roderick Kiewiet, "Sociotropic Politics: The American Case," *British Journal of Political Science* 11 (1978): 129–61.
9. Arthur H. Miller, "The Majority Party Reunited? A Comparison of the 1972 and 1976 Elections," in *Parties and Elections in an Anti-Party Age,* ed. Jeff Fishel (Bloomington, Ind.: Indiana U. Press, 1978), p. 130.
10. Robert H. Entman, *Democracy Without Citizens: Media and the Decay of American Politics* (New York: Oxford U. Press, 1989), p. 126.
11. Ibid., pp. 125–26.
12. Thomas E. Patterson, *The Mass Media Election: How Americans Choose Their President* (New York: Praeger, 1980), pp. 120–25. Also see Sidney Kraus, *Televised Presidential Debates and Public Policy* (Hillsdale, N.J.: Lawrence Erlbaum Associates, 1988), pp. 73–74.
13. David O. Sears and Steven H. Chaffee, "Uses and Effects of the 1976 Debates: An Overview of the Empirical Studies," in *The Great Debates 1976: Ford vs. Carter,* ed. Sidney Kraus (Bloomington, Ind.: Indiana U. Press, 1979), pp. 240–58.
14. Warren E. Miller and Teresa E. Levitin, *Leadership and Change: Presidential Elections from 1952 to 1976* (Cambridge, Mass.: Winthrop, 1976), p. 189.
15. Ibid., p. 211.
16. Everett Carll Ladd, Jr., with Charles D. Hadley, *Transformations of the American Party System,* 2d ed. (New York: W. W. Norton, 1978), pp. 225–39.

17. Miller and Levitin, *Leadership and Change...1952 to 1976,* pp. 199–202; Arthur Miller, "The Majority Party Reunited?" p. 138.
18. J. David Gopoian, "Issue Preference and Candidate Choice in Presidential Primaries," *American Journal of Political Science* 26 (August 1982): 523–46.
19. Bartels, *Presidential Primaries and the Dynamics of Public Choice,* p. 83.
20. David W. Abbott and Edward T. Rogowsky, "Voting Behavior in the 1976 Election: A Preliminary Report," in *Political Parties,* 2d ed., eds. David W. Abbott and Edward T. Rogowsky (Chicago: Rand McNally, 1978), pp. 208–15.
21. Arthur Miller, "The Majority Party Reunited?" pp. 129–30.
22. Abbott and Rogowsky, "Voting Behavior in the 1976 Election," pp. 211–13. Also see Herbert B. Asher, *Presidential Elections and American Politics,* 3d ed. (Homewood, Ill.: Dorsey, 1984), p. 157.
23. Miller and Levitin, *Leadership and Change...1952 to 1976,* p. 189.
24. Pamela Johnston Conover and Stanley Feldman, "Candidate Perception in an Ambiguous World: Campaigns, Cues, and Inference Processes," *American Journal of Political Science* 33 (November 1989): 912–40. Also see Miller and Levitin, *Leadership and Change...1952 to 1976,* pp. 220–21.
25. Arthur Miller, "The Majority Party Reunited?" pp. 133–34, 138.
26. Morris P. Fiorina, *Retrospective Voting in American National Elections* (New Haven, Conn.: Yale U. Press, 1981), p. 125.
27. Kristen Renwick Monroe, *Presidential Popularity and the Economy* (New York: Praeger, 1984), p. 140.
28. Ibid., p. 142.
29. Arthur Miller, "The Majority Party Reunited?" p. 132.
30. Bartels, *Presidential Primaries and the Dynamics of Public Choice,* pp. 183–84.
31. Miller and Levitin, *Leadership and Change...1952 to 1976,* pp. 219–20.
32. Fiorina, *Retrospective Voting in American National Politics,* p. 175.
33. Kathleen A. Frankovic, "Public Opinion," in *The Election of 1980,* ed. Gerald Pomper (Chatham, N.J.: Chatham House, 1981), pp. 97–102.
34. Diamond and Bates, *The Spot,* pp. 276–79. Also see Jamieson, *Packaging the Presidency,* p. 384.
35. Diamond and Bates, *The Spot,* p. 276; Jamieson, *Packaging the Presidency,* p. 382.
36. Diamond and Bates, *The Spot,* pp. 270–71.
37. Herbert E. Alexander, *Financing Elections,* 3d ed. (Washington, D.C.: CQ Press, 1984), p. 125; Frank J. Sorauf, *Money in American Elections* (Glenview, Ill.: Scott, Foresman; Boston: Little, Brown, 1988), pp. 208–9; and Jamieson, *Packaging the Presidency,* pp. 417–28.
38. Quoted by Myles Martel, *Political Campaign Debates: Images, Strategies, and Tactics* (New York: Longman, 1983), p. 20.
39. Michael J. Robinson and Margaret A. Sheehan, *Over the Wire and On TV: CBS and UPI in Campaign '80* (New York: Russell Sage Foundation, 1983), pp. 73–75, 244–47.
40. Frankovic, "Public Opinion," pp. 113–17.
41. Arthur H. Miller and Martin P. Wattenberg, "Throwing the Rascals Out: Policy and Performance Evaluations of Presidential Candidates, 1952–1980," *American Political Science Review* 79 (1985): 359–72; Walter Dean Burnham, "The 1980 Earthquake: Realignment, Reaction, or What?" in *The Hidden Election: Politics and Economics in the 1980 Presidential Campaign,* eds. Thomas Ferguson and Joel Rogers (New York: Pantheon, 1981), pp. 109–10; and Frankovic, "Public Opinion," pp. 113–17.

42. Robert S. Erikson, "Economic Conditions and the Presidential Vote," *American Political Science Review* 83 (June 1989): 567–73.
43. Gregory B. Markus, "Political Attitudes During an Election Year: A Report on the 1980 NES Panel Data," *American Political Science Review* 76 (September 1982): 538–60.
44. Jamieson, *Packaging the Presidency,* p. 412.
45. Diamond and Bates, *The Spot,* pp. 258–62.

Chapter 7.   The Politics of Retrospective Approval: 1984

1. Gary C. Jacobson and Samuel Kernell, *Strategy and Choice in Congressional Elections,* 2d ed. (New Haven, Conn.: Yale U. Press, 1983), pp. 94–109. The figures on party assistance to House candidates are cited on p. 105.
2. John C. McAdams and John R. Johannes, "The Voter in the 1982 House Elections," *American Journal of Political Science* 28 (November 1984): 778–81.
3. Paul C. Light and Celinda Lake, "The Election: Candidates, Strategies, and Decisions," in *The Elections of 1984,* ed. Michael Nelson (Washington, D.C.: CQ Press, 1985), p. 90.
4. Scott Keeter, "Public Opinion in 1984," in *The Election of 1984,* ed. Gerald M. Pomper (Chatham, N.J.: Chatham House, 1985), pp. 93–99.
5. Detailed descriptions of Glenn's image-building strategy are provided by Gary R. Orren, "The Nomination Process: Vicissitudes of Candidate Selection," in *The Elections of 1984,* ed. Michael Nelson, pp. 57–59; Edwin Diamond and Stephen Bates, *The Spot: The Rise of Political Advertising on Television* (Cambridge, Mass.: MIT Press, 1984), pp. 3–32; Richard F. Fenno, *The Presidential Odyssey of John Glenn* (Washington, D.C.: CQ Press, 1990), pp. 125–210.
6. Benjamin Ginsberg and Martin Shefter, "A Critical Realignment? The New Politics, the Reconstituted Right, and the Election of 1984," in *The Elections of 1984,* ed. Michael Nelson, p. 16; Orren, "The Nomination Process," pp. 58–59; and Diamond and Bates, *The Spot,* pp. 29–32.
7. Orren, "The Nomination Process," pp. 52–53. Also see Larry M. Bartels, *Presidential Primaries and the Dynamics of Public Choice* (Princeton, N.J.: Princeton U. Press, 1988), p. 128.
8. Kathleen A. Frankovic, "The Democratic Nomination Campaign: Voter Rationality and Instability in a Changing Campaign Environment," in *Elections in America,* ed. Kay Lehman Schlozman (Boston: Allen & Unwin, 1987), p. 266.
9. Michael J. Robinson, "News Media Myths and Realities: What the Network News Did and Didn't Do in the 1984 General Campaign," in *Elections in America,* ed. Kay Lehman Schlozman, p. 157.
10. Bartels, *Presidential Primaries and the Dynamics of Public Choice,* pp. 103–7, 262.
11. Orren, "The Nomination Process," pp. 40–41.
12. Ginsberg and Shefter, "A Critical Realignment?" pp. 16–17; Orren, "The Nomination Process," pp. 66–67; and Bartels, *Presidential Primaries and the Dynamics of Public Choice,* p. 225.
13. Bartels, *Presidential Primaries and the Dynamics of Public Choice,* pp. 259–61. Frankovic, "The Democratic Nomination Campaign," p. 278, agrees

with Bartels that momentum was the key factor in Hart's rise and fall, but disagrees when it comes to an assessment of the role that ideology played in the Democratic race. According to Frankovic, ideology was not related to the vote in the 1984 Democratic primaries.

14. Bartels, *Presidential Primaries,* pp. 263–67. Also see Paul R. Abramson, John H. Aldrich, and David W. Rohde, *Change and Continuity in the 1984 Elections* (Washington, D.C.: CQ Press, 1986), pp. 41–42. For a more detailed discussion of Jesse Jackson's base of support in the 1984 campaign, see Adolph L. Reed, Jr., *The Jesse Jackson Phenomenon* (New Haven, Conn.: Yale U. Press, 1986); Lucius J. Barker and Ronald W. Walters, eds., *Jesse Jackson's 1984 Presidential Campaign* (Urbana, Ill.: U. of Illinois Press, 1989); and Lorenzo Morris, ed., *The Social and Political Implications of the 1984 Jesse Jackson Presidential Campaign* (New York: Praeger, 1990).

15. Gerald M. Pomper, "The Nominations," in *The Election of 1984: Reports and Interpretations,* ed. Gerald M. Pomper (Chatham, N.J.: Chatham House, 1985), p. 19. Also see Thomas E. Patterson and Richard Davis, "The Media Campaign: Struggle for the Agenda," in *The Elections of 1984,* ed. Michael Nelson, pp. 116–17.

16. Bartels, *Presidential Primaries,* pp. 84–88.

17. Orren, "The Nomination Process," pp. 69–70.

18. Abramson, *Change and Continuity in the 1984 Elections,* p. 139.

19. Ibid., p. 58. Also see Michael J. Robinson, "Where's the Beef? Media and Media Elites in 1984," in *The American Elections of 1984,* ed. Austin Ranney (Durham, N.C.: Duke University Press, American Enterprise Institute, 1985), pp. 196–200.

20. Edwin Diamond and Stephen Bates, "The Ads," in *The Mass Media in Campaign '84,* eds. Michael J. Robinson and Austin Ranney (Washington, D.C.: American Enterprise Institute, 1985), p. 51.

21. Internal Republican tracking polls.

22. For a discussion of the gender gap in 1984, see Light and Lake, "The Election: Candidates, Strategies, and Decisions," p. 105; and Keeter, "Public Opinion in 1984," pp. 101–6. For an analysis of the roots of the gender gap, see Jane J. Mansbridge, "Myth and Reality: The ERA and the Gender Gap in the 1980 Election," *Public Opinion Quarterly* 49 (1985): 164–78.

23. Light and Lake, "The Election: Candidates, Strategies, and Decisions," p. 86.

24. John Kenneth White, *The New Politics of Old Values,* 2d ed. (Hanover, N.H.: University Press of New England, 1988), pp. 70–73.

25. Light and Lake, "The Election: Candidates, Strategies, and Decisions," p. 107; Abramson et al., *Change and Continuity in the 1984 Elections,* chaps. 6 and 7; Donald R. Kinder, Gordon S. Adams, and Paul W. Gronke, "Economics and Politics in the 1984 American Presidential Election," *American Journal of Political Science* 33 (May 1989): 491–515; Gerald M. Pomper, "The Presidential Election," in *The Election of 1984,* ed. Gerald Pomper, pp. 142–44.

26. White, *The New Politics of Old Values,* p. 70.

27. Ibid. Also see Abramson et al., *Change and Continuity in the 1984 Elections,* pp. 194–95; and Keeter, "Public Opinion in 1984," pp. 91–92.

28. Light and Lake, "The Election: Candidates, Strategies, and Decisions," p. 74.

29. White, *The New Politics of Old Values,* p. 57.

30. Abramson et al., *Change and Continuity in the 1984 Elections,* p. 175.
31. Martin P. Wattenberg, *The Rise of Candidate-Centered Politics: Presidential Elections of the 1980s* (Cambridge, Mass.: Harvard U. Press, 1991), pp. 111–13.
32. Abramson et al., *Change and Continuity in the 1984 Elections,* pp. 169–72; and Warren E. Miller, "The Election of 1984 and the Future of American Politics," in *Elections in America,* ed. Kay Lehman Schlozman, pp. 300–301.
33. Abramson et al., *Change and Continuity in the 1984 Elections,* p. 171.
34. Miller, "The Election of 1984 and the Future of American Politics," p. 300.
35. Theodore J. Lowi, "An Aligning Election, A Presidential Plebiscite," in *The Elections of 1984,* ed. Michael Nelson, pp. 281–84.
36. John H. Aldrich, John L. Sullivan, and Eugene Bordiga, "Foreign Affairs and Issue Voting: Do Presidential Candidates 'Waltz Before a Blind Audience'?" *American Political Science Review* 83 (1989): 123–41.
37. Abramson et al., *Change and Continuity in the 1984 Elections,* p. 203.
38. Ibid., p. 175; William Schneider, "The November 6 Vote for President: What Did It Mean?" in *The American Elections of 1984,* ed. Austin Ranney, p. 225.
39. Abramson et al., *Change and Continuity in the 1984 Elections,* p. 203.

Chapter 8.   The Triumph of Issue-Based Images: 1988

1. Paul Taylor, *See How They Run: Electing the President in an Age of Mediaocracy* (New York: Knopf, 1990), p. 5.
2. Peter Goldman, Tom Mathews, et al., *The Quest for the Presidency 1988* (New York: Simon & Schuster, 1989), p. 13.
3. Marjorie Randon Hershey, "The Campaign and the Media," in *The Election of 1988: Reports and Interpretations,* ed. Gerald M. Pomper (Chatham, N.J.: Chatham House, 1989), p. 96. Also see Thomas E. Patterson, "The Press and Its Missed Assignment," in *The Elections of 1988,* ed. Michael Nelson (Washington, D.C.: CQ Press, 1989), pp. 63–92.
4. Hershey, "The Campaign and the Media," p. 98.
5. Ibid., p. 100.
6. Martin P. Wattenberg, *The Rise of Candidate-Centered Politics: Presidential Elections in the 1980s* (Cambridge, Mass.: Harvard U. Press, 1991), pp. 134–55.
7. Charles S. Bullock III and Burdett A. Loomis, "The Changing Congressional Career," *Congress Reconsidered* 3d ed., eds. Lawrence C. Dodd and Bruce I. Oppenheimer (Washington, D.C.: CQ Press, 1985), pp. 68, 77–78. Gephardt's Washington orientation is evident in his election as House Majority Leader, next-in-line to the Speaker.
8. Taylor, *See How They Run,* p. 15.
9. Goldman, Mathews, et al., *The Quest for the Presidency 1988,* p. 124.
10. Ibid., p. 65.
11. *Newsweek,* October 19, 1987.
12. Taylor, *See How They Run,* p. 201. The behind-the-scenes strategizing in the Bush camp prior to the Dan Rather interview is described in detail by Taylor, pp. 196–201; and Goldman, Mathews, et al., *The Quest for the Presidency, 1988,* pp. 198–201.

13. Roger Simon, *Road Show: In America Anyone Can Become President, It's One of the Risks We Take* (New York: Farrar, Strauss, Giroux, 1990), pp. 3–30, tells the story of the Straddle ad and the 1988 Republican campaign in New Hampshire.

14. Peggy Noonan, *What I Saw at the Revolution* (New York: Random House, 1990).

15. John Cassidy, "From Wimp to Winner," *(London) Sunday Times,* November 6, 1988. The details of the Paramus focus group are also recounted by Goldman, Mathews, et al., *The Quest for the Presidency 1988,* pp. 299–303; and Simon, *Road Show,* pp. 214–17.

16. Taylor, *See How They Run,* p. 190.

17. Cassidy, "From Wimp to Winner."

18. See Chapter 2 for a review of the role played by "independent expenditure" campaigns in presidential elections as a result of the Supreme Court's *Buckley v. Valeo* decision.

19. When Ronald Reagan first ran for governor of California in 1966, an ad on behalf of incumbent Edmund "Pat" Brown parodied Reagan's lack of credentials for office by showing clips of Reagan in a number of his old television and movie roles—as a cowboy, a salesman, and a down-and-outer. The ad was too sophisticated. Many television viewers saw Reagan's picture so often that they thought it was an ad for Reagan. See Ernest D. Rose and Douglas Fuchs, "Reagan vs. Brown: A TV Image Playback," in *The New Style in Election Campaigns,* ed. Robert Agranoff (Boston: Holbrook Press, 1972), pp. 350–63.

20. Ross K. Baker, "The Congressional Elections," in *The Election of 1988: Reports and Interpretations,* ed. Gerald M. Pomper (Chatham, N.J.: Chatham House, 1989), pp. 153–76.

21. Paul R. Abramson, John H. Aldrich, and David W. Rohde, *Change and Continuity in the 1988 Elections* (Washington, D.C.: CQ Press, 1990), p. 3.

22. Ibid., p. 167.

23. Ibid., p. 173.

24. Wattenberg, *The Rise of Candidate-Centered Politics,* pp. 121–23.

25. Jean Bethke Elshtain, "Issues and Themes in the 1988 Campaign," in *The Elections of 1988,* ed. Michael Nelson (Washington, D.C.: CQ Press, 1989), pp. 117–18.

26. Barbara G. Farah and Ethel Klein, "Public Opinion Trends," in *The Election of 1988: Reports and Interpretations,* ed. Gerald M. Pomper (Chatham, N.J.: Chatham House, 1989), p. 115.

27. Hershey, "The Campaign and the Media," p. 99.

28. Taylor, *See How They Run,* p. 223.

29. Ibid., p. 224.

30. John Kenneth White, *The New Politics of Old Values,* 2d ed. (Hanover, N.H.: University Press of New England, 1988); Farah and Klein, "Public Opinion Trends," p. 118; and Gerald M. Pomper, "The Presidential Election," in *The Election of 1988: Reports and Interpretations,* ed. Gerald M. Pomper (Chatham, N.J.: Chatham House, 1989), pp. 137–44.

31. Wattenberg, *The Rise of Candidate-Centered Politics,* p. 146.

32. Ibid., p. 130.

33. Ibid., pp. 151–52. Also see Wattenberg's discussion, *The Rise of Candidate-Centered Politics,* pp. 123–29.

34. Kathleen Hall Jamieson. From her participation in a panel on "The Ethics of Political News Reporting and Advertising on Television," Ripon

College, Ripon, Wisconsin, October 20, 1989. Taylor, *See How They Run,* p. 214, also discusses the false inferences contained in the Revolving Door ad.

35. Taylor, *See How They Run,* p. 191.
36. For a review of the Reagan administration's environmental record, see Jonathon Lash, Katherine Gillman, and David Sheridan, *A Season of Spoils* (New York: Pantheon, 1984); Sheldon Kamieniecki, Robert O'Brien, and Michael Clarke, *Controversies in Environmental Policy* (Albany, N.Y.: State U. of New York Press, 1986); and Norman J. Vig and Michael E. Kraft, *Environmental Policy in the 1980s: Reagan's New Agenda* (Washington, D.C.: CQ Press, 1984).
37. Goldman, Mathews, et al., *Quest for the Presidency 1988,* pp. 362–63.

Chapter 9. The Future of American Politics

1. Thomas E. Patterson and Robert D. McClure, *The Unseeing Eye: The Myth of Television Power in National Elections* (New York: Paragon Books, 1976), p. 103.
2. Ibid., pp. 102–3.
3. Ibid., p. 108.
4. Richard Joslyn, *Mass Media and Elections* (Reading, Mass.: Addison-Wesley, 1984), p. 199.
5. Richard Joslyn, "Political Advertising and the Meaning of Elections," in *New Perspectives on Political Advertising,* eds. Lynda Lee Kaid, Dan Nimmo, and Keith R. Sanders (Carbondale, Ill.: Southern Illinois U. Press, 1986), pp. 139–83.
6. Ibid., p. 174.
7. Ibid., p. 175.
8. Martin P. Wattenberg, *The Rise of Candidate-Centered Politics* (Cambridge, Mass.: Harvard U. Press, 1991), pp. 121–23.
9. Alexander Heard, *Made in America: Improving the Nomination and Election of Presidents* (New York: HarperCollins, 1991), pp. 59–63; Leslie A. Tucker and David J. Heller, "Putting Ethics Into Practice," *Campaigns and Elections* 7 (March-April 1987): 42–46.
10. Ibid., pp. 59–65.
11. Ibid., p. 66.
12. Kathleen Hall Jamieson, *Packaging the Presidency* (New York: Oxford U. Press, 1984), p. 449, observes: "The difficulty in relying on news to correct distortions in advertising is, of course, that comparatively few people consume news while many are exposed to ads."
13. Jamieson has done extensive work on the unspoken and often misleading inferences contained in political ads. In *Packaging the Presidency,* p. 449, she complains about "[p]olitical argument by visual association." Her more recent work deals with the manipulation of picture quality (the use of freeze frames, different shadings, etc.) and the audio track (i.e., playing with tonal quality) to affect viewer response. While news reporters are likely to criticize an ad for a misstatement of facts, they are less likely to seize upon these more subtle video and audio distortions.
14. The story of the FCPC, its potential, and limits is told by Tucker and Heller, "Putting Ethics Into Practice," pp. 44–45. See note 9 above.

15. Kathleen Hall Jamieson has made this argument. See David S. Broder, "Who Should Play Cop for Campaign Ads?" *Washington Post National Weekly Edition,* February 13–19, 1989, p. 9.

16. Paul Taylor, *See How They Run: Electing a President in an Age of Mediaocracy* (New York: Knopf, 1990), pp. 268–80.

17. Everett C. Ladd, "Like Waiting for Godot: The Uselessness of Realignment for Understanding Change in Contemporary American Politics," *Polity* 22 (Spring 1990): 520–21. For a more detailed discussion of the changes in voting alignments that resulted from America's transition from industrial to postindustrial society, see Everett Carll Ladd, Jr., with Charles Hadley, *Transformations of the American Party System,* rev. ed. (New York: W. W. Norton, 1978), pp. 181–388.

18. Everett Carll Ladd, "On Mandates, Realignments, and the 1984 Presidential Election," *Political Science Quarterly* 100 (Spring 1985): 12–13.

19. The importance of "inoculation" by a candidate in fending off an attack campaign is detailed by Michael Pfau and Henry C. Kenski, *Attack Politics: Strategy and Defense* (New York: Praeger, 1990).

20. Wattenberg, *The Rise of Candidate-Centered Politics,* pp. 10–11.

21. Ibid., p. 11.

22. John G. Stewart, *One Last Chance: The Democratic Party, 1974–76* (New York: Praeger, 1974), pp. 106–12. Also see Wattenberg, *The Rise of Candidate-Centered Politics,* pp. 107–9.

23. Kevin Phillips, *The Politics of Rich and Poor* (New York: Random House, 1990). Especially see the book's "Introduction" and pp. 3–52.

24. Ibid., esp. pp. 57, 78, and 84.

25. Ibid., p. 201. Also see pp. 190–94.

26. Robert Cameron Mitchell, "Public Opinion and the Green Lobby: Poised for the 1990s?" in *Environmental Policy in the 1990s: Toward a New Agenda* (Washington, D.C.: CQ Press, 1990), pp. 81–99.

27. Poll data from various 1989 and 1990 NBC News/*Wall Street Journal,* CBS News/*New York Times,* Gallup Organization, and Opinion Dynamics Corporation polls, presented by Everett Carll Ladd, *The American Polity: The People and Their Government* (New York: W. W. Norton, 1991), pp. 271–75.

28. C.B. Holman, "Go West, Young Democrat," *Polity* 22 (Winter 1989): 323–39.

Name Index

Subject Index

PRESIDENTIAL CAMPAIGNS AND ELECTIONS

Composition by Point West, Inc., Carol Stream, Illinois
Printed and bound by McNaughton & Gunn, Inc., Ann Arbor, Michigan
Edited by Dana R. Gould, Hoffman Estates, Illinois
Designed by Willis Proudfoot, Mt. Prospect, Illinois
Production supervision by Robert H. Grigg, Chicago, Illinois
The text is set in Baskerville; display in Poster Bodoni
The paper is 50 lb Champion Pinehurst White Offset